D0031718

GHOST
DANCES

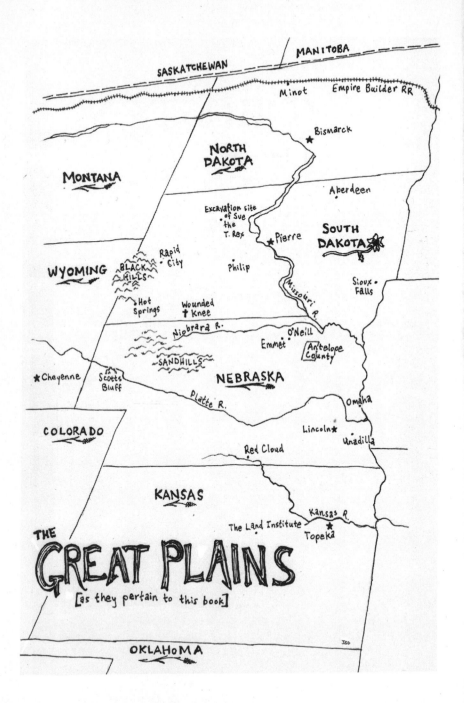

THE
GREAT PLAINS
[as they pertain to this book]

GHOST DANCES

Proving Up on the Great Plains

Josh Garrett-Davis

LITTLE, BROWN AND COMPANY
New York Boston London

Little, Brown and Company
Hachette Book Group
237 Park Avenue, New York, NY 10017
www.hachettebookgroup.com

First Edition: August 2012

Little, Brown and Company is a division of Hachette Book Group, Inc., and is celebrating its 175th anniversary in 2012. The Little, Brown name and logo are trademarks of Hachette Book Group, Inc.

The publisher is not responsible for websites (or their content) that are not owned by the publisher.

The Hachette Speakers Bureau provides a wide range of authors for speaking events. To find out more, go to www.hachettespeakersbureau.com or call (866) 376-6591.

Some names have been changed in consideration of the subjects' privacy.

Library of Congress Cataloging-in-Publication Data
Garrett-Davis, Josh.
    Ghost dances : proving up on the Great Plains / Josh Garrett-Davis.
        p. cm.
    Includes bibliographical references.
    ISBN 978-0-316-19984-1
    1. Great Plains—History.   2. Great Plains—Social life and customs.
3. Great Plains—Environmental conditions.   I. Title.
    F591.G26 2012
    978—dc23   2011043621

10 9 8 7 6 5 4 3 2 1

RRD-C

Printed in the United States of America

For my family, broadly

CONTENTS

GHOST
DANCES

Prologue

Theoretically, the American bison at the Bronx Zoo could stampede north from their corral to a shallow enough spot in the Hudson River to cross, swarming through New York State, decimating lawns and forests and golf courses along the way, a herd metastasizing over the land, reclaiming its former territory: practically everything west of the Appalachian Mountains and east of the Sierra Nevada.

That is, since they live in the Bronx, the lone tongue of mainland New York City, these bison still inhabit the same continent they always have. If they were in island exile in the Central Park Zoo or Rikers, or marooned in Brooklyn or Queens somewhere, they'd have bits of sea between them and their home on the range. Probably the most common metaphor for the bison's aboriginal Great Plains habitat is an "ocean of grass"—it's unavoidable, and I use it plenty myself—but to put an actual ocean between these roughs and North America would be cruel. Whether it's the salt or tides or the Plainslike vastness of it, the sea would seem to inflict a starker displacement.

It is August, hot and humid. The eleven animals I count are

taking turns looking out through inch-wide gaps between the planks of their high corral fence. They resemble the tourists studying smaller zoo animals—the caged birds, bats, or rodents—but they are in fact ogling the scrap of range that is their own during grazing hours. Their famous figure is enchanting: the thick skin, thick fur, thick shoulders, thick footfalls, and thick dry snort. After several seconds one bison moves away and another presses an eye to the fence, or if the first dillydallies the second feints a charge, stirring a puff of dust. Even penned, they keep a herding tradition, ganging up near the fence or toward the cinder-block dugout at the back end of the corral. They're built like woolly brown baseball players, heavyset with nimble lower legs, surprisingly unsluggish but definitely not lithe runners like the zoo's cheetahs and gazelles. I wouldn't want to play catcher as one charged home.

Of all the animals here, the bison look most ill at ease, restless and alien in a dirt pen no bigger than the zoo's carousel (children here ride praying mantises and grasshoppers instead of ponies). They don't seem exotic enough for a zoo, seem to demand more space. Somehow, the bison's summer-shed fur dangling this morning looks like a T-shirt half torn off in a fight—it is the Bronx, after all—and the agitated tails sweeping city houseflies away remind me of broken windshield wipers with the rubber blades whipping pointlessly.

Buffalo clearly aren't as charismatic to most visitors as they are to me. Except for the two guys in khaki Wildlife Conservation Society shirts fixing the guardrail I am leaning against, I am alone spying on the bison from above, from a zoo parking lot off Fordham Road. Earlier, I barely glimpsed the Bengal tiger rolling on its back like a house cat before I was stampeded by day campers. ("Matthew! Concrete! Stop playing around!"

"I *am* on concrete." Pause. "Matthew! Fully on the concrete!") Here there's no competition.

In a way I feel we're kin, that I've become like the zoo buffalo peering back at the range through the fence boards, as I read about Plains history and go back to explore places I never appreciated as a kid in South Dakota. I ended up living in New York City not by any design but by chance, following my college sweetheart to Brooklyn. Now in island exile in Manhattan, I felt the urge to take the 6 train back to the mainland to see these city cousins of the bison in Wind Cave National Park, the purest herd in South Dakota.

New York has a large population of human refugees from East Backwater, Square-State, each with his or her strange story of getting here; every so often I meet someone at a Brooklyn party or through friends or work who grew up in Beatrice, Nebraska, or Elko, Nevada, or Lone Wolf, Oklahoma. The Bronx Zoo's buffalo herd arrived similarly piecemeal from the last remnants of their species that had survived out west. Shortly after the zoo opened in 1899, it acquired bison from a Wyoming ranch via a Massachusetts wildlife advocate; from one of the Kansas buffalo skinners who had helped cause the virtual extinction of the bison but who later captured and raised a few on his ranch; from the Page Woven Wire Fence Company in Michigan, which had taken the animals on tour to demonstrate the strength of its fences.[1]

Up the hill from the bison, I sit down to ruminate outside a plywood-fenced construction site without any gap to peer through. COMING SOON: MADAGASCAR! EXPERIENCE UNIQUE, EXOTIC HABITATS! a sign promises. THE NEXT BEST THING TO BEING THERE. I'm unable to fool myself into thinking I've left the Bronx. (As I sit there, one construction worker inside the fence bellows at another, "You're a what-the-fuck kind of guy!") The tiny, corralled bison herd and their pitiful pasture cannot truly conjure the grassland Plains of my imagination. I'm not sure it's the next best thing to being there. In fact, it is the leaves of grass in a Walt Whitmanish sense—the visitors, the whole bubbling scene—that make up the richest expanse at the zoo, as in New York at large. "Sensational Kids" and Ming Yuan Chinese School students from Queens with their Bluetoothed teen counselors. Tourists sipping Fla-Vor-Ices and Capri Suns. College girls asking if the wagging tail of the one-humped camel means it is happy.

I still dream about South Dakota, of course. Beyond traveling and reading, that's another way to plumb a place one knows intimately. On a night not long ago I was standing on the western bluffs above the Missouri River, looking across at the bluffs on the other side. They were much more rocky and dramatic in the dream than they are in waking life, with towers of swallow's-nest sandstone and piles of boulders as if this were farther west. It was a calm day, mercifully windless, typically sunny.

The Missouri River cuts a backward solidus through South Dakota's middle, dividing the state into West River \ East River. I was born East River, spent my early adolescence West River, and graduated from high school *on* the river, in Pierre. Then I left for the East Coast, except in my memories, studies, and dreams. The Missouri follows the foot of where the Laurentide Ice Sheet stopped during the last ice age, and consequently marks the boundary between a flat, Midwestern glaciated landscape (East River) and rolling grasslands (West River). By coincidence, the divide between East River and West River is roughly parallel to, and then crosses, the hundredth meridian of longitude, which marks the threshold of average rainfall, about twenty inches per year, that is sustainable for cropland agriculture. In short: East River farms, West River ranches. Transitional landscapes like this witness a frisson of species called an *edge effect*, a vital generative meeting of landscapes and also human cultures. In a sense, this dream view was like the Great Plains in miniature, West and Midwest, both and neither.[2]

All of a sudden my dream-self noticed a large chunk of rock break off the eastern bluffs and fall toward the shore. From the distance across the river, this lurch of decay, a geologic time-lapse, was oddly silent. I thought of the time I was driving past a school and saw one of the letters on its sign fall off—*What are the chances?* We usually see the eroded cliff, the gap-toothed sign, but never the midnight moment when the glue that holds the world together finally lets go. In a staid place, a touch of dynamism or decay.

In fact this moment was even more momentous. After a beat, other boulders started to fall, and sandstone fragmented and cracked and tumbled down to the riverbank. A thought struck me: It was an earthquake. (This was a night in early 2010, when temblors hit Haiti, Chile, and Baja in close sequence, so that must have been the Freudian "day residue.") We are not known for our earthquakes, for good reason, but even unconscious I thought of the New Madrid earthquake of 1811.[3] In the seismic zone around the borders of Missouri, Illinois, Kentucky, and Arkansas—seemingly as unlikely as South Dakota—a massive earthquake struck in December 1811, and another couple of jolts followed in early 1812. Supposedly, chimneys crumbled in Maine and bells rang in Washington, DC, but the most indelible image from that quake was that it produced a sort of inland tsunami that made the Mississippi River flow upstream for a while.

The reversal of a river is a catastrophic, even apocalyptic, event. The definition of *down* vanishes, along with faith in a predictable world. Now a place I know so well and have such strong ideas about was different in its very compass and gravity.

Soon, in the dream, the water levels before me began to inch up, and I realized what was happening. The Oahe Dam, just upstream of Pierre (if there was an *upstream* anymore), was preventing the water from flowing north, so I was standing on the bed of what would soon be a reverse reservoir. I started scrambling up the bluffs.

This book is a chronicle of some currents in the ocean of grass. At its center is the narrow channel of my own life, which touches every other narrative here at least glancingly. I had an atypical, sometimes lonely upbringing in South Dakota, shaded by secrets and a general sense of not belonging in the place where I was from. I left as soon as I could, moving to Massachusetts and then New York, but could not truly leave the Great Plains, its culture, or its mythology behind. Yet there was something alienating about the history I was always taught, of vanishing bison and a vanishing Indian race, of a single influx of agricultural pioneers in the nineteenth century and the development of a culture that endured long enough to exclude me. There was only one *downstream.*

As the book progresses, I move from my own story to the stories of some of my ancestors and relatives on the Plains, and from there to a new personal mythology of the place, a collection of stories I've found on journeys around the region—travels both literal and imagined. I've read bunches of books about the

Plains and visited places that struck a chord. Some of the stories here are not strictly about knowing the physical and historical Plains—the Bronx Zoo bison and a dream-time earthquake, for starters. Some, like my own, begin on the Plains and end elsewhere. Others begin elsewhere and end on the Plains. Like any portrait of a place, this is idiosyncratic and biased and certainly not comprehensive, but it's true and complete in its own way. I've come to understand the Plains as a particularly porous landscape, where plenty of strangers and exiles have had great influence. In fact, I ultimately realized that I belong to that country precisely because I don't belong there: The currents in and out, the streams and storms and contamination, define the ocean of grass.

This is also an attempt to *rewild* the Plains, to use an ecological term: to reintroduce extinct, exotic, or forgotten species and stories to the prairie. Ultimately, through a distinct collection of currents, this is how I navigate home.

PART ONE

Strangers about to Meet, Buffalo and Spanish Bull.

Scotty Philip's bison fighting a bull in Ciudad Juárez, Mexico, 1907.
(Photo courtesy of the State Archives of the South Dakota State Historical Society)

ONE

Superstition vs. Investigation

1.1

My dad and I were driving home, from Rapid City to Pierre, tunneling east 180 miles through the huge glass brick of Plains sky, which dulled the light on a June afternoon so that the edges around the horizon were a hypnotic white. Now that I'm long gone from South Dakota, I would describe the mixed-grass prairie out the windshield as golden and singularly majestic, an ocean of fiber and rich carbohydrate, a subtle ecological masterpiece; back then it looked like dead brown straw.

The emptiness of the Plains can strike a puny human either way: as profound, or profoundly tiresome.

I had had a lifetime of drives like this — OK, sixteen years, but *my* lifetime — and I found the trip punishingly boring, endless. The only solace was my rightful every-other-cassette on our little sage-colored Tercel's stereo to override three hours of tape hiss outside, waiting for the album, any album, to start. That's what the Great Plains sound like, whether you're standing still and the wind is whooshing ceaselessly through grass and the clouds are careering almost audibly in the big blast of sky, or you're driving fourscore-and-ten miles per hour and your tires are somersaulting and your windshield is plowing up its own wind: It's tape hiss, or that moment after you've dropped the needle on a record and it has yet to find its music. That sound, drawn out over hours, or years.

At the end of our drive this day, the tape would be eaten in the deck, the needle scratched roughly over the record.

Rapid City was our regional watering hole, home to a mall with more choices than J. C. Penney's and Kmart; to the airport from which I flew to Portland, Oregon, three times a year to visit my mom; and importantly to a punk rock scene and a real record store, Ernie November. I had accumulated a few dozen seven-inch records and cassettes and about eighty CDs, which I arranged and rearranged on a small wooden shelf, either alphabetically or by date of purchase, or even by the color of their spines. It had taken almost a decade to assemble this humble library, since I'd first heard Mötley Crüe at the hardcore age of seven.

We left the Black Hills and passed the pinkish moonscape of the Badlands, then turned off I-90 onto U.S. Highway 14. The first town there was Quinn, hardly a town at all, with a single-digit population. I remembered the two of us stopping there late one night six years earlier, when I was first moving in with Dad after that hard summer of my parents' custody fight over their only son. Dad's twenty-year-old bronze Dodge pickup had overheated hauling a load of our boxes, so we stopped at the Two Bit Saloon, a real false-front Western bar and the only business in Quinn. While we waited for the engine to cool, I sat on a vinyl stool and drank a plastic cup of orange juice, feeling alien being ten and in a cowboy bar.

The halfway point on our trip was Philip, named for Scotty

Philip, one of the visionaries of the late nineteenth century who saved the American bison from extinction, preserving a remnant of this landscape's iconic species. But that's the thirty-year-old Plains scholar in New York City talking, not the bored-to-tears sixteen-year-old. Scotty Philip was a prosperous rancher, one of the first white men to live in western South Dakota—then the Great Sioux Reservation—by virtue of being a "squaw man," brother-in-law to Crazy Horse, no less. I'll get to his story here by and by.

The last real town on our route was Midland, a colorless Plains village with a Main Street, a rodeo ground and a football field, a few gray-green trees. Its distinguishing feature is the hot artesian well water trapped between two solid layers of rock underground; when tapped, it spews out under its own pressure like the steam from an overheated radiator. There is a latent fury in this monotonous landscape, ready to unleash a tornado or a shrill blizzard or a boiling, sulfury geyser if punctured. The place can turn nasty, can turn on you in a way that feels targeted and predatory but is actually enormously indifferent.

In seventh grade, I'd had a social studies teacher from Midland who told us that athletes there had to race each other to the showers to get the first water; anything after that was scalding. Ms. Hueber had a husky voice and a Billy Ray Cyrus haircut, which led us students to the snickering conclusion that she was a lesbian. I wondered if there was some code I could use to telegraph her that I was cool with it, that I knew lots of lesbians, including my own mother.

At last, in the middle of the afternoon, Dad and I descended the shale bluffs into the Missouri River valley and home into Pierre (pronounced "peer"). The state capital boasts a population of thirteen thousand, a natural gas "flaming fountain" beside the rotunda, and a single high school whose mascots are the Governors and Lady Govs (we've never elected a lady gov, in fact). Dad and I turned onto Pierce Street at the white sky-scraper of the grain elevator and pulled up at our yellow stucco house, a century-old farmhouse surrounded by half-century-old GI Bill Levittown boxes, now fading and undesirable. Our house's stucco and foundation were cracked. Thin plastic shut-ters had replaced the old-fashioned kind beside our windows, and they, too, continually cracked and blew off in the wind.

Stiff and yawning from the drive, I walked to the side door to wait for Dad to unlock it. We locked the house only when we left town; the front key didn't even work. The door was already ajar. We hadn't shut it tight, and the damned wind had blown it open.

I climbed the stairs two at a time to my room. I reached toward the bulb to turn it on, then spotted the black shoelace that usually hung from the pull chain, fallen and coiled on the carpet. A half dozen Delta Airlines UNACCOMPANIED MINOR buttons were pinned along the spine of the lace.

My room was a fun house, with low walls and slanted ceil-ings that I had painted pumpkin orange with green trim. The carpet was a red-white-and-blue tin-soldier design the previous owners had installed for their boy in the 1970s. Built into the walls were a bureau and shelves I'd converted with paint from Old Glory to pumpkin patch. Being in the top corner of an old house, the room required plastic film over the windows in win-ter, and it was probably best I wasn't there for the oven summers—Dad didn't "believe in" air-conditioning. I slept on a mattress on the floor inside a kaleidoscope of clashing souvenirs I had vigilantly cataloged in my memory. Now some shapes were missing.

"Dad," I called loudly but calmly, "I think you better come up here." It was a surgical theft: my CD library, a few seven-inch records, and the portable CD player that had been plugged into my parents' old silver Sanyo stereo receiver. It must have been somebody who knew me, but it couldn't have been somebody I liked.

There was a perverse sort of vindication in being robbed. *This* was why I was going to leave South Dakota as soon as I got my diploma. This place was so hostile: the drives that clamped my skull in boredom (we had yet another drive to an airport coming up for me to fly to Portland); the wind that never, ever stopped pushing me back; the billboard that said, WE SOUTH DAKOTANS REJECT ANIMAL ACTIVISTS, and all the times at some Kozy Korner or other when I'd eaten potato salad and french fries because they were the only vegetarian items on the menu; the fact that I had never kissed a girl and the worry that people thought I was queer in one way or another—Lord knows what they would have said or done if they knew Mom actually was; and now the theft of the few valuable things I owned.

The next day I came down with a fever of 103 degrees. I had to leave soon for Mom's for the summer, but I was disoriented in my fun house, overheated in the 90-degree days of June. I wasn't getting to hang out with my friends in my last days at home, and I wouldn't be around to solve this crime. The fever and Tylenol gave me a strange sensation like I was hearing two people argue through a wall, barking unintelligibly at each other. I had bought a tinny, frantic punk CD called *Destroy*

What Destroys You in Rapid City, and since it was all I had left, I sat on the lumpy antique couch and listened to it over and over on Dad's stereo, which was untouched in the burglary. The music was seemingly 78 rpm; it only echoed the barking. I could never stomach that album or Tylenol after that week.

I began to assemble a catalog of loss for the insurance company, and began to guard my memories of songs and liner notes and facts as belongings that couldn't be stolen. I was never sure I'd noted every single album because I'd keep thinking of one more to add to the list. From then on, when I bought used CDs, I left the price tags on the jewel cases (jewel cases!) to remind me of the times and places I acquired them, constructing a little fort of memory around each one. Partial list in hand, I flew west to Portland.

Artist	Title	Notes
Jane's Addiction	*Ritual de lo Habitual*	My third CD ever; censored cover (Tipper Gore era), with First Amendment cleverly replacing a nude painting; Dad bought used from Ernie November when he had a work trip to Rapid City; surprised me.
Nine Inch Nails	*Pretty Hate Machine*	Fourth CD ever; $7 at a pawn shop in Hot Springs, SD, circa 1992, sixth grade; impressed by the "Head Like a Hole" video and the "industrial" genre.

Artist	Title	Notes
Rancid	self-titled 7-inch ("Idle Hands," "Battering Ram," etc.)	$3; amazing show at tiny JJ's Rose Arcade in Box Elder, SD; guitarist Lint actually talked to us afterward, and I (wearing a yellow Jujyfruits T-shirt over a purple rugby shirt) told him I liked his leather Operation Ivy jacket.
Sublime	*40 oz. to Freedom*	$5; bought because I liked the cover; realized I had heard it between bands at a ska-punk show; a couple of years later, singer OD'd and they got popular.
Magnified Plaid (MxPx)	*Pokinatcha*	Evangelical friend Peter sold to me for $5; he had a thorough Christian rock collection; he once asked about the rainbow ribbon pinned to my backpack, said his apostate bisexual sister in Denver had told him it was a symbol; "They can't own a rainbow."
Hellbender	self-titled	Watershed CD, ostentatiously literary punk band whose guitarist and bassist were the writers Wells Tower and Al Burian; show happened to be going on when I was visiting Rapid City; October of ninth grade; I learned the word *mantra* from "Clocked Out."

19

1.2

Per my parents' custody agreement, I flew west toward Denver or Salt Lake City and on to Portland, or east toward Minneapolis to fly west to Portland, and then I flew back, east from Denver or Salt Lake, or west from Minneapolis, into South Dakota. I saw green-and-white Rocky Mountain peaks drop to seared August grasslands with spiderweb-thin fencerows and specks of black Angus and the smudge of dust behind a pickup truck on a gravel road. I saw, in January, square sections of Midwest farmland like white dominoes with farmhouse dots; as I flew west from Minnesota into South Dakota the land got drier, the farms got bigger, and the dominoes turned gradually from double-fours to double-ones; and finally around the hundredth meridian and the Missouri River, it got too dry for farming and the dominoes deliquesced into ranch land. We hunkered in that drab stripe of no-man's-land between the fertile Middle West and the spectacular Mountain West. With the distance travel brought, I also saw the dry, conservative culture I was growing up in as opposed to the culture in Portland, which seemed much closer to the left-wing values both of my parents taught me: antiracist, feminist, environmentalist, brightly artistic.

Those airplanes—and the frequent-flier miles and UNACCOMPANIED MINOR buttons accrued while jetting away from the dimpled, dun Plains and bumping back toward them in thirteen-seat prop planes and half-empty jets—refracted my perspective on the region in a way I've come to understand as essential. Through a tiny multipane oval, the Plains land spreads out to the horizon as a giant, flat disk—a record, say, Side B—and you can see something of the big picture of how water flows, where roads go, where are clustered what few inhabitants the place allows. Yet probably almost anybody who is reading this has flown over the Plains states and would agree that the bird's-eye view is limited— *It's so barren and dull, and at night there are almost no lights! What is out there?*

Even speeding across on I-70 through Kansas, I-80 through Nebraska, I-90 through South Dakota, or I-94 through North Dakota without leaving the truck stops and rest stops is not much better for seeing the Plains as a real place. At least, though, in a car you can glimpse the A Side of the record, that ever-changing winged sky that plays over the region. And then driving a bit slower on smaller roads, and walking around, and growing up in the culture the grassland created, the worm's-eye view: That's the rest of the A Side perspective, but one that's sometimes as limited as flying above it, whether you love the place wholeheartedly or resent it, as I often did.

It was common for punk rock bands to release split seven-inches, with a couple of songs by one band on Side A and by the other on Side B, potentially drastically different. It's impossible to listen to both at once. It's also impossible to see the Plains from the ground and from the air at the same time, but by leaving and returning you turn the record over and over, even after you've left seemingly for good.

So, taking off and landing. Homesteading and pulling up stakes. Paradoxical as it sounds, I've come to understand that *coming* and *going* are perhaps the only things native to the Great Plains.

1.3

That August I flew back to Pierre. My list won me a large check from the homeowner's insurance, something like $800, probably more than I'd paid for my collection. The police had not found any evidence. The night before junior year started, my own band, Stickman, opened for Hellbender at the red-carpeted Pierre Elks Lodge, where we'd begun hosting punk rock chautauquas the year before. There being a paucity of teenage amusements, we'd ordered up an anarchist subculture native to London or New York—or, at that time, Berkeley and Gainesville—and we assembled it ourselves as if it were a pre-made house ordered from the Sears catalog (at a younger age, I had yearned fruitlessly while scanning the pages of guitars and drum sets in the back of the J. C. Penney catalog). In fact, as I realized after coming east, our ragtag gatherings were truer to the punk ideals and blueprints than the scenes many of the bands we loved came from. It was impossible to be a poseur or a wannabe in Pierre, because there was no hierarchy or history or code to tell us what to pose as or want to be: If you showed up, you *were*.

In Stickman I played bass guitar and sang bouncy, earnest punk songs like "The Mighty Lobsters of Maine Revolt" and the quasi-communist "Potluck Society." Today I swell a bit with pride thinking about the latter one, as if a little brother had written it—how as a sixteen-year-old I couched my own leftist punk ethics (*from each according to her ability…*) in terms of a South Dakota church-basement dinner: *And even assuming a few don't contribute / The wealth is abundant as long as we share / Plenty of shelter and plenty of food / In the absence of greed there is plenty to spare.*

Before the show, I shot pool with Hellbender in a room beside the Elks Lodge bar. They were from Chapel Hill, North Carolina, but lately lived in Portland. I'd miraculously hung out with the bassist and drummer there (I'd written the band letters, and they wrote back) for an afternoon when I first arrived at my mom's house in June. Portland had refreshingly calm days, towering trees, rock festivals, STRAIGHT BUT NOT NARROW buttons—crucially, a lack of fear about the secret of Mom's sexuality and an abatement of the loss that fact implied.

Al Burian (the bassist) and I had walked down a moss-trimmed sidewalk in a hip quarter of Southeast Portland, and I explained how harsh the climate was on the exposed, treeless Plains. From this distance, I could start to see that harshness as noble and romantic in a way that I couldn't back home. Life in South Dakota had a poetic heft. Al nodded knowingly. "So there's nothing to keep the elements at bay." I kept mulling over the sophistication of that phrase, *at bay*.

Over billiards at the Elks Lodge in Pierre, amid the awkwardness of a teenager conversing again with his twenty-five-year-old heroes, discussing record thefts and their tour, I asked, "So, do you guys have any extra copies of that first album that I could buy?"

They all laughed ruefully, and the guitarist, Wells Tower, said, "Those things are long gone."

I mail-ordered what I could. One band from Gainesville sent me a free split seven-inch with a note that said, "Sorry about your CDs."

A few weeks later, I went to Capital Pawn, a dingy stucco storefront on Main Street where a leathery proprietor sold hot VCRs and pairs of woofers boxed to fill a car's trunk. I clacked through his box of scuff-cased CDs, working to spend the insurance check. Wal-Mart, Kmart, and Dakotamart sold only major-label alt-rock garbage or at best some heavy metal. I was only half surprised to find four CDs that were unmistakably mine: a split album of the Rudiments with Jack Kevorkian and the Suicide Machines, the Mighty Mighty Bosstones, Urban Dance Squad, and the Vampire Lezbos. With the possible exception of the Bosstones, nobody else in Pierre could have owned these. I felt a nervous thrill in solving the crime and then anger that the cops hadn't already done so while I was gone. Who knew what had already been sold? Pretty quickly, though, the seller's code (17348-8), written to this day on the jewel cases' black bindings as a reminder of all this, led the Pierre police through a couple of intermediaries to the three young culprits and most of the missing discs. Maybe the wind *had* initially blown the door open, and they were stoned, drunk, or tweaking on meth and just walked in. Maybe I was wrong about the drugs and they just didn't like me.

Greg was a pudgy kid with glasses. He was about thirteen and lived three blocks away—also with a single father. I knew who he was only because his older brother had been in my General Music class in junior high and was best friends with my friend Seth. Greg's brother and I had played Nirvana songs together on school-issue classical guitars. The second thief, I had never met or heard of, though I guess he came to Stickman shows. He was also named Josh. I later heard he went to juvie for a meth offense.

The third kid was probably fourteen, a pale redhead named Aaron whom everyone called "Beater" after some fictional masturbation incident. When I was in ninth grade he was in seventh, and we had gym class at the same time. He was even less graceful and sporty than I was. Sometimes he sat on the benches because he hadn't brought athletic clothes. I cringe now at the meanness, wish I could say I never called him Beater. I wonder if he remembered me from that time, if that raced through his tweaking head when he was loading my record collection into a paper bag. Or maybe he knew me only as the singer and bass player of one of two local punk bands.

A couple of years later, Beater joined in an epidemic of suicides, a preternatural and horrific meteor shower that struck Pierre in the late 1990s. I don't remember whether he shot or hanged himself or what. My senior year, a *New York Times* reporter and photographer came out to our school in the "gullet of the Great Plains" to try to explain our slow calamity in an article titled "In Little City Safe From Violence, Rash of Suicides Leaves Scars." The only explanations seemed to be the abundance of guns (though a few were hangings), the anxious atmosphere of a one-industry (government) town headed by a rather authoritarian governor, and the fact of being "remarkably isolated, ringed by a vast, grassy moonscape and bracketed by the Bad River and whistles of water with names like No Heart Creek, Whisky Gulch and Tall Prairie Chicken Creek."[1]

We all found this description a bit overwrought, to say the least. If teen suicide is a fatally shortsighted act, a failure to recognize that *this too shall pass*, then the urban journalist's perspective was almost fatally farsighted, an airplane that never actually lands. Yet both the teens and the journalist were onto something: Life as an unattractive, poor teenager in a cruel town *is* truly unbearable, and conversely there *was* something poetic and almost supernatural in our humdrum lives, the artesian wells waiting to burst — *Beater* — that strangers could see better than we could.

How to reconcile these two perspectives, the cracked windshield of an old car cruising Euclid Avenue and the telephoto lens? Side A and Side B? Superstition and investigation?

1.4

"Superstition vs. Investigation," reprinted from the *Red Cloud Chief* of June 13, 1890, is a xeroxed printout the Catherland boosters give to tourists in Red Cloud, Nebraska. It is the text of Willa Cather's high school graduation speech.

Willa was one of three graduates, the only girl, and she indisputably fit the description *punk rock*, avant la lettre. I could scarcely have imagined a classmate or comrade who was so hardcore. She glowed with a ferocious genius and individual sensibility. She blazed around her little Plains town of five thousand, attaching herself to grown-ups who had wood to feed her mind's fire: French-German Jewish neighbors with a library of European art and books; the founder of Red Cloud, former Nebraska governor Silas Garber, and his elegant wife, Lyra; an old slacker British store clerk who shared with her his love of Latin and animal dissection; a host of less-educated European immigrants (Bohemians, Norwegians, and others) who lived and told great stories; the theater companies that, like touring punk bands with fur coats and lapdogs, came to play at the opera house.[2]

Everything I did as a sour, ambitious adolescent in Pierre in the 1990s, Willa outdid in Red Cloud in the 1880s. I, too, scouted for culture, though I wouldn't read her work until I went east to college. I was enchanted by my dad's Mennonite anarchist friend Michael Sprong, who stayed on a cot at our house when he came to Pierre to lobby the state legislature for the South Dakota Peace and Justice Center and who gave me dubbed cassettes of radical punk and hip-hop and old copies of a Christian anarchist zine, *A Pinch of Salt*. I went to the Rawlins Municipal Library after school to read *Rolling Stone* and discovered *Harper's*, which was oh so much smarter. I became pen pals with Al Burian from Hellbender—he of *at bay*—who put out a funny, cerebral slacker zine, *Burn Collector*.

I dressed like an old man, sporting polyester polo shirts from my mother's father in California and from Value Village. Willa dressed like an old man in 1880s Red Cloud—infinitely more badass. She cropped and shingled her dark brown hair and wore a starched shirt, suit, and tie with a bowler hat. She had a babyish face and gray-blue eyes and looked like an iconoclastic Oliver Twist.

Her graduation speech, which she delivered in the Red Cloud opera house as a sixteen-year-old, is high-flown and abstruse; it's also hard to make sense of without knowing her frictions with her town. Perhaps her mother convinced her to wear at least a skirt for the occasion, or maybe she just went up there in pants and anarchist hair and rocked it. The speech begins, as any adolescent pronouncement should, "All human history...," and grows from there. She disdains the superstition of the ancient Hebrews, who "delved into the mystical and metaphysical, leaving the more practical questions unanswered, and were subjected to the evils of tyranny and priestcraft." The Greeks, by contrast, "allowed no superstition, religious, political or social, to stand between them and the truth, and suffered exile, imprisonment and death for the right of opinion and investigation." Sadly, history sank into the Dark Ages, when the "Earth seemed to return to its original chaotic state, and there was no one to cry, *'Fiat lux.'*...All the great minds were crushed." Superstition had conquered. But the philosopher and scientist Francis Bacon rekindled the *lux* of investigation by proposing scientific experimentation in the *Novum Organum:* "Thus we went painfully back to nature, weary and disgusted with our artificial knowledge, hungering for that which is meat, thirsting for that which is drink, longing for the things that are."

At sixteen! In the hinterland, the "parish," as she would later call it! Willa had a command of all Western civilization, of Latin and natural science. Here I thought I was courageous when I wrote a school research paper on the hypocrisies of American Protestant churches defending slavery before the Civil War and then condemning it, silencing women before suffrage and then ordaining them. I proposed implicitly in this essay that a similar shift might occur in the church's treatment of gays, but kept secret the fact that my mom fell afoul of the current doctrine, not to mention the mores and prejudices of South Dakota. Willa was likewise marshaling her grand argument toward an unspoken quibble with her fellow townsfolk. (That she, too, would later probably fit the category of lesbian was not yet an issue, despite her dressing in drag, since that category did not yet exist in Nebraska.[3])

The fact was, she had gotten hold of a set of doctor's tools from a dead uncle and had developed an enthusiasm for dissecting animals, to the sniffs of more proper Red Cloudians. She fancied herself an apprentice doctor, and she followed a couple of local doctors around on house calls and even dosed a boy with chloroform before his leg was amputated. She had taken to signing her name "William Cather Jr. M.D." — though her father was Charles, not William — and her friends called her Willie, Will, or Billie. On her own, she apparently killed, dissected, and embalmed stray cats and dogs and maybe other creatures. She filled out an "Opinions, Tastes and Fancies" survey in a friend's scrapbook with the data that her favorite amusement was "vivisection" and her idea of perfect happiness was "amputating limbs."[4]

Instead of sneaking around researching and reading, even timidly consulting a conservative minister as I did on my project, Willa fired her message point-blank at the squares. Except that she didn't outright mention her vivisections in her speech. After her synopsis of Old World darkness and light, she spoke in the abstract about a male alter ego. "Scientific investigation is the hope of our age, as it must precede all progress; and yet upon every hand we hear the objections to its pursuit. The boy who spends his time among the stones and flowers is a trifler, and if he tries with bungling attempt to pierce the mystery of animal life he is cruel," Willa complained. Then she revealed "his," and likely her, ambition: "Of course if he becomes a great anatomist or a brilliant naturalist, his cruelties are forgotten or forgiven him; the world is very cautious, but it is generally safe to admire a man who has succeeded."

Her expansive mind ridiculed the small minds of Red Cloud right to the faces that shielded them. It doesn't get any punker than that. I was a relative milquetoast confronting Pierre, trying to invent messages like "Potluck Society" to challenge and blandish at the same time. Willa socked it to them.

But Willa Cather didn't become a great anatomist or a brilliant naturalist; she became a great and brilliant novelist. When she lived among those who knew only Side A by Superstition, she confronted them with Side B by Investigation. When she moved away, first to college in Lincoln and then to the East, Cather evidently found Investigation, that empirical bird's-eye view, to be insufficient on its own to represent the Plains. Her artistic triumph would be to overlay her epic visions on these very townsfolk's lives to the degree that biographies of her often read like the end credits of a movie (Ántonia Shimerda was Annie Pavelka, Dr. Archie was Dr. McKeeby, Marian Forrester was Lyra Garber...). The classics of literature and philosophy she read as a teenager in her "Rose Bower"—her wallpapered attic bedroom about half the size of my pumpkin-patch fun house—would be fused in her fiction with that drafty bedroom itself.[5] Even her graduation speech would be delivered, by another male alter ego, Jim Burden, in *My Ántonia*. "I thought my oration very good," Jim says. "It stated with fervour a great many things I had lately discovered." Afterward, Ántonia tells him, "There ain't a lawyer in Black Hawk"— er, Red Cloud—"could make a speech like that." And there wasn't.[6]

The Nebraska of Cather's novels and stories is a romantic place where a falling out between two businessmen over the Nebraska Populist presidential candidate William Jennings Bryan in 1896 (a "great leader" to one and a "great windbag" to the other) triggers a young person's existential vertigo, a tragic loss of the belief "that there are certain unalterable realities, somewhere at the bottom of things."[7] In her fiction, suicide is as common as it was in Greek tragedies, or in the Pierre of my high school years: Ántonia's father shoots himself in the barn in winter, and his body stays there frozen for four days before the priest and coroner can get there; eventually the villain of *My Ántonia*, Wick Cutter, gruesomely shoots his wife and himself; one tramp throws himself into a wheat thresher, another into a town's standpipe; when his hogs die of cholera, a farmer garrotes himself with binding twine and the spring action of a bent stick; a pretentious, effeminate teenager robs his employer and lives large in New York City for a week before jumping under a train; a stroke victim who had to leave his post as second violin in a Prague orchestra only to play second fiddle to his mean, thrifty son in Nebraska breaks his violin and pulls the shotgun trigger with his toe, Kurt Cobain–style.[8]

These stories have the quotidian dignity of being rooted in real people but also the archetypal resonance the *New York Times* projected on Pierre's moonscape suicides in 1998. I think back and remember this guy Jeremy who sat behind me in social studies class when I first moved to town and flicked my ears and called me "skater fag," then drew a map showing me how to get to Beckwith's, the local bike and skateboard shop. He was a handsome jock who had grown muscles and a mustache before anybody else and consequently had carte blanche around the junior high for a while. His was a hanging, I think with a belt. There was James, the pothead who sat at my lunch table in junior high with all the long-haired headbangers wearing black T-shirts, and who later shot his ex-girlfriend, the hottest headbanger girl, and himself. I also remember Ryan, who was in my homeroom class when we watched Channel One News, during which another friend and I made juvenile, provincial jokes about "Tutsi-rolls" and "Hutu stew" as Anderson Cooper reported the faraway genocide in Rwanda. I can't remember if Ryan laughed at us, but he was so kind and mild I couldn't believe it when he shot himself. Then there was Aaron, "Beater"—I felt responsible for his death more than any of the others. There is something gained by stepping back and turning them into epic tragedies, valiant but failed struggles against a pitiless landscape or a hidebound culture. But there is also something exploitative about doing so; we were just kids.

Cather was a quintessential plainswoman; she moved from Virginia to Nebraska at the age of nine in 1883, struggled against it until she left at age twenty-two, and it defined her all her life. It's significant that her character's name in *My Ántonia* is Jim Burden—what many of us who leave the Plains carry. Cather's coming and going, I think, allowed her finally to balance the individual dignity and truth of the land, of Superstition, against the bird's-eye objectivity of Investigation, which she'd championed so stridently as a punk rock girl.

After I left, landing ultimately, like Cather, in New York City, I often went back to visit places where I lived as a child and to explore new ones. In Red Cloud, Nebraska, I slept in a tent at an RV park, a pilgrim in this literary Bethlehem, with the roar and clang of a demolition derby as an evensong. I'd seen the Willa Cather Memorial Prairie and the stained-glass windows she donated to Grace Episcopal Church and her little Rose Bower with the sloped ceiling. I did and did not want to see the sparkling scrim of art over it all, or to imagine her as a punk rocker, a constructive rebel perhaps lonely in her hungers. Were her and her friends' DIY theater productions like our Elks Lodge shows? Cather turned out to have two sustained (if not sexual) relationships with women as an adult out in Pittsburgh and New York. I wonder how those proclivities shaped her view of Red Cloud, much as I wonder if any of Pierre's suicides were gay. Was she silent and alone behind the punk exterior? Did she take the loneliness of this great, mythic landscape and turn it inside out, into bluster and self-regard?

Even back then, after her brash defense of Investigation (and vivisection) to the Red Cloud audience, young Willa backed off a bit and restored wonder to her equation. I imagine her bold but still girlish voice taking a pause after asking about vivisection, "Ah, why does life live upon death throughout the universe?"

Then she finished, "The most aspiring philosopher never hoped to do more than state the problem; he never dreamed of solving it.... Our intellectual swords may cut away a thousand petty spiderwebs woven by superstition across the mind of man, but before the veil of the *'Sanctum Sanctorum'* we stand confounded, our blades glance and turn and shatter upon the eternal adamant." A less than punk rock note to end on, but anyway, amen. Amen, Willie.

1.5

Not long after my sleuthing at the pawn shop, I sifted through a soiled paper bag holding most of my CDs at the police station and took them home. One of the thieves had hidden the loot somewhere out in the moonscape, in the wind and elements *(not so beauteous and mythic then, were they, Writer?)*, and had fetched it when the cops came. There was one CD in the bag that wasn't mine, a grunge album called *Dirt*, along with plenty of grunge and dirt that wasn't mine either.

Later, Greg's probation officer asked me to meet with Greg, so the delinquent could face his victim. Dad dropped me off at the granite courthouse on Capitol Avenue one fall afternoon, and I walked in the front door with a pit in my stomach as if *I* were in trouble. I already knew in a vague way that my perspective gave me an intangible privilege Greg didn't have, even if our material privilege as children of single fathers on the poor side of town was comparable. My dad had an Ivy League education and worked as a legal aid lawyer for little money, more or less by choice. I had seen quite a bit of the outside world. I knew this too would pass. Greg and the other two thieves didn't have the books, the band, the travel, or the distance, lacks most painfully exemplified by Aaron's eventual suicide.

The hallway was much dimmer than outside, the floor tiled in institutional fashion. I turned a corner and saw Greg sitting in a wooden chair, looking to my eyes a little haughty. But I wasn't angry, or at least I felt guilty being angry. The probation officer asked me to sit down. Greg and I didn't shake hands.

"Is there anything you want to say to Josh?"

Greg looked down and to the side. "Yeah, I wanted to say I'm sorry for taking your CDs and stuff," he said. "'Cause I know you like music. If somebody did that to me, I would have been mad."

I couldn't tell if he was sincere, or if it changed anything. I don't remember what I said in reply. Maybe I just nodded and left, kept it all at bay, flying away again in my head.

Artist	Title	Damage
Jane's Addiction	*Ritual de lo Habitual*	Intact, except for broken jewel case lid; once the nude cover art was reinstated, the First Amendment version became more collectible.
Nine Inch Nails	*Pretty Hate Machine*	Lyric sheet glued shut by water; didn't listen for years until the beeps of a dump truck in reverse gear brought to mind "Something I Can Never Have."

Artist	Title	Damage
Rancid	self-titled 7-inch	"Stickman Forever" carved in vinyl with something sharp; unplayable and out of print; bought again five years later in Amherst, MA, for an appalling $10.
Sublime	*40 oz. to Freedom*	Missing, perhaps sold by Capital Pawn; rebought used only six blocks from the Portland record store where original was bought; $8.
Magnified Plaid (MxPx)	*Pokinatcha*	Cover virtually destroyed from sitting in paper bag in the moonscape; disc still playable.
Hellbender	self-titled	Cover waterlogged; lyrical lyric sheet still readable.

Two

Landscape of Motion

2.1

Neither of my parents was from the Plains.

A few Euro-American families have stayed on the same land for generations, buying up sections of property as their neighbors moved away, since nobody could make a living on just 160 acres. Many American Indian families have stayed on reservations continuously. Some Plains folk moved into town. But a good share of them come and go, even if they don't go far; and many of the anomalous dynasties there receive subsidies from elsewhere to sustain them. An environmental history describes the region as a "landscape of motion," most of whose native peoples were always nomadic and whose large animals (bison and elk, chiefly) were migratory.[1] It's changed in many ways, with Plains towns looking superficially more or less like any old small towns—except flatter in space and color—but ultimately we can't ever outgrow this ecological fate.

My dad was born in 1952 to a Harvard graduate student with Nebraska and Colorado roots, and his wife, a New England Yankee. The oldest of three children, Dad was raised primarily in Ithaca, New York, in a stylish house he later described as "a modern, oblong structure that resembled a green ice cube." His parents sent him to boarding school near Princeton, New Jersey; then he attended Brown University. By that point his family had fallen apart, his father moving with a new wife to teach at Yale and his mother moving to California.

Dad had fixated on the West since age twelve, particularly an imagined house on mountainside stilts overlooking Casper, Wyoming. Then there was the thrill of the road trip he and his father took through Wyoming and South Dakota in the summer of 1966, when he was fourteen, on which my granddad used the wide-open straightaways to see what it would be like to drive a hundred miles per hour. A child's cowboy fantasy, a sense that the East ill suited him, the rift in his family. After his freshman year in college, Dad registered voters in blazing Tulsa, Oklahoma. He was slight and awkward, and had a round, tanned face and thin brown hair that split and stopped growing when it reached his collar. He was enchanted by the fact that he would have to walk for *weeks* across grasslands, deserts, and forests to get to an ocean. There was a solidity to this land and its culture, and despite his experiments with marijuana and LSD, despite his ardor for liberal Democratic politics and against the Vietnam War, he longed for a traditionalist plot of America.

The next summer Dad worked on the campaign for the man who would become the most liberal Democrat and the first Arab in the U.S. Senate, South Dakota's James Abourezk, a Lebanese-American who had grown up on the Rosebud Sioux Indian Reservation. A week after graduating from college, Dad returned to this state he found even better than Oklahoma — for good, it turned out. South Dakota had a Democrat in its modest governor's mansion, a union meatpacker (Morrell's) in its largest city (Sioux Falls), some top-shelf local country music (Red Willow Band), and plenty of cheap Grain Belt, Blatz, and weed.

My mom was born on the opposite coast, in Southern California, in 1955, the first child of an Air Force veteran from Oklahoma and an ambitious, college-educated working woman, the daughter of a department store owner in La Crosse, Wisconsin. Both had left their small towns at the first chance and splashed into Los Angeles. The family moved north to the Bay Area, where my grandpa earned his college degree at Berkeley and then worked as a probation officer, and my grandma worked as a welfare caseworker. They settled in Hayward, a working-class suburb of Oakland. In eight years they had six children.

Though she was mostly oblivious to the social revolutions popping around her in San Francisco, Oakland, and Berkeley, Mom decided on instinct to go to college in the humid coastal woods at the experimental University of California at Santa Cruz during its idealistic first decade. She suspected she might be a lesbian, but that term didn't describe an especially definite lifestyle. She was naive, with squinting green eyes and pretty honey-colored hair, a lapsed Irish Catholic, chastened by her mother not to be "shanty Irish." Her new classmates were feminists and hippies, and the scene at Santa Cruz was wondrous if a bit scary. She took short courses in auto mechanics and skydiving and began a major in "community studies."

After her sophomore year, in the summer of 1975, Mom found a job knocking on poor and working-class doors twelve hours a day in Sioux Falls, South Dakota, for the newly formed Association of Community Organizations for Reform Now.

ACORN had started in Arkansas, and its second state was South Dakota, another poor rural state, the "Mississippi of the North." Senator Abourezk had persuaded ACORN to come; it was only later that the organization would realize it thrived best in big cities. Many of ACORN's target neighborhoods in Sioux Falls were ripe with the salty, fecund smell of Morrell's, the largest employer in those years. Dad was another ACORN canvasser, soliciting local civic activism—getting poor folks to serve on community boards and such. Mom tended, it seemed, to drift into situations and out of them without much volition. She never returned to Santa Cruz.

Both of my grandfathers, the Okie and the Yalie, had married up, and raising their children on one coast or the other represented an improvement over their own childhoods. From Mom's father's point of view, a ticky-tacky childhood in a Northern California suburb, even stretched thin, was a damn sight better than growing up the son of a presser in a tailor's shop in Norman, Oklahoma, in the Depression. Dad's father had been packed along as his peripatetic journalist father moved yearly from Denver to cities around the country, so it was a rise to marry my grandmother, who came from a Connecticut family where the boys went to Yale and the girls went to Vassar. Dad, too, received the finest oaken education in America.

By tumbleweeding into South Dakota from different directions, one with little intention and the other with more, both my parents were incomprehensibly and ungratefully refusing the advantages they'd been fed, rolling against the centrifugal force that spins the ambitious children of the middle out to the edges of the country. They were reintroducing to the Plains, which once had such centripetal gravity, an endangered species: the idealistic young homesteader.

They first rented an upstairs apartment in an old white brick house on a hill north of downtown Sioux Falls, and lived with almost no furniture. In the background of their cadre of young Democrats lingered a faint pungency of tobacco and pot smoke and the rough twang of "progressive," or "outlaw," country and western. Within a year they moved farther afield, to Mission, on the Rosebud Sicangu Sioux reservation, where they rented a red double-wide trailer infested with field mice that tunneled through the homemade bread they learned to bake. Dad worked at the welfare office, and Mom worked as an elementary school teacher's aide. They took classes in Lakota Sioux culture at Sinte Gleska College and canoed the Niobrara River across the Nebraska line.

They moved to the rez in 1977, in the immediate aftermath of the most tense and outright violent period of racial unrest in South Dakota in the twentieth century. A scattered movement broadly called Red Power had started in 1969 among American Indians who had "relocated" from rural reservations to urban centers, either through direct federal policies that encouraged assimilation and the political "termination" of tribes, or by the migration of Indian GIs to cities far from home once they were out of the service. Federal Indian policy seemed to shift every couple of decades from "self-determination" to paternalism and assimilation, and its caprices, strangely, recapitulated the Plains history of nomadism and population shifts around the landscape of motion. Gradually Red Power activism—which called for permanent self-determination and an end to policies like relocation but which was also an unchanneled eruption of rage among poor, young Indians—moved back to the reservations, culminating in a series of fracases and insurrections, especially in South Dakota: a 1973 riot at the Custer County Courthouse in the Black Hills after a white man stabbed and killed a Lakota man and was charged only with manslaughter; two takeovers of a pork-processing plant on the Yankton Sioux Reservation and then the murders of two FBI agents and one young Indian activist in a firefight on the Pine Ridge Reservation in 1975, the summer my parents were knocking on doors for ACORN; and most famously a seventy-one-day armed standoff in 1973 at Wounded Knee, the ignominious site of a massacre of Sioux in 1890.[2]

2.2

Bill Janklow owned a bazooka. After he was elected governor of South Dakota in 1978, he built a berm around the governor's mansion in Pierre so people couldn't see his nefarious doings. He had killed an Indian. He could start his car remotely from inside his house. He was radically unhandsome, with thick glasses and a permanent sneer. None of these statements are wholly true, but as allegations and rumors they animated a Lex Luthoresque villain in my childhood conception of a Smallville.

Janklow's was another coming-and-going story. He was born in Chicago to a South Dakotan mother and a Jewish father who took the family to Germany while he was a prosecutor at the Nuremberg trials. Not long after Janklow's father died, the family returned to South Dakota. Janklow left high school early to join the Marines, reputedly to avoid being sent to reform school for shooting a gun at a water tower and for sexually assaulting a seventeen-year-old girl (he later said it wasn't rape—"It didn't go that far"—and his juvenile records were sealed). After serving, he returned to South Dakota for college, then law and business school.[3]

His political career started before I was born, thanks in large part to the Indian-white tensions caused by the Red Power movement, and he would continue to be the central pole in South Dakota politics well after I left home. Beginning in the late '70s, those politics shifted to the right from the days of electing George McGovern and James Abourezk to the U.S. Senate. Most white South Dakotans did not share my parents' contempt for Janklow or their sympathy for the American Indian Movement, the Black Panthers of Indian country. In 1974, after the Wounded Knee standoff, Janklow was elected attorney general with two-thirds of the vote, largely due to his fierce response to AIM. But—since AIM's "terrorism" by and large took place on Indian reservations outside state jurisdiction—he relied mostly on tough talk and symbolism. *Put a bullet in a guy's head, and he won't bother you anymore.*[4] He drove eighty practically everywhere he went, was said to own a private arsenal, including supposedly the bazooka, and had been accused of raping his children's fifteen-year-old Indian babysitter when he was a legal aid lawyer on the Rosebud Reservation, several years before my parents moved there. Democratic leaders brought the girl forward to publicly accuse Janklow during his 1974 campaign for attorney general. A few months after he was elected, the accuser was found dead in a ditch; this was the Indian I somehow came to believe he had killed. When the writer Peter Matthiessen repeated the rape allegations in his book *In the Spirit of Crazy Horse*, Janklow unsuccessfully sued him and one of the few bookstores in South Dakota brave enough to carry the book.[5] The charge will probably always remain in the realm of speculation, with conspiracy-minded lefties guessing it was true and conservatives dismissing it as a "canard."[6]

Janklow's wild popularity was not in spite of all this but because of it. Though a tribal judge found enough grounds to charge Janklow with rape, multiple investigations cleared him of the charge, and most voters deemed it a vicious smear. It worked to secure his landslide victory. White South Dakota loved him for getting things done. In his first term as governor, he quickly pushed the legislature to reinstitute the death penalty and then repeal usury laws in order to draw businesses such as Citibank to the state. He used prison labor to build necessary infrastructure. South Dakota also loved—thrilled at—his frankness, a rare trait in our state. He *called a spade a spade*. After hearing a student curse in the hallway at a high school he visited, he said a teacher should have disciplined the student by slamming his head into a locker, then "apologize... as you took the blood off his forehead, that he'd startled you when he shouted like that." In 2001, in his fourth term, he threatened to take down all the organization credits on Adopt-a-Highway signs to thwart an ACLU lawsuit after the state initially refused a sign to a gay rights group. As a sort of vigilante philanthropist, he would quietly buy equipment for an Indian reservation baseball team, or pay some kid's college tuition. He also organized an efficient and Marinelike cleanup after a tornado leveled a small town in 1998—many people thought of him as a "pirate saint."[7]

Almost as if he were the flesh-and-blood version of some inchoate fury we'd repressed but not abandoned when the lawless nineteenth century gave way to the progressive twentieth, the people voted for him again and again, for a total of sixteen years as governor, then as a U.S. congressman. Long-standing racial conflict between Indians and whites did not move him; in 1995 he opposed the ultimately successful effort to rename Columbus Day as Native American Day in South Dakota, declaring, "We talk about reconciliation more than necessary."[8] I don't think it's an outlandish stretch to say he contributed to the Pierre suicides in his third and fourth terms. Our town was small enough that the terrifying, hostile climate Janklow created among state employees chilled all corners as if by a cold draft—with so many parents working for the government in our company town, their fear about apparently random firings doubtless trickled down to us teenagers.

In 2003, Janklow's first term in Congress and his long career as an elected official ended abruptly when his Cadillac hit a white motorcyclist while going through a rural stop sign at seventy miles per hour. The politician who had, a few years earlier, tried to make possession of drug paraphernalia an imprisonable felony served a hundred days in jail for manslaughter.[9] Upon release, he built up a successful law and lobbying practice in Sioux Falls, and continued to speed when he regained his driving privileges (he was pulled over in June 2011 driving ninety in a sixty-five-mile-per-hour zone).[10] On January 12, 2012, he died at age seventy-two of brain cancer. He was only the third politician to lie in state in the Capitol Building, and all his allies and opponents paid respectful tribute to perhaps the most important man in state history. I can now regard him with enough academic distance to see him as an artifact, a curious incarnation of the violence underlying our placid landscape and culture back home, like the voracious tornadoes and scalding artesian wells. But I can never fully shake my childhood sense of him as a superhuman terror.

2.3

During the summer of 1978, Mom took a three-week class at Black Hills State College in Spearfish, South Dakota. Since it was nearby, my parents decided to get married at the Butte County courthouse in Belle Fourche, the geographic center of North America. They were married by a deputy sheriff who, as Dad put it, "wouldn't have appreciated the congratulatory spliff we got as a wedding gift from one of our witnesses." She wore a green cotton dress, and he wore a Methodist-red corduroy sport coat. With their spliff and a six-pack, they celebrated with their two witnesses in the city park, posing for grainy, square pictures as they poked their heads out from behind a tree and hung off the back of the same bronze Dodge that, years after the whole thing had fallen apart, would overheat in Quinn outside the Two Bit Saloon. As a display for Dad's bumper stickers, that pickup truck would have as long a life in South Dakota politics as Janklow, lasting to proclaim, HE's STILL A JERK (no identification necessary), into the twenty-first century.

In 1977, Dad received some money from his mother, and my parents invested in a record store in Aberdeen, the third largest city in South Dakota, a sheet of graph paper dropped on a tiled floor of wheat fields at the flat eastern edge of the Plains. For the first few years they were mostly absentee owners of Prairie Dog Records, while some friends, the other investors, managed it.

They spent those years between the rez that had once been Janklow's home and Wisconsin, where Mom was finishing her college degree. Mom graduated from the University of Wisconsin in the last days of the 1970s. When my parents moved to Aberdeen to run the record shop—which my dad thought of as a "counterculture sanctuary"—Mom was four months pregnant.

THREE

Ghost Dances

3.1

From the Good Samaritan to the Salvation Army, Christianity has had a way of enfolding the outsider and comforting the down-and-out with a covenant for paradise.

In the late nineteenth century, American Indian tribes across the Plains and the West endured near-apocalyptic losses. The eradication of bison, the passage of the Homestead Act, the invasion of homesteaders and gold rushers that pushed Eastern tribes west, the nixed treaties, the shrinking reservations, the alcoholism, the diseases, the military campaigns against tribes that resisted—all these came essentially at once and spelled a brutal end to Indian life in anything like the forms that previously existed in the region. Though tribal armies won battles against whites (Custer at Little Bighorn), they lost the war. The only real hope for redress or restoration would be supernatural.

Far from the Plains, where so many of the crucial Plains stories begin—in this case, in the western Nevada desert— the Paiute tribe had neighbored more or less amiably with white ranchers through the 1880s. There, David Wilson, a farmer, adopted an orphan Paiute boy, Wovoka, and rechristened him Jack. Like Joseph Smith's, Jack Wilson's plain-Jane name belied a destiny for celestial prophecy. The Wilsons were Christians, and Jack picked up just enough of their faith to shape something new with it. The meek shall inherit the earth; the last shall be first and the first shall be last. God assures Isaiah of a socialistic leveling off: "Every valley shall be lifted up, and every mountain and hill be made low; the uneven ground shall become level, and the rough places a plain."[1] By 1890, Wovoka/Jack's prophecies would spread through a dozen Great Plains tribes like a wall of flame and would come to their most magical and tragic climax in South Dakota, on the Pine Ridge Reservation.

Around the end of 1888, the teenage Jack came down with a severe feverish illness. I imagine him sweating through a grass-filled tick mattress in the Wilsons' frontier cabin, thrashing and hearing paranormal sounds like the ones I heard the summer my record collection was stolen. Who knows what wilderness medicine they gave him. On New Year's Day, 1889, during his long febrile bed rest, Nevada also witnessed a solar eclipse, the kind that turns the world's colors inside out and sends people into a panic. Jack/Wovoka visited the spirit world, where God instructed him to bring a new religion to his people. God deputized him and entrusted him with Western affairs, leaving the East to president-elect Benjamin Harrison and retaining spirit-world duties Himself. Jack's spirit world resembled a Christian heaven—everlasting youth, happiness, and abundant game—and the new religion alchemized Paiute beliefs with Christianity and strains of a religious revival that had appeared among some West Coast tribes fifteen or twenty years earlier: Live in peace, including with whites, without lying or stealing, and soon all friends and relatives living and dead would unite in the spirit world. Following his vision, Jack taught the Paiutes a dance, the Ghost Dance, to hasten the millennium.[2]

The times were rife with prophetic sects: Swedenborgians, Shakers, Mormons. (Mormonism was the only Judeo-Christian faith to explain the existence of Indians at all, as a lost tribe of Israel, previously "white, and exceedingly fair and delightsome" but marked, for their sins against the believers, with a "skin of blackness."[3]) And among American Indian peoples in particular, similar semi-Christian revitalization movements had appeared after epidemics and wars since at least the eighteenth century. Predictably, the new Ghost Dance religion swept through several tribes, and to Wovoka's prophecy was added— if he had not intended it to begin with—the promise that whites would vanish from the land and that the bison and elk would return with all of the dead from the spirit world. One Arapaho Ghost Dance song declared, *"I'yehe'! my children— Uhi'yeye'heye'! / I'yehe'! we have rendered them desolate— Eye'ae'yuhe'yu! / The whites are crazy—Ahe'yuhe'yu!"*[4]

Ghost Dance devotees generally sought peace with whites while they waited the anticipated two or so years until the Apocalypse, which would come in one of a number of forms. The Indians would ascend high mountains before a great flood washed whites from the land. Indians would fall into a deep sleep before a typhoon, and their dance feathers would loft them, still unconscious, to the new world. A new earth would slide from the west over the old one as the right hand slides over the left.[5]

In 1890, the Ghost Dance spread almost overnight through the Sioux tribes of the brand-new states of North Dakota and

South Dakota after a party of Sioux pilgrimaged to see Wovoka in Mason Valley, Nevada (despite his deific deputy position over the West, he never left home). Not surprisingly, considering the Sioux's recent wars with white invaders, their versions of the Ghost Dance religion acquired an aspect of Armageddon. The ancestors, they believed, would ride in driving a stampede of bison like the Four Million Horsemen of the Apocalypse and would conquer the whites in battle, aided by a landslide, a flood, and/or a wall of fire to smother, drown, and/or drive the enemies back across the ocean to their proper homeland.[6]

Sioux Ghost Dancers also added a Ghost Shirt to the ritual of the dance, a white cloth vestment supposed to be bulletproof—possibly an adaptation of Mormon temple garments. Many Mormons accepted the Ghost Dance prophecy as valid, since they themselves expected an 1890 Apocalypse in which the uncursed Israelites frozen in Canadian tundra would rejoin their cursed cousins.[7] "The people," said Oglala Sioux chief Red Cloud, "snatched at the hope. They screamed like crazy men to Him"—the Son of God, Wovoka—"for mercy."[8] Over several months in 1890, government agents and military leaders at Sioux reservation agencies moved from disdain for "such absurd nonsense" to terror.[9] "Indians are dancing in the snow and are wild and crazy," an Indian Service agent wrote in a frantic telegram to Washington (each culture used *crazy* to describe the other; Red Cloud used it to describe his own). The Ghost Dancers danced to exhaustion, fainting, and visions. They were emboldened to stand up to reservation police, they stopped shopping at the trading posts, children stopped attending school.[10]

They were perhaps less inclined to actually rise up than they had been before Wovoka's prophecies; they were confident that the whites would disappear and their ancestors would return with the green grass the next spring. But the prophecy certainly shook white power on the reservations. The irony was that this was in part nativized Christianity, which whites had been pushing on Indians for decades (one federal agent thought the Ghost Dance no more harmful than Seventh-day Adventism[11]). Now it seemed to have the revolutionary potential that had resulted in Jesus's Crucifixion by the Romans.

On December 15, 1890, Indian police killed Sitting Bull, one of the greatest Sioux chiefs still living, in a botched attempt to arrest him at his home a couple of hundred miles north of Pine Ridge. The government wrongly suspected him of being the rabble-rouser behind the Ghost Dance, and his death only heightened tensions. Two weeks later, a band of Minneconjou Sioux Ghost Dancers led by Spotted Elk (known to whites as Big Foot) began heading from a fugitive camp in the Badlands moonscape back toward Pine Ridge to surrender. Spotted Elk was the next targeted "fomenter of disturbances" to be hauled in, but he was immobilized by pneumonia, pulled in a wagon by his followers.[12]

The northern Plains at that time of year are wan—the blanched short-grass matted and dusted with dry snow that won't stay in place, the wind whipping and always threatening a blizzard. Trudging across it must have been like treading water across the Arctic Ocean, Spotted Elk prostrate and coughing blood in a dory. When the Sioux espied some cavalry, it might have been half reassuring, like spotting a large armored ship on the open ocean. The Indians raised a white flag. The Ghost Dancers, around 120 men and 230 women and children, went willingly to a camp on Wounded Knee Creek, arriving just at dark.

In the morning, the cavalry posted firing lines and four

Hotchkiss revolving cannons around the camp, as if surrounding the captives with galleons in frigid seas. The Ghost Dancers placed their guns in a large pile, but the troops weren't satisfied. They ransacked the tents where the Indians had slept, looking for more weapons — knives, clubs, pistols. Yellow Bird, a medicine man, began urging the Indians to resist, telling them they were bulletproof, and one young man held his Winchester high and spun around as if he'd been the only one to hear Yellow Bird, though he was in fact deaf. I can only imagine that time slowed for a moment — everyone sunken underwater, even the bitter wind pulling back — as a gunshot popped from somewhere and Yellow Bird enigmatically picked up a handful of earth and tossed it into the air, where it dispersed.[13]

Within minutes scores of Indians were dead. The Hotchkiss cannons, like early bazookas with a mile range, felled fleeing survivors. About 250 of the Ghost Dancers died. One survivor, Louise Weasel Bear, later said, "We tried to run, but they shot us like we were buffalo. I know there are some good white people, but the soldiers must be mean to shoot children and women."[14] That night, before any of the dead could be buried, a blizzard indeed came on. The most famous photos from the event show Spotted Elk after the storm with snow blown into all the crevices of his clothes. He is propped up on his elbows, his hands and forearms frozen in the air as if he were finally lifting himself from his sickbed.

The massacre was the coup de grâce in the Indian wars. There would be no more substantial Sioux military campaigns or uprisings, at least until the 1970s, when AIM held their standoff at the very same spot. The buffalo were long gone. South Dakota now had the beginnings of a state capital in Pierre, my sometime hometown. Homesteaders were uprooting the prairies—former Indian land—that the federal government had given them for free. It is no wonder that the Sioux were enchanted by Wovoka's Ghost Dance religion, known to the frightened settlers and Indian agents, perhaps in the same terms Rome used for Christianity, as the "Messiah Craze."

In retrospect it appears that the Ghost Dance religion was the purest version of the myths that console those of us bereft by the continual displacement in a landscape of motion. The Sioux tribes had in fact lived primarily on the Plains only since the eighteenth century, when European-introduced horses made their way north through Indian trade routes. (The dominant Indian tribes on the Plains in the hunting-bison-on-horseback era—the Sioux, Comanche, and Blackfeet—all came from elsewhere when the horse opened more opportunities for a reliable existence there.[15]) Yet the destruction of this relatively recent way of life was in some sense the end of the world. James Mooney, the first anthropologist to study the Ghost Dance (beginning just before the Wounded Knee Massacre), found in its prophecy our universal longing for the "dreamland of youth."

"As with men," he wrote, "so it is with nations."

Every civilization looks back on a "golden age, before Pandora's box was loosed, when women were nymphs and dryads and men were gods and heroes."[16] Impossible as it is, each secretly wishes for that imagined past to return somehow, as easily as one hand sliding over the other.

3.2

My earliest memory is of a silver paper punch swinging from a piece of jute twine behind the counter of Prairie Dog Records on Main Street in Aberdeen. Records against one wall, the long counter facing them. A dusty glare comes through the front window, and everything is an early-'80s shade of brown, like the stained plywood shelves or the way things must have looked through the big amber-tinted glasses people wore then.

There was something hopeful in that tone, a world the colors of burlap and carob. But in retrospect it looks doomed, and foolhardy. My parents appear as pioneers of a land that wouldn't yield, thinking rain would follow the plow. Mom tried to stock "women's music," feminist folk anthems such as "We Are a Gentle, Angry People," and Dad loved the Dead, Dylan, and the Stones, and progressive country. What sold best was REO Speedwagon's *Hi Infidelity*. More profitably than records, Prairie Dog also sold bongs, pipes, and rolling papers. It was the only head shop between Sioux Falls and Fargo, between Minneapolis and Rapid City. Kids came from as far as two hundred miles away to load up on glassware. Once I learned to crawl, they had to watch that I wouldn't beat the stoners to the paraphernalia.

"You were a nuisance," Dad later told me. I pulled records off the bottom shelf and perhaps batted at the paper punch with my paws.

At two months, I made my first political pilgrimage, three hundred miles west to the Black Hills International Survival Gathering, the largest protest in South Dakota history. Twelve thousand people camped out on a ranch near Ellsworth Air Force Base east of Rapid City to oppose uranium mining, military buildup, and continued treaty violations against Indian tribes. Russell Means, the most charismatic of the AIM leaders from the Wounded Knee occupation and other actions around the country, declared there, to my uncomprehending pink ears, among others, "The natural order will win out, and the offenders will die out, the way deer die when they offend the harmony by overpopulating a given region. It's only a matter of time until what Europeans call 'a major catastrophe of global proportions' will occur. It is the role of American Indian peoples, the role of all natural beings, to survive. A part of our survival is to resist."[17]

It was a ghost dance religion for the Cold War, when the land all around us was pocked with Minuteman nuclear missiles entombed deep in the mesh of native grassland roots.

One morning there, after Mom nursed me, my parents set out over the parched July rangeland for some seminars on alternative energy. Before we made it up the hill from the campground, I spit up over her only shirt. "You just covered her with puke," Dad said. They drove an hour into the Black Hills to find a Laundromat and missed an entire curriculum on photovoltaic cells or something. "It was an early indication of how having a child could change all of your plans," he said. Mom had not accepted that idea. When people told her that her life would change as a mother, her response was "That's old-fashioned thinking." Not long after, she took me to the movie theater to see *The Killing Fields*, thinking I would sleep through it.

Prairie Dog Records epitomized their hopes, and they seeded traditions and values for me, the "prairie puppy," as they worked to prove up on their progressive homestead:

"The birds will use it for their nests," Mom would say as she let her hair out the window of our red Datsun named 'Mata (pronounced "may'-tuh" for a child's pronunciation of *tomato*). I imagined lucky robin chicks growing with a golden braid of her hair coiled around them, that rich, dark blond that mine would be if I grew it out.

She had the vision that she would "raise a little feminist," and had assumed I'd be born a girl. I wasn't supposed to be born in the hospital; it was only that I was two weeks early, and the midwife was from out of town and wasn't able to fly to Aberdeen in time. They planned to name me Niobrara, after the river they had canoed in the rez days.

"Joshua Nathaniel Davis was born under sunny skies on the Dakota prairie . . . to Kathleen Garrett and Jeremiah Davis, our joy and our hope for the future."

Mom's last name would be hyphened on five years later.

Our gags and games had moral lessons. A major-key nursery rhyme for baritone, alto, and prairie puppy:

> *Oh, the peach pit said to the apple core,*
> *"The color of your skin doesn't matter anymore!*
> *Yo-ho-ho, can't you see?*
> *The color of your skin doesn't matter to me!"*

Though I always understood this to be a joyful antiracist ditty, it was much later that I recognized it as specifically appropriate to South Dakota, where racial tension was between peach whites and red Indians.

Mom and I used to play a sort of tickle torture where I sat on her lap, squealing and squirming in her embrace, yelling, "Mrs.! Mrs.! Mrs.! Mrs.!" When I couldn't take any more, instead of "Uncle" I yelped, "Ms.!"

"Ronald Reagan is mean; he gives money to rich people." This was the prairie puppy's populist analysis of the president's efforts to lower the top income tax rate from 70 percent to 28 percent. I was not yet three.

T-shirts I was given over the years:

PRAIRIE DOG RECORDS: IT'S A DOG'S LIFE

JANKLOW SUCKS

ONLY ELEPHANTS SHOULD WEAR IVORY

THRASH NOT TRASH (a skateboarder's
Earth Day message)

The one time I saw Janklow in person was at a cracker-barrel Quonset-hut political meeting. He was wearing an ordinary gray business suit like any politician, but my little chest tightened in my sweatshirt thinking of the bazooka, the berm, the dead Indian, the remote car ignition. I was glad there were so many farmers around as witnesses.

No G.I. Joes, camouflage clothes, He-Men, Star Wars (Reagan again), Autobots, or Decepticons, except with my own money, twenty-five cents per week. Even though we didn't have a TV to watch the cartoons and ads, I would save for months to buy a single macho figurine, and I found a plastic Castle Grayskull at a rummage sale for two dollars. With motley militias I set up battles of good guys and bad guys.

Once, as I was dealing Dad a play-by-play history of my war, he interrupted and explained that he didn't like war, didn't believe in good guys and bad guys.

"Well, you're in one."

"What's that?"

"The 'lection."

He wrote our conversation down in the brown leather

binder with the horse on the cover—my baby book—alongside my earlier anti-Reagan stump. The good guys (and gal) in this case would have been Walter Mondale, Geraldine Ferraro, and our local Aberdeen Democrat Tom Daschle; the bad guys were Reagan, George H. W. Bush, and Governor Janklow.

"Before you go to sleep, say a little prayer," one or the other would sing, rubbing my back. I lay stomach-down in the creaking twin bed Dad had used as a boy. I had my own room perched on the second floor of our aging box house. As I fell asleep at night, one of them would finish John Lennon's lullaby, exchanging my name for Sean's: "Darling, darling, darling, darling Josh."

Another of their favorite lullabies was "The Baby Tree" from the Jefferson Starship album *Blows Against the Empire*, in which prospective parents visit an island full of infants and choose to take home *only babies that smile, smile.*

Dad read me the canon he'd grown up with: two old Horatio Alger rags-to-riches books, an 1871 British boys' adventure called *Out on the Pampas*, the original *Winnie-the-Pooh*, the nineteenth-century *Real Diary of a Real Boy*, *Johnny Tremain*, *Treasure Island*, *The Adventures of Tom Sawyer*. Mom's tastes ran toward the New Age, toward singing *Free to Be . . . You and Me* and Raffi songs together. She convinced me for many years, with the help of E. H. Shepard's androgynous drawings, that Christopher Robin was both a boy and a girl, since s/he had a boy's name, Christopher, and a girl's, Robin.

Our own nest had a long garden parallel to the driveway, fertilized with a pickup load of sheep manure from my godparents' farm outside of town. The garage had white plywood doors that swung open, barn-style. Inside the house were books and records stacked like cordwood: a whole wall of books on planks suspended between hexagonal terra-cotta bricks; records in three long wooden crates that looked like cowboy coffins. We had a closed-in porch where I could be locked for time-out (one time I shattered the front-door window pounding on it in protest). The porch roof had a low-tech "solar collector": a large, flat box with a plexiglas top and a black bottom that built up hot air and blew it into the house in the sunny but frigid Dakota winters.

I realize now these facts made our home a model of aesthetic virtue in Dad's eyes. Mom has since shown herself to have more upscale, contemporary-artsy tastes: strident wall colors, sculptural cupboard knobs, simple furniture. Dust and clutter make her claustrophobic, so Dad's collections (beyond books and music, there were buttons, postcards, steamer trunks, files, art he'd found as a college student cleaning dorms, and a whole cabinet of knickknacks) must have tormented her.

Baby book, about age three:

Knows all colors; knows letters and numbers to 10; writes *JOSH*; starting to dress himself (socks, shoes, coat); has had several imaginary friends: Ronald, Quick, Melissa, Chris, and the pinching dinosaur; really likes church and Jesus; likes folk songs for children, Joan Baez, and Tom Petty; enjoyed his all-natural Easter basket from the food co-op; memorizes lengthy itineraries; believes Grannie has her own airplane to fly in; he knows we're poor.

Prairie Dog Records went belly-up when I was two. Dad got odd jobs selling radio ads and hail insurance to farmers, and Mom went back to school to get her master's in counseling.

One day the next year, some lawyer friends of my parents' came over for a visit. When they knocked, I answered the door, "Come on in! Want to smoke a bowl?"

Bowl-smoking was thereafter confined to the basement.

3.3

The homesteaders of the previous century had to stick together to survive, and their values became moral and collectivist. By our time literal survival was not in doubt, and from the tax cuts and the repeal of usury laws on the "mean" end of the political spectrum to the bongs and *Free to Be ... You and Me* on our end, individualism reigned in the 1980s. After the family business failed—and the last chord of that rock-and-roll homestead rings forever in my ears as what might have been, *the golden age, before Pandora's box was loosed*—both my parents progressed toward their individual interests. They were not moving in the same direction.

Dad got a job as the sole administrator, organizer, and lobbyist for United Family Farmers, a group of aging yeomen fighting to preserve the progressive farm society their forebears had tried to establish and resisting the consolidation and industrialization of agriculture. He went to Pierre and even to Washington to lobby against overambitious irrigation projects that would pollute local rivers and put farmers further in hock to the government and big agribusiness; UFF promoted rural domestic-water pipelines instead. The man who at age twelve had knocked on doors in Ithaca, New York, for Lyndon Johnson with a saucer-size button covering his chest was thrilled to be in the thick of politics, fighting for the earth and its salt. On specific issues—stopping a couple of big irrigation projects and promoting the domestic-water pipelines—UFF was successful.[18] But as the farmers grew old, their children (those Dad's age or so) declined to take over the farms, and corporations such as ConAgra and Cargill gained ever more dominance over ever fewer farms. In terms of maintaining their family-farm culture, UFF was doing a ghost dance of its own; the farmers might as well have tried to halt the wind, bucking the boom and bust of the landscape of motion.

Yet in many ways Dad was becoming one of the pioneers who stayed. Early on, he'd acquired a fold-up road map of South Dakota and begun highlighting in red every route he took. It had the pattern of a network of blood vessels gradually filling until he'd traveled every paved highway and every major gravel road, and been to every town with more than a hundred people. He also broke with his agnostic upbringing to become a Methodist, baptized the same day I was, and he attended church nearly every Sunday thereafter. He even opposed abortion, though he rarely got a chance to support a pro-life candidate who shared enough of his other pro-life values (health care, social welfare, environmentalism, abolishing the death penalty) to be worth voting for.

Mom got her master's and started working as a counselor at a local mental health center. She joined a Methodist women's group that took a feminist read on the Bible—she was staunchly pro-choice. I attended a small Montessori preschool and kindergarten, whose child-directed education leaned more toward her sensibility than toward Dad's *Johnny Tremain* traditions. I learned some reading, writing, and arithmetic but mostly just stood at an easel painting all day.

In the end Mom couldn't or wouldn't, or in any case didn't,

"stick." According to the rules of the 1862 Homestead Act, settlers could pay a small filing fee and claim up to 160 acres of
federal land for free provided they made "proof of settlement
and cultivation," improving the land by building a home and
farming it for five years. At this point they could "prove up," as
it was informally called, and gain full title to the land. Mom
met the letter of the (now extinct) law; she was a homeowner
and had been a business owner. But like many members of the
earlier generation of settlers, she never proved up in a deeper
way. She had drifted into South Dakota and she was liable to
drift out at the first good opportunity. Back in the '70s, she'd
match the guys bottle for bottle, seeing it as a feminist triumph
to keep up. But she could never claim the terrain; she was only
finding a niche to survive there. She didn't want to fight con-
stantly against the society she lived in, a battle instinct homesteading seemed to require. She had also tired of fighting Dad
all the time over little differences. In 1987, just after she
divorced him, she wrote a letter to the future me: "I think I've
learned a lot about happiness in the past few years. I read a lot
of inspirational books and find I am continually searching for
the meaning of life. Happiness seems to come from enjoying
whatever you are doing. Life is not meant to be tolerated with
an attitude of 'I'll just get through this.'" She wanted a place that
was spiritual rather than religious, nurturing rather than combative. A softer world of self-help and New Age flourished on the
West Coast. She also began to understand what being lesbian
meant. None of these seemed to be options with Dad, and she
wasn't able or willing to *just get through this* to preserve the family.

So they divorced. Mom and I got an apartment in the
neighborhood, and I slept on a pallet at the foot of her bed. The
shuttling back and forth was at first minimal. Then Dad's job

with UFF ended—its concrete raisons d'être were largely finished—and he decided to go to law school five hours' drive away at the University of South Dakota. He could find no one to buy our house (the 1980s farm crisis affected folks in town as well), so he gave it back to the bank. The eventual next owners tore off the solar collector, as Reagan did at the White House around the same time. My nomadic life began, slowly, amid the pulled-up stakes there, and shoots of disillusionment invaded the ideals my parents had seeded. Leaving that homestead, I first developed my bird's-eye view of South Dakota.

3.4

It was at that time I discovered music for myself, the dirty-boy Sunset Strip spectacle of glam metal. It hooked me via a few entrancing hours of MTV at a babysitter's house in 1987, between second and third grades. Cable TV was expert at sowing in provincial kids the desire for an expensive big-city life. I wasn't old enough to make sense of the sexual energy and innuendo in Mötley Crüe and Poison (let alone the paradox of cocky virility costumed in lace garters and eye shadow, which remains fascinating to me even after twenty-five more years of rock-and-roll fandom), but I adored its textures. The appeal was really the cough-syrup-red sleekness of spandex tights and Porsches, starkly against the frayed earth tones of my world; the overblown snare-drum reverb like a Learjet taking off, against my parents' laid-back, organic music; the crisp money against our austerity. Rock and roll was also simply a pattern, a 4/4 taint that infused my brain stem and has never left.

Almost immediately I fled into the space that heavy metal

opened. I took the difficulty of our homestead falling apart hard but mostly silently and alone. Shortly after my parents divorced, I began wetting the bed again following some consistent dry years. Neither of my parents seemed to connect the two events, and they hypothesized several physiological sources for the wet sheets. Perhaps I slept too deeply. Or maybe it was a milk allergy; for a summer I poured mucky beige Soy Moo over my Oatios. Then there was some hospital test of which all I remember is having to drink a bottle of castor oil the night before to clear out my system. That summer, Dad had come back to Aberdeen to work at some friends' law firm, and he and I lived in an efficiency apartment he imagined, charitably, as a "tree house." I remember it as a hothouse where I sweated nights in a pissy sleeping bag on an Army cot and choked down amaranth crackers, Soy Moo, and castor oil.

Another hypothesis for the bed-wetting was a weak bladder. I was back at Mom's during the school year, in a bigger apartment, the middle floor of a white house that had been split in three. I was prescribed an exercise where I drank a large plastic cup of water and held my pee until I almost wet my pants. In the end we solved my problem with a loud buzzing alarm connected to a metal screen under my sheets that went off at the first drop of moisture and woke me.

It was a passive-aggressive war, in which I caused headaches and extra trips to the Laundromat for my parents and they in turn put me through a battery of discomforts to punish me for acting out. I remember a few outright aggressive moves on my part, screaming, *I hate you*, in a tantrum. Once, around the time my parents first separated, I smashed a window at the United Family Farmers office with a hammer. Afterward I remember counting out dollar bills from my allowance like a game of solitaire to pay for the glass. The summer before Dad left for law school, he and I drove to Arizona to visit some friends who had left town. One day I scared everybody in our party by making as if to jump into a red-rock canyon. At Thanksgiving the next year, I kept running away into the streets of Sioux Falls, where Dad and I were visiting—my face in a photograph from that day is excruciatingly dark and sad. The only palliative that could keep me in the house before turkey dinner was the rare dose (for a TV-free kid) of MTV playing Aerosmith videos. It's no wonder I fell for heavy metal, a metered and melodic analog of my abrasive alarm, of *I hate you*, of a hammer through glass—a howl on the Plains.

But calling these common traumas war or heavy metal or a howl simultaneously exaggerates them and defuses them by reasoning them out or placing them inside a metaphor. Analogy is tricky that way. It seems to draw unfamiliar experiences nearer by linking them with familiar ones, and to heighten everyday experiences by linking them with exotic images or deep traditions. Yet categorizing and making metaphors can be done only from that airplane-window view, and thus by removing oneself from one's own life. It is connection that is actually disconnection.

This was the response I was beginning to learn in lieu of flailing a hammer or leaping into a canyon. I didn't have any confidants, and suicide and rebellion began to seem pointless and expensive, ghost dances that would result in massacre rather than a real return of the dreamland of youth. It's easy to emphasize the *ghosts*, the Apocalypse, and to neglect the *dance*. But certainly part of the lure of the Ghost Dance, and of ghost dances in general—these expressions of longing and nostalgia— must be the art, the rhythm, the poetry, of the breast-beating dance. It helps us forget, sure. But it also creates a new world for the one that was lost. Songs for a ghost dance keen and then they rouse: From memories they move to an aptly named *bridge*, in which imagination ferries us to a new place. For me, metaphor and distance from raw emotion—searching for restoration in the form of well-placed notes or lyrics, for instance— became viable defenses.[19]

One of my first songs, written for keyboard and vocals, was "We Are the Children of This World." It was a pretty bald rip-off of a ballad by White Lion, "When the Children Cry," except mine reversed the perspective from a guilty adult's to an innocent child's. Both songs lamented the destruction adults had wrought: implicitly, the Cold War, the burning of the Amazon, the hole in the ozone layer. But our verses were indistinct enough that the *fighting* and *hurt* could just as easily have referred to—and did refer to—the damage done to individual children by divorce, fights, and abuse. My song was silly but a little heartbreaking, if anyone had stopped to listen to it (I can remember the tune of the refrain but none of the words other than the title and something about *fighting ... every day*). Its lament over the state of the world was a clichéd displacement of a more particular, lonely despair. A ghost dance or a shattered window is at least quick with a spark of resistance, however futile. Metaphor seems like giving up, but it was the best option. Without intending to, I've cultivated it ever since in one way or another, mostly through music.

There were a couple of teenagers who had hung out at Prairie Dog Records, asking my parents to spin early heavy metal and hard rock on the store stereo and buying cassettes and LPs they liked. Dan Reed was a guitarist and singer who had a crush on one of the record-store employees, and Dan Pred was a drummer whose parents owned a coat store a couple of blocks up Main Street. Both were growing their hair long, and Dan Reed later spoke of driving around the straight rural roads outside Aberdeen, smoking bowls and blasting AC/DC. Six or seven years later, in 1988, the Dan Reed Network released their self-titled debut on Mercury Records. Reed and Pred had moved to Portland, Oregon, where Reed was born, and started a band with two black guys, a guitarist and a bassist, and a Japanese-American keyboardist—a strikingly cosmopolitan troupe (not to mention that Dan Reed was part American Indian, and Dan Pred was a rare South Dakota Jew), wearing scarves and fingerless gloves. The sound was markedly more synth pop than metal, more Prince 'n' Queen than Guns N' Roses, but here were Aberdeen kids who had become worldly rock stars. They had videos, "Ritual" and "Rainbow Child," on MTV. They were warming up for Bon Jovi, and then the Rolling Stones. Their example was an early inkling that I might leave for the sharp urban outside.

I was growing more removed from the world around me. Athletic talent was starting to matter, and promising athletes began to distinguish themselves around third and fourth grade; money, too, was becoming more important as trends caught on. I had not much of either. Mom believed I needed extra brain food and lobbied my teachers to give me "enrichment" and "gifted" work, which often involved me leaving my normal classroom or sitting in the back. We still didn't have a TV, and I was afraid someone would notice my plastic bedsheets and alarm box, so I didn't bring friends over much. I was the only kid obsessed with Warrant, White Lion, and Def Leppard; my peers were into the New Kids on the Block, Larry Bird, and Ninja Turtles. I lorded esoteric bits of knowledge over classmates in an unbecoming and antisocial way.

In the back of my third-grade classroom I saw a classified ad in *Boys' Life* where I could send for a free catalog of skateboarding gear. The California Cheap Skates catalog, a glossy half magazine of decks, trucks, wheels, and sneakers that came in the mail every few months, became my first foray into my own generation's subcultures. The consumer culture of skateboarding wasn't much edgier than glam metal: I was at least as attracted to the graphic design and fresh polyurethane as I was to the sport's radical repurposing of corporate landscapes for play and its anticapitalist slacker ethos. But more than the MTV music, skateboarding and its community led me, ultimately, to underground culture. I soon bought, for two dollars, a shredded Vision Shredder deck with blue grip tape from the high school brother of a neighborhood skater my age (the board's former owner later became a charismatic local punk rock guitarist under the name Jolt Revolta). Then I got a brandnew Santa Cruz deck for Christmas. I was wavering between my old Montessori friends, who were becoming jocks, and the neighbor kids who went to a different school and wore earrings and Anthrax T-shirts, but I didn't fit with either group.

Mom had a new friend who was stopping by more and more. Linda was the younger sister of one of Mom's good friends who had moved to Omaha. She had red-brown hair that hung straight and plain, and a deep, quiet voice that came out like a ventriloquist's, with her mouth nearly closed. I remember her riding up on a blue Cannondale with a startlingly thick frame—it was called a "mountain bike," she told me. She had other bikes, too, and had ridden cross-country; she had lived in Portland for a while before coming home to Aberdeen. Soon she started staying over, ghosting around the apartment and making me uneasy. Her meticulousness exceeded even Mom's, and I was forbidden to leave any clutter around. Mom continually asked me to turn down my little mono tape deck, even when it seemed almost inaudible.

Tarnishing the old ideals, Linda contrabanded a TV into Mom's bedroom; I didn't complain when it later moved to the living room. I was put on a quota of ten hours per week, and the three of us began spending many nights watching *Jeopardy!*, *Wheel of Fortune*, *MacGyver*, and *Matlock*. If I didn't want some hanging-out time to count against my quota, I had to sit alone in my room or the kitchen. I could hear the two of them laughing and would peek in to see them holding hands and drinking beers on the couch, a vintage L-shaped affair. I explained vaguely to Dad that Mom had just "decided" to get a TV after a decade without one.

One day, our landlady, Katie, left a note in thin, old-person slant script saying she wanted to speak with Mom about our water usage, which had increased. Our rent was based on just two of us living in the apartment. When Katie came over Mom sent me to my room, because she didn't trust me not to give a secret away with a face or a twitch. It seemed that Katie had all the power over us implied by her title *landlady*, and I was further intimidated by her snowy Republican coiffure and her suspicion. I listened with my door cracked as Mom explained that no, she didn't have anybody else living with us, it was just that I had dandruff and had to take extra baths with a special shampoo.

3.5

Even before I was told, I understood I was keeping a secret, from Dad, from my classmates, from anybody in town. As with the L.A. metal, I had a hazy comprehension of sexuality. But even the fact that Linda's bike saddlebags were called *panniers* seemed to sexually charge the situation—the word was French, and sounded like *panties*.

Finally, Mom took me for a walk to explain something. It was winter; I guess I was eight and a half. The trees were naked, and we walked by one of my classmates' houses.

"Honey, do you know what *gay* means?" Mom asked me.

"Um, happy?" I was playing dumb. I had heard the insults *gaywad* and *gaylord* thrown around at recess like dodgeballs. Plus, the previous summer—that of the tree house and castor oil—Dad and I had driven to New York and stayed with one of his college friends in a steamy SoHo loft, and the friend and his boyfriend slept in the same bed in their underwear. (On their roof I also posed wearing my prized black denim jacket for a photo I planned to submit to a "Who looks the most metal?" contest in *Metal Circus* or *Metal Edge* magazine.) Through some combination of intuition and whispered school-yard explanations, I knew pretty well what *gay* meant and what Mom was about to tell me.

She explained that some women love women and some men love men, that this was OK and natural. This dovetailed with the feminism she'd always instilled in me, with androgynous Christopher Robin. It was the next logical step from men and women being equals. Maybe she explained somehow that gays were discriminated against, that Katie could evict us for Mom's relationship with Linda, that Dad could take me away if he found out. Anyway, that was what I understood.

I was already losing my place as the object of Mom's attention, and this was a further threat. It stands to reason, looking back, that I must have been angry with both of my parents for creating this situation, but I really only remember fear. Did our neighbor in the basement have theories about the two women living upstairs? He was often gone, working on the Burlington Northern, but he was around enough to see something. During hunting season he hung and gutted a deer in our shared garage, leaving a blood mark on the cement and a ziplock bag of venison jerky for me. Might he tell Katie?

Linda's parents lived not far from us, and we would go over to eat homemade cake doughnuts or to watch the Super Bowl, whose halftime show that year featured 3-D images you could see only if you put on the glasses Coca-Cola had supplied to Kessler's supermarket. Did their daughter's friendship with Mom jump out at them?

I spent the next summer with Dad in Vermillion, the university town. One week I went out to a Methodist camp in the Black Hills. We all rode in a yellow school bus 350 miles from eastern South Dakota to Storm Mountain, and we stopped once along the interstate to pick up a couple of ranch kids. I remember they were named Quinn and Wyatt, and they said they lived thirteen miles apart and were thus "practically neighbors" — they could ride horseback to play together. The rest of us questioned these hicks incredulously as if they were from another country, which the thinning populace of rural America in essence was. I have been referring to my parents as homesteaders and playing with the history and mythology of South Dakota and the Plains more generally, but it's somewhat tongue in cheek. The cowboy-and-Indian period and the homesteader era, strong as their pull on our imaginations remains, had vanished. Strangely, though our lives differed little from those of our contemporaries in various parts of America, the grassland and its ghosts lingered powerfully, if peripherally. Quinn and Wyatt proved the rule; as I recall, they were already self-conscious about the precious rarity of their agricultural lives— *practically neighbors*, with a canny grin. I was probably more innocent of mass culture than they were, since I'd had a TV for only a few months at ten hours per week and had played video games only a handful of times at other kids' houses.

The next year would be my last with Mom, though only the moody Gaia of the landscape of motion knew it. Mom was now working at an alternative program at Aberdeen Central High School, where she wore Birkenstock sandals, carried a back-pack instead of a purse, and was known as the "granola lady." She and Linda began making plans to move to Portland, where such a getup would not be untoward.

We subscribed to the *Sunday Oregonian*, with its fertile forest of microprint classified ads: dreamed-of jobs for Mom and Linda, drums for me. Mom showed me tantalizing green brochures and researched schools. It turned out there was an arts magnet school called Buckman Elementary, where I could go for my last year before middle school. I had to write an essay and get teachers' recommendations for admission—it was like applying to college, which was when I had imagined my rock-star future would really get under way. Both Mom and I were thrilled when I got in, but I was not to tell Dad about any of our plans.

Portland promised to rocket me from the carob-tone early '80s to the sleek purple '90s. It seemed we would have more money there, and Mom was already acquiring nicer things: a vintage chrome table, a sparkling green Plymouth Volaré with a white soft top. I remember a can of USDA surplus commodity peanut butter that turned up from somewhere (a sign of poverty that was tastier than co-op peanut butter, if a bit shameful), but overall we seemed to be moving up. At the end of that year, for my tenth birthday—and perhaps as a reward for keeping our secrets?—I received as a gift one of the first children's mountain bikes in South Dakota, I'm sure: red like a Porsche and newer than anything I'd ever owned.

Portland was going to be a dream, a progressive paradise, home of the Dan Reed Network, an end to the secrecy and fear about Mom's lesbianism.

Dad's house, meanwhile, was frozen in amber (and remains so). He drove 'Mata into the ground and then bought a white Renault (aka White Rabbit) with high mileage but classy spokes on its hubcaps, the latter of which, of course, held no interest for him. I had no clue, since Linda disappeared every time he came to pick me up, but Dad had heard gossip about her living with us. He did not know about our plans to move over the summer. He'd spotted a copy of the *Oregonian* once when he fetched me for the weekend but hadn't put the pieces together. He found out about the move, rather unpleasantly, that spring when a deputy sheriff interrupted his law school graduation-day party to serve him with papers challenging their joint-custody arrangement and showing Mom's job prospects and my admission to Buckman Elementary. She was leaving in two weeks, and I was to follow at the end of the summer.

She ought to have known him well enough to predict that he would not roll over before her purported fait accompli. In fact, he had already begun researching custody cases involving lesbian mothers in the law school library and thinking about fighting for custody once he had settled into a lawyer job in the coming years. Instead of a simple move west to greener pastures, the summer became a disaster, with vicious fighting all around, lawyers, a psychologist, Dad studying for the bar exam and looking for jobs and not wanting to be bothered, as well as one glorious and peaceful month staying with my grannie (Dad's mother) in St. Paul, Minnesota, while I waited to find out where I would live the next year—to find out which parent and which place would "win" me.

FOUR

The Three Guys Who Knew

4.1

River Street, the winding main drag of Hot Springs, South Dakota, has businesses on only one side. They inhabit lovely, century-old red-sandstone-block buildings with pressed-tin ceilings and often vacant apartments upstairs. The buildings face crumbly cliffs of the same rusty quartzite color, streaked with white lime. Sunk in a trench between the street and the cliff, the Fall River runs clear like a weak broth—steaming in the winter—at 87 degrees Fahrenheit. Blake Stevens, my first friend in Hot Springs, lived with his mom and sister above Donnell's Art Supply, whose sandstone bricks were painted silver, on River Street. You entered the apartment from a long wooden staircase in the side alley.

Dad and I moved to Hot Springs that fall, at the start of my fifth-grade year, toward the end of my parents' brief but vicious fight over whether I should move to Portland with Mom and Linda, or to whichever South Dakota town had a law firm ballsy enough to hire a thirty-eight-year-old fresh out of USD

Law after a thirteen-year run of antinuclear, pro–family farm, pro-Indian, pro-environment hell-raising around South Dakota.

By way of a babysitter, a fellow skater, I graduated from hair metal to punk rock that summer, listening to Dad's two Dead Kennedys records so many times that he never played either of them again. The defiant weirdness of punk iridesced like a religion to me from my first exposure to its good word, the way reason and investigation did to teenage Willa Cather. It had the energy and anger of metal, but also ideals that were like our old ideals but snottier and more fun.

Late that summer I also scraped a few layers of skin from the left side of my body, face to shin, sliding like a needle sideways across an LP while trying to skateboard down a long hill—just weeks before Dad, ranked fifth in his law school class, was finally hired at a salary of $18,000 by a feisty Hot Springs lawyer who, years later, got into some trouble for, among other things, castrating a neighbor's bull that strayed onto his ranch, this surgery being technically legal under an obsolete but unrepealed law from early statehood days. (When it looked like this defense might not hold up, the surgeon-lawyer sent a ringer to do his overbidding when the now-steer was sold at auction, thus ruining his foe's claim of property damage.)

Hot Springs is in the southwest corner of South Dakota, in the southern Black Hills, nearly the farthest point in the state from Aberdeen. (Including Vermillion, in the southeast corner, I lived in three of the state's four corners in a matter of months.) It lay less than an hour's drive from Wyoming to the west, the Nebraska panhandle to the south, and the Pine Ridge Reservation to the east. Built in the Fall River valley and along various tributary creek beds where ponderosa pines grew like grizzled whiskers out of red mountains, Hot Springs had numerous hills almost impossible for a ten-year-old to bike up and too dangerous for him to skate down. I climbed 155 stairs up the bluffs on my walk to school each day. Many of the town's 4,300 residents lived in the State Veterans Home up Minnekahta Avenue or frequented the VA hospital atop another little mountain, and the weedy lots on VA Hill off the hospital campus shone with fragments of liquor bottles. The elderly cast to the town meant that the local school, and my pool of potential friends, was even smaller than the population would suggest.

Blake's mom, Mary, was the Welcome Wagon greeter and gave us an envelope full of coupons for local businesses. We went over to the apartment above Donnell's Art Supply for dinner a few times — once for a thick elk stew, a cream sauce with gamy sinews. Unlike us, the Stevenses had a television (my brief life of rationed TV was now history) and even cable and a Nintendo, so Blake and I played *Duck Hunt* or watched *SK8-TV* after dinner. He was two years younger but not much smaller, and soon we became good enough friends to fight, stretching T-shirts and straining headlocks over who played next — as close as I could come to sibling rivalry. I ignored the fact that he said "skate-eight TV," missing Nickelodeon's clever spelling, and rode a Variflex poseur board, the cheap kind from Pamida that was impossible to do tricks on. I pretended he had more than a fleeting interest in the rock bands I was discovering.

I stayed over at Blake's apartment once, early in the year. Mary was delighted to have me — her wagon gave an extra welcome to another single parent in town, a family that was neither the VA doctors with their nuclear families nor the moms in the trailer park on the east side of town who let their kids loiter around the hill of vets' broken Stolichnaya liters. Standing over a pot of macaroni and cheese, with her dark hair and blushed cheeks, she looked to me like a fortune-teller, though she was in fact a florist and a massage therapist. Blake and I sat on the old couch and slurped the macaroni with our eyes locked on Nickelodeon. The pro skaters on sunny West Coast half-pipes seemed terribly far away from my green Monopoly house on Cold Brook Avenue, one of three small houses in a red ravine, its yard a mass grave of dry Miller moths and box elder bugs with orange chevrons on their black backs, exoskeletons crunching underfoot. After eating some Hostess dessert I could never have convinced Dad to buy, Blake and I set to playing *Contra* on the Nintendo. Enthralled, bouncing when my "guy" jumped, I was oblivious to the connection between the guerrillas we picked out of the pixelated trees with M16s and Dad's red T-shirt that said, MY COUNTRY INVADED NICARAGUA, AND ALL I GOT WAS THIS LOUSY T-SHIRT.

It wouldn't be long before my own political peach fuzz sprouted. The Dead Kennedys, with their surfy leftist satire ("Kill the Poor," "Let's Lynch the Landlord"), were the beginning. That same year, in the space of a two-paragraph essay on the freedom of speech, I would defend Eugene V. Debs, 2 Live Crew, and flag burning. The next year I would interrupt sixth-grade geography to ask if we should really be talking about God in a public school. When the same teacher, Coach Raabe, later mentioned offhand how American Indians lived in free houses paid for by our tax dollars (a couple of Native students were in class at the time), I unwisely relayed the line to Dad. The next day, Coach Raabe held me after class and, sitting on the edge of his desk, arms crossed, sternly clarified that he had no racist intent, that I'd misunderstood. I trembled and nodded before bolting out the door, terrified and unapprised of Dad's quick call to chew him out.

When Mary told us it was time to get ready for bed, we reluctantly bade our freedom fighters night-night, changed into baggy Kmart wannabe skateboard pants, and went to brush our teeth. As I brushed beside the dull white sink, Blake took off his glasses and started combing the front of his brown hair into a breaking California wave. This struck me as absurd.

"Why are you combing your hair *before* bed? It's just going to get messed up." I was not immune to vanity; in fact, I was dying with impatience waiting for my bangs to grow long enough so I could flip them from my left eye with a skaterly toss of the head like the shredders out west, not to mention the two years I had to wait before Dad would let me get my ear pierced. "Is it for all the girls in your dreams?"

"I don't know. Yeah," Blake replied, examining his work in the mirror from different angles. Both of us were runty and not particularly interested in girls yet (we had ignored his sister, who was my age, all evening), but primping for girls seemed like what boys were supposed to do. Watching cable and playing Nintendo and eating Hostess dessert, I felt a soothing normalcy about the evening. It was a relief after the last year in Aberdeen with Mom and the secrets we kept.

Now, by autumn, I was brushing junk food off my teeth at a sleepover, a calming sign.

Blake and I returned to his room, where I sat on my sleeping bag on the brown carpet and he sat on his bed. We talked about what we should name our band. I favored the Vegetarian Cannibals or the Styrofoam Zebras, and he halfheartedly assented to whatever. He was the first real bandmate I'd had, but in his apathy was not entirely unlike the imaginary bandmates I had drawn for my cartoon band, Toxic. I had already written a handful of new songs on my keyboard ("Save the Elephants": *So say you're very sorry / For taking their i-vorry...*), and eventually my enthusiasm, and the Styrofoam Zebras, would win out with Blake. I, the only child, would play keyboard and sing, and he would, well, sing along.

In a lull, out of nowhere as he sat on his bed, Blake cocked his head, looked down at me on my sleeping bag, and asked, "Is it true that your mom ran off with another lady?"

My eyes widened a bit and my guts clenched, though I tried to look relaxed. I already had a year of practice evading Dad's general questions about my life with her.

"No," I said. He must have been satisfied with my answer; or maybe he sensed how I froze, and knew that he would shortly be choking in a headlock, his California wave being yanked out by the roots, if he pushed it further. The question never came up again.

From that night on, I knew people might be talking, even though in years to come nobody in South Dakota would ever leak the gossip to me or confront me with an awkward question about my mom. We are a polite people. Yet Mary Stevens had given Dad a button to hang on his button collection—a crowded masterpiece of brown burlap on our living room wall—that said, IN A SMALL TOWN, IT'S NO SOONER DONE THAN SAID. It hung there, hidden among NO NUKES, the six-inch LBJ-for-president pin, and F*CK CENSORSHIP.

I believed that Mom and Linda had moved to Portland because talking about this subject in South Dakota was completely off-limits. That crucial summer, once the battle began and I was sent to a psychologist to tease out my reluctant opinions on the situation, nobody prepped me for Dr. Arbes's question, out of nowhere like Blake's, "How do you feel about your mother's relationship with Linda?" I think I gasped. I didn't know if I had slipped and given something away; otherwise, how had Dad, and thus Dr. Arbes, found out? Perhaps to preserve some semblance of the secret, I lied and told him that Mom had never talked to me about her relationship with Linda. It felt like an interrogation, and when Dr. Arbes concluded at our final appointment that it seemed I was not in fact comfortable with Linda, it was an indictment. I was implicitly guilty of prejudice (a grave sin in our family) and of not being comfortable with my own mother; as punishment, I would lose her.

After the question came up again at the sleepover with Blake, I was furious with Dad. He had clearly gossiped to Mary, even justified his divorce with my secret. But I wasn't about to confront him, to bring up the subject that had finally uprooted and overturned my entire life. Though I didn't know it, my parents were still fighting (by mail, without actually speaking) over the agreement they'd begun when Mom decided her chances in court were hopeless. She finally signed under threat that he would not send me on my first trip to Portland that Christmas.

The Styrofoam Zebras gradually broke up, or Blake and I stopped hanging out. The final break came when he crowed the chorus of "Save the Elephants" in a sarcastic nasal tone in front of his sister when we were over at his apartment for dinner.

"You said you liked it," I said.

Soon I befriended kids in my own grade, particularly a skateboarder who was a doctor's son and a jock, and two girls: the daughter of a rancher and a VA employee; and the daughter of a biker and a Mormon. The smallness of our town democratized social groups in a way that would have been unlikely in Portland. The application process at the arts magnet school, for instance, would have filtered out much of the social diversity that being in a city presumably provides.

By sixth grade, I hung out with the few high schoolers in Hot Springs who wore flannel shirts and Chuck Taylor sneakers. We were a mélange of subcultures: a blond skater boy who painted BASS on the rearview mirror of his gray Grand Prix and listened to the Geto Boys; my hero, a senior girl who went to punk shows in Rapid City and counted the days before she moved to Seattle; the older sister of the rancher's daughter, a Danzig fan; an evangelical skater who introduced me to Australian Christian death metal (Mortification) and Christian punk rock (One Bad Pig, Crashdog); and my jock friend's older brother, a Depeche Mode fan whose effeminacy resulted in him moving to Denver after the BASS skater spray-painted FAG on his house in pink letters. He actually was gay, it turned out, and almost twenty years later I learned that my hero's mother had lived with a lesbian partner before we moved to town. My dad tells me there were plenty of other gays in Hot Springs as well. Had I known any of this, the stab of fear I felt about friends like Blake finding out about Mom might have relented. But of course if we had lived in a culture where such information was available to everyone, and wouldn't result in hate crimes, there would have been little to fear.

Under the umbrella of "alternative," there was a ragtag community I fit into, and an ethos on which I could hopefully build the sort of *take that* guts that Willa Cather got from investigation. We rebel adolescents hung around the parking lot of the shuttered Piggly Wiggly, practicing rail slides on slick yellow cement parking blocks or just sitting around for hours after school doing nothing. Once, we found a box of fluorescent light tubes and dropped them from an embankment into the parking lot to hear them pop. Another time we hunched through a four-foot drainage tunnel under downtown Hot Springs to the Fall River. After five o'clock we sometimes skated over to Norwest Bank to use the curbs at the drive-thru for other trick attempts.

In sixth grade, for a short period, some other friends my own age got on a shoplifting kick at SunMart, Bison Barn, Coast to Coast, and other businesses. Mostly candy, which we sold at school. By the time I finally got the nerve to steal something myself, somebody at school told his parents, who told Dad, who scared the bad out of me when he confronted me. I told him that all I stole was a fishing lure from Coast to Coast (I stuck to this lie so faithfully that I don't remember what I actually stole, though it was truly minimal). He took me to the store to confess, and they rang up the twenty-nine-cent lure that I, trembling, pointed out on the shelf. I paid for it with a dollar bill. Again, antisocial behavior seemed not to be worth the terror, and I began learning to play the drum set after school in the band room instead.

4.2

Partway through seventh grade, Dad and I moved on to Pierre; things with the bull-castrating boss didn't work out after all, and Dad found a job at Dakota Plains Legal Services as the lawyer in their only off-rez office. Pierre was three times the size of Hot Springs; it also curled around a river, but here it was the Missouri, a giant rattler to the Fall River's garter snake. Pierre was dead center in South Dakota, on that dividing line between East River and West River, central and mountain time, wholly exposed to the wind and weather—*nothing to keep the elements at bay.* It could be 110 in the summer and 35 below in winter. Purple hailstorms galloped up from West River ranch land and trampled East River crops for five minutes before continuing east.

On my first day of school in Pierre, a rugged-looking girl passed me a note requesting that I check the box of which group I fit into: jock, prep, geek, or headbanger. Pierre was big enough to have more rigid castes than Hot Springs; plus, being the capital gave it a bureaucratic, political culture unlike the libertarian free-for-all of Hot Springs. I declined to choose officially but was initially about two-thirds headbanger, one-third geek, with a sliver of prep thrown in by my good grades and behavior. My life revolved around skateboarding and alternative and punk rock. I spent most afternoons skating with various new friends, again primarily at banks. It was odd that these most sterile of businesses, with gray carpets and fake plants in their lobbies, could become pagan dance grounds with the addition of an imperceptible veneer of wax on the curbs. Bill Janklow had legalized usury, but we still clattered together a culture in its midst. The best skate spot was the "Advantage," an early ATM hut on an irregular concrete island in the middle of the Sooper Dooper grocery parking lot. Within weeks of my moving to Pierre, my photo made the front page of the *Capital Journal,* picturesquely mid-ollie, arms raised like goose wings, on the capitol steps.

By this time I'd spent two summers, Christmases, and spring breaks in Portland, which in the early 1990s teemed with youth wearing long johns under army-green cutoff shorts and T-shirts for lush Northwest bands like Pond, Seaweed, and Soundgarden. The Dan Reed Network had turned out to be a rather dim flash in the pan, and now the sleek synth-rock late '80s—even synthesizers themselves—seemed obsolete compared with real angst. We'd leapt from clean transistor amplifiers to Humbucker pickups and warm, gritty tubes. The summer following seventh grade, after half a year in Pierre, Mom took me to Lollapalooza, where she read a novel in the grass behind the Forum tent (Timothy Leary was speaking inside, but she wasn't interested in that part of the counterculture anymore) and made me check in after each set: Rage Against the Machine, Babes in Toyland, Dinosaur Jr., Arrested Development, Primus, Alice in Chains.

Portland was a cornucopia of foliage and culture, and my experiences there made me something of a Johnny (Rotten) Appleseed at Pierre Junior High. I brought the first seven-inch records of various subgenres—ska, emo, pop-punk—into town like a pioneer making the desert bloom, and introduced my new friends to the scene in Rapid City.

I felt a homesteader's satisfaction after importing Operation Ivy or vegetarianism to one of the best pheasant-hunting locales in the country (I didn't know that the Chinese pheasant, too, was exotic, despite being our state bird). But some things I withheld. I'd attended, for instance, the Portland Gay Pride parade a couple of years in a row and been thrilled by the release of chanting, "Two, four, six, eight / What makes you think your teacher's straight?" with Mom and the other Educators for Equity. I'd made rainbow-bead necklaces out of Fimo clay and earned almost a hundred dollars selling them at a protest against Measure 9, a proposed constitutional amendment that would have required Oregon's government to discourage "abnormal, wrong, unnatural and perverse" sexual behavior. I'd met kids who had grown up since birth with two moms, who had rock-climbing footholds riveted to their bedroom walls. I'd gone to a New Age church camp called Unique You with kids who thought it was cool to say they were bisexual. What would Quinn and Wyatt have thought?

At Unique You, Mom came along as a chaperone, not wanting to lose an entire week of my visit, but she gave me a measure of independence there. I soon attached myself to alt-hippie teenagers as I'd done in Hot Springs; they adopted me as their elfin punk mascot, calling me by my camp-designated "Native American name," Laughing Star. (I still associate the term *Native American* with such blasé pillaging of some misty notion of Indian culture—all-white sweat lodges, Chief Seattle quotes, day-camp dream catchers—and thus usually avoid it nowadays.) They consoled a crying star when the talent show organizer forbade me to sing my favorite Red Hot Chili Peppers song, "Give It Away," because of its lecherous lyrics.

When we returned to Portland from camp, I rode the light rail to visit my two teen friends in the suburbs. We watched *Hair* and made Fimo beads on tin TV trays. After a couple of hours, the three of us walked to 7-Eleven for a Slurpee break, and the girl held my hand while I balanced on a parking lot curb. Suddenly, she looked at me and asked, "How come your dad is a homophobe?"

"Huh? I don't know," I said. More impossible questions. I'd only just learned the word *homophobe*, and I flushed with shame. Dad had recently written Mom snidely that he would "spare you any disparaging remarks" about her New Age megachurch, and my Sunday school teacher there with AIDS, so the charge wasn't entirely inapt. But I couldn't summon toward Mom the fury I'd felt for Dad after Blake asked about her running off with another lady—though she had now apparently bad-mouthed Dad to some teenagers. I could never muster an ounce of blame for her; I couldn't shake the sense of my own culpability for mishandling the secret. Stone-faced, I tried to stanch her crying each time I got on a flight back to drab South Dakota. Living in a supposedly homophobic house most of the time, I was evidently not Portland material; but it was clear I wasn't South Dakota material either.

James Farrell was the second guy in South Dakota who knew. He wore his straight brown hair cut into an alternative wedge (having recently graduated from a bizarre calico dye job), accessorized with plum-colored Doc Martens and Smashing Pumpkins T-shirts. He was a year ahead of me at Pierre Junior High, and he had the freest living arrangement of anyone in school. Though I never talked about it with him, I had heard rumors about his broken family *(in a small town, it's no sooner done than said)*. He and his siblings had been distributed to foster homes.

James was placed with two young Romanian Seventh-day Adventist foster parents—a dentist and his wife—who lived on the rich side of town in a blue house shaped like Pizza Hut. Being cooler than middle-aged parents, they allowed our motley crew to descend on the Pizza Hut house. Diseased, a grindcore quartet with which my own bands would later share many bills, played one of their first shows in that basement. During a break I played a bass guitar in public for the first time, trying the cursive bass line from the Breeders song "Cannonball." Another friend, Anthony, and I used to wrestle incessantly at the Pizza Hut house until one time when he punched the top of my head and broke his hand. Anthony's dad was a nationally known hunting and fishing guide who, despite being a Republican, had worked with my dad on some environmental campaigns. The red cast on Anthony's trigger hand left him with nothing to do on a hunting trip, so he brought me, the vegetarian friend, along for the weekend to ride four-wheelers around a farm north of Bismarck, North Dakota.

We also hung out a lot with Jackie and Jenny, two girls who had recently crossed into the territory of alternative. Once, I persuaded Jackie to bring me a jar of blue Manic-Panic hair dye from Rapid City. We were about to dye my hair in her white, columned faux-classical house, but her mother stopped us. We decided the solution was to go to the YMCA and dye my hair in the women's bathroom near the front doors. Just as she put the dye in my hair, some young girls walked in, pointed at me, and said, "That's not a girl!" I darted out into the January sub-zero, laughing hysterically with the blue glop freezing into cake icing on my head. The dye set while Jackie drove me home in her minivan, and I snuck in and rinsed it in my upstairs bathroom, ending up with green hair before Dad was the wiser.

James's foster parents always enjoyed my willingness to try seitan and ersatz meatballs. They were vegetarians for religious reasons, and I had become one at Unique You. James wouldn't touch the stuff; they stocked a cabinet with SpaghettiOs for him. All of this I think of as a spotty reliquary of teen counter-culture in Pierre: assembled from whatever idols (records, dye, seitan) were smuggled in, and expressed as band names scribbled on Anthony's cast, the YMCA punk hair salon, and Christian sect meals turned alt-veg. If a "counterculture sanctuary" like Prairie Dog Records was bound to fail in a town so small, then we would worship provisionally and almost illicitly.

In the summer of 1994, after I'd finished eighth grade and James ninth, he asked to join me on my annual summer commute to Portland. It was, after all, princess to the bounteous alternative queen, Seattle, and he had some relatives nearby. I yearned to connect my two worlds (hence the punk rock evangelizing), to show someone the awesome record stores and Hawthorne Boulevard, where everybody you passed was either a hippie or a punk, but I was terrified. If he was staying at Mom and Linda's house for a week, he'd have to know why they shared a bedroom and had issues of *Just Out* on the coffee table.

Dad, in his romance for the America of yore, suggested that James and I hop a westbound Amtrak and offered to drive us three hundred miles north to Minot, an Air Force town in desolate upper North Dakota—the Empire Builder's nearest stop. We pulled into Minot late the evening before the train passed through town and ate a Country Kitchen supper more suited to James's eating habits than mine. Once the three of us retired to a motel room, Dad (the democrat) allowed the majority to watch MTV; we heard the new alternative single, an Offspring song with an ominous snake-charmer guitar lick. Then we watched the news to learn that Bill Janklow had won the Republican primary for South Dakota governor and, after an eight-year hiatus from elected office, would likely be moving back to Pierre for at least four—as it turned out, it would be eight—more years. I would be living less than a mile from my old bogeyman.

I kept setting deadlines to tell James. First it had been before we left Pierre, then before we boarded the train. We stretched our legs playing Hacky Sack on the station platform, the Empire Builder pulled in, and I still hadn't done it. I didn't want to tell him in front of Dad, who may have been concerned about this disclosure, too, but never said anything. For all he knew, I'd told all my friends already; I was audacious with my wardrobe (Hawaiian shirts, a T-shirt depicting a purple-Mohawked punk puking, "utility" pants with ten inches of slack in the waist, a paisley jester's hat) and at times with my opinions, so it was possible I'd blasted through South Dakota teen prejudices on this subject.

Once we settled in our seats, I'd do it. We had twenty-six hours to discuss the fact as we traversed the northernmost tier of the continental U.S. from North Dakota to the wide-open Hi-Line of Montana, along the Canadian border, gilt wheat fields and prairies so big you could see the curve of the earth. (Surveyors have added doglegs every twenty or so miles on the straight north-south roads on the Plains to account for the narrowing of the meridians. They're often the only curves on these roads.) At Havre, Montana, that afternoon, we stepped off the train for a twenty-minute break. Just north of us lay the Cypress Hills region where the writer Wallace Stegner lived as a child, a "flat, empty, nearly abstract" world where any human was "a challenging upright thing, as sudden as an exclamation mark, as enigmatic as a question mark."[1] Though I didn't have words for it, I was familiar with that lonely, punctuating sense.

James and I rolled on into the Rockies, the western wall of the Plains, then Glacier National Park at sunset, Coeur d'Alene and Spokane in the middle of the night, and daybreak again in the Columbia Gorge. Here was the story of Western expansion forged into two rails, false as it was—my triannual shuttling back and forth from South Dakota to Portland was a more apt distillation of the region's nomadic settlement and unsettlement than a one-way "Empire Builder." The train's namesake was James J. Hill, the railroad baron who sparked the land rush to the Hi-Line; most of the settlers, Wallace Stegner's family included, failed and left, so the empire Hill built was pretty fleeting.[2] The myth wasn't. Riding the Empire Builder myself, I couldn't admire the wondrous West or even mock the drunk, washed-up glam dude with a long frosted perm walking the aisle and talking about "monkey tentacles." I felt like I had an ulcer.

The seats in coach were comfortable, with leg rests and a greater recline than airplane seats. (I was by now familiar with the quicker routes to Portland, and had been stranded in Denver and Salt Lake City in blizzards, eating personal pan pizzas with the other Unaccompanied Minors.) Still, I couldn't sleep. I tried right side up, then with my head on the blue vinyl footrest and my feet elevated, which strangely seemed better proportioned. I faked sleep through the dark, dry-mouth hours. At last the sun came up over eastern Washington, but I still hadn't told James. He seemed to sleep all right.

We pulled into Union Station in Northwest Portland a little ahead of schedule, pulled our backpacks and my bass in its pleather gig bag from the overhead bins. I lagged a little as James crossed to the century-old train station, sandstone bricks and cathedral ceilings under a looming clock tower. He walked through the doors into the public hall. Now it was too late.

But Mom wasn't there yet. We sat on a long oak bench to wait.

"There's something I should tell you about my mom." I hesitated. "She's, like . . ."

"Strict?" James asked, a little bemused.

"Well, yeah, a little bit. But she's also—she lives with . . . She's, like . . ."

James laughed nervously.

"She's, like, um . . . She's, like, gay."

"Really? That's funny, man." His mouth stretched over his braces in a stifled smile. He asked if she lived with a girlfriend, and, relieved, I nodded yeah. The adrenaline fuel shut off and my face started to cool. The fact that he didn't say it was disgusting, didn't start looking for a ticket back to Pierre, was a relief, but there were still two months after he left Portland when I wouldn't be around to control the damage if he decided to tell my friends, for whom *faggot* and *queerbait* were routine slams.

Other than Linda's quiet and nerve-racking presence, Mom's neat bungalow, with its tended lawn and tasteful decor, even the television, was more normal and presentable than Dad's and my house. Linda pruned the rhododendrons, pulled stems of clover out of the grass by hand, and edged sharp outlines to the yard around the sidewalks. Instead of Dad's HINCKLEY FOR PRESIDENT poster (a bizarre piece of his collection of Americana, featuring the slogan "He's had a shot at the man; Let's give him a shot at the job"), his dusty, forty-year-old stuffed wallaby, and the button collection, Mom's house had a fireplace and a couple of landscape watercolors on the wall. The outdoor trim *was* purple, but that seemed hip, like James's Docs. Mom wasn't butch-looking; she was still the granola lady with long hair and "flowy" clothes. She was socially charming and knew how to bake. One had to go looking for her eccentricities, unlike Dad's: She used a deodorant crystal, which lay in a velvet bag in a homeopathic- and herb-stocked medicine cabinet; she kept Goddess Cards and Animal Spirit Cards tucked into a bookshelf.

James seemed unfazed when Linda came home from work that afternoon. She was like a silent draft that made me uneasy in their house, and I kept the yard-sale boom box they put in my room there almost inaudible as I had years before. But James was cordial and easygoing, and he charmed Mom and Linda—as well as a lesbian tech-ed teacher who worked at the middle school where Mom was a guidance counselor, and her partner, when they came over for barbecued salmon and Gardenburgers. James's week in Portland turned out to be anticlimactic after my epic and perilous psychic Oregon Trail journey west. Mom had already become Portland's biggest cheerleader (which often felt like pressure to speak up and ask to move there) and made a splendid tour guide. As planned, we explored alternative Portland, 2nd Avenue Records, the 24-Hour Church of Elvis, and a Victorian house–coffee shop called the Pied Cow.

Never another word about Mom after James flew back to Pierre. We never erased the trip from history, just left it like failed settlers and let grasses and weeds grow in around the wagon ruts. Three-fourths of a prairie's mass hides in its roots, buried around old rusted ranch tools, arrowheads, and fossils. It is this high ratio of underground to aboveground that maintains the ecosystem in dry years—when roots are unearthed we risk a Dust Bowl, or slower erosion that is cumulatively as dramatic. My secret stayed unexcavated, protected from the hooves of teenage cruelty or wildfire gossip, as far as I knew. It was odd that James was the first person I told. He was not my closest friend, just the one who had the inclination to visit Portland. After he started high school that fall, the two of us grew into different social circles, both decidedly more mainstream than our skater-headbanger clique in junior high. It was clear that I wouldn't be a leper when I got home, but it was somehow unsettling to know I wasn't the only person who could dig up the secret. I felt the sharp point of James's knowledge any time we saw each other, but I suppose he was sympathetic to keeping family business private. That was what we did.

When I returned from Portland, something amazing happened. A couple of guys from my grade, Eric and Mike, were starting a band and had heard that I played bass. They weren't veteran punk rockers but had jumped on the bandwagon after Green Day sold out—I would have described the band signing to a major label just so matter-of-factly back then—and the Offspring and Rancid had major hits. Nonetheless, I was overjoyed to be in a band, for the first time after five long years of hypothetical songwriting in my bedroom, mimicking guitar parts with a *jzzhhh* sound and beatboxing drum parts.

In Mike's basement, Stickman wrote a set's worth of songs fairly quickly that year, learning to play our instruments as we went. Before he learned chords, Eric played single-note guitar lines. I practiced to play and simultaneously sing my absurdist or secretive lyrics. Our big early hit was "Someday, Sometime": *Someday I hope to be a real live logger / So I can be just like a small Paul Bunyan / I'll get up at the crack of dawn and rush to the kitchen / And indulge myself in a big dish of flapjacks / Flapjacks, flapjacks, I could go on forever eating flapjacks / Flapjacks, flapjacks, enough for me and my twin brother, Simon.* The idea of having a twin brother had intrigued me for years, from the imaginary friends when I was three to a book I wrote and illustrated in fourth grade about teenage twin brothers who were skateboarding FBI agents. Perhaps the singular weirdness of my existence begged the *Is this real?* confirmation an alter ego could provide, or maybe I felt the split of who I was in Portland versus who I was in South Dakota as a sort of twinship.

Stickman played its first show at a classmate's birthday

party at the Elks Lodge, where her dad was a member. The next year, we collaborated with Diseased and shelled out seventy-five dollars to rent the lodge ourselves to put on a real show. It was miraculously successful, with kids from all the castes moshing like equals. Stickman replaced skateboarding in my heart, and my bandmates and their circle became my not-so-anti-establishment friend group. I was more timid and diplomatic than I had been at eleven, less audacious than at thirteen—in politics, wardrobe, and so on. I still stood out, but I almost never confronted or offended.

4.3

The only one of the three guys who could be considered a con-fidant was Isaac "Boo" Vogel. I told him my mom was gay when I had just six months left in Pierre before leaving for college. This was as far as my courage developed there, after lying to Blake, telling James under duress, and berating myself for my cowardice compared with my dad's political stridency and my mom's liberation: one voluntary confession.

Boo and I became best friends in a troupe of teenage boys who got good grades and didn't drink, but who drove around listening to punk and inventing pranks. We'd take the loop north of town along the roads numbered 1804 and 1806 for Lewis and Clark's ascent and descent of the Missouri, and cross the Oahe Dam, a colossal earthen berm holding the river back almost to Bismarck. Our group made outlandish home movies about fallen and redeemed rock stars or about romances with an oscillating fan (I missed some of the best high jinks when I was in Portland on school breaks), and a grinning trio of us called the Guitar Bandits busked for change at the exit to the state capitol at five o'clock one Friday afternoon as state workers left their offices. A confused, buffalo-chested security guard sent us packing, so we *went across / to the Joe Foss*—another state office building. *I guess we showed that guy who's boss,* we related in our eponymous theme song, which we later performed at a couple of city concerts and talent shows by storming the stage (with permission) wearing kerchiefs over our faces: *Just three honor roll teens / On a roll for fun.*

Boo and I also had a "deep" side, when the two of us would hang out and dissect the hypocrisies of our classmates or complain about our friend Matt giving us monkey bumps and wedgies or farting in the car and child-locking the power windows. Once, in my living room, sitting in Dad's antique rocking chair with the Navajo tapestry on it, Boo broached a subject that was close to every teenage boy's heart, or hand, but that everyone else avoided as if even discussing it would make them go blind. "So... I'm not the only one in this room who...?" he ventured, after we tacitly acknowledged that I knew what he was talking about.

I think it was Boo's inability to let sleeping dogs lie and his notion of confession as intimacy—anomalous characteristics in our town—that gave me an itch to confide in him. It marred the closest friendship I'd ever had to keep this from him, but I didn't want to lose the friendship either. Boo's dad was deputy secretary of Social Services in Janklow's administration, a laconic hulk who seemed to sit in his recliner every night watching the Atlanta Braves. My own dad had told me that Mr. Vogel favored cutting welfare and had the power to do it, and I figured Mr. Vogel knew Dad's politics from his bumper stickers and frequent letters to the editor. I interpreted his silence as disapproval.

Boo himself never left a silence to be interpreted. In one of the summaries of my parent-teacher conferences that Dad sent to Mom, he reported that my trig teacher had noted my "slight tendency to talk in class, mostly with his friend Boo Vogel (who never shuts up), but Mr. Drube says Josh will quiet down if he asks him to." We endlessly imitated Drube's *Prairie Home Companion* voice, sighing, "Josh and Boo, would you *cut* it out?" Like almost everybody, Boo had no aversion to using *fag* as a rough substitute for *dipshit*, or *gay* for *lame*. But since there were no *out* gays in town—just a few dozen speculation cases—it was hard to say how he might feel toward them.

Once, Boo and I had been riding in the maroon Mitsubishi of the third Guitar Bandit, Mike (also the drummer of Stickman and of our newer band, His Trusty Steed), and somehow Mike and I had gotten in an argument about whether homosexuality was a sin. I may have started it, feeling for cracks in my shell of silence. We cruised east on Capitol Avenue. Boo was riding shotgun, and I leaned up from the middle of the backseat as the melodic jackhammer of NOFX's skate-punk blared from the speakers. "They're born that way," I insisted. "How could it be a sin?"

"They don't have to act on it," Mike said.

"They can't help it. It's like being born with six fingers," I said, hating myself for being so cowardly and abstract and hoping at the same time that this analogy seemed to show enough distaste that he wouldn't suspect *me* of being gay myself.

"Just 'cause you have six fingers doesn't mean you have to jack off," Mike said, as if there were any possibility that any of the three of us didn't. I don't remember Boo joining in this argument. Boo was the only one of the Bandits who had kissed a girl or drunk a beer. He was handsome and charming—he

looked like a small Leonardo DiCaprio with dark blue eyes—
but with his impulsive and critical tongue he had burned so
many bridges that his dating prospects in a one-school town
were limited. I supposed Mike's purity came from having conservative Catholic parents as old as most people's grandparents.

The summer before senior year, Dad and I had taken a
wildlife trip to Tanzania with some money his mother gave
him. While driving back eight hours from Minneapolis, the
closest international airport, Dad and I were debating some
theoretical or political point related to homosexuality. Often
such debates served as nonthreatening surrogates for the more
painful struggle long past, the way my songs often did. Neither
of us had ever mentioned Mom's lesbianism in seven years living together.

"You know," Dad said, "we've discussed sexuality before,
but one thing we've never discussed is your mom's sexuality."

"Yeah, we *haven't* talked about it," I responded a bit sharply.
Dad interpreted this as *What took you so long?* but it may have
simply been the first directionless pressure bursting out of a
sealed emotional chamber. At some unspoken level I resented
both of my parents for the secret I had to keep. I resented the
blithe confidence both of them had in their rightness. I resented
that during the custody fight Dad had hoisted a sail to take
advantage of antigay westerlies he didn't really believe in. But
in this momentous discussion—a first break—I couldn't artic-
ulate how I felt about the whole situation. I'd never talked it
out, but this was a start.

Once school began, I staged a tentative challenge to the
unspoken antigay climate when I "came out" about Mom to
our minister at Oahe Presbyterian Church. Pastor Jeff was helping me research my not-Catheresque-enough paper comparing

the Protestant Church's shifting doctrines on slavery and women clergy, and implicitly predicting a similar shift in its current prohibitions on homosexuality. I figured Dad had already told Pastor Jeff about Mom anyway, and he confirmed this. Jeff patiently told me that he himself had once had long hair, that Jesus was a radical, and that it was natural to question our elders. He believed our society overemphasized sexual sins as worse than other common sins (lying, coveting, idolizing money)...*but* sin was still sin. He advised me that "sometimes our elders *do* know something."

(When I turned eighteen later that year, Pastor Jeff proved his longhair bona fides, writing a letter and sealing it for his files to the effect that I was registering for selective service with serious moral qualms about war. Presumably if the draft had ever restarted, I could have used this in a conscientious-objector petition.)

I waited a few days after returning from Portland at Christmas our senior year to tell Boo. I knew in my head it would be fine, we were almost adults, times had changed (Ellen DeGeneres had just come out on TV), and Boo was open-minded; but the fear was primal, in my muscles. The first time anybody ever found out, I lost my mom. I was just about to reach for the occasion to confess, and my hand drew back like something would burn it.

"I have something I need to tell you," I said one January day. I led him up to the third bedroom of our old yellow house—Dad's office, which, like my pumpkin-patch room, had a slanted ceiling and a bare bulb with a pull chain hanging from it. Isaac found this setting peculiar; we had never hung out in that room before. As the chain snapped against the porcelain fixture, the room lit up yellow, the stain-yellow paint

Dad had chosen for the walls and ceiling and the buffalo-grass shag carpet we'd inherited from the house's previous owner. Dad had bought a used amber-and-black-screen computer without Windows (although this was already 1998) and a dot-matrix printer, a recent upgrade from his nonelectric typewriter. All of the markers of my foreignness that Isaac already knew about and accepted, even admired, hung like a funk in the close room.

"There's something big you don't know about me," I began. I detected worry and confusion on his face. There was no going back: "I never told you this before, but my mom is gay."

"So?" he said without hesitating. "I don't care. It's no big deal."

I relaxed a little and nodded. Again, nothing even close to what my stomach had warned me might happen. I would have been ready for a physical attack. We faced each other for a second like boxers.

"I thought you were going to tell me *you* were."

Starting to gain my composure and the preachiness that called my friends out when they impugned the Indians on welfare or "objectified" (in Portland lingo) girls too crassly, I rejoined, "Would that have mattered?"

"Sort of," he allowed, wrinkling his nose. "It would be sort of weird."

This was the other part of what gunned the adrenaline when the prospect of "coming out" arose: that people would think or say *I* was gay, or even that deep down I actually was. After being a bit of a prepubescent lady-killer in Hot Springs, I'd had only one girlfriend in Pierre, and it had taken roughly the same sort of *heave-ho* to ask her out that it took to tell James or Boo about Mom. Eva and I had passed each other triangle-folded notes and held hands once at James's Pizza Hut house when his foster parents weren't home; we never kissed. She dumped me, she wrote in a last note, because I was so timid and we were already just friends anyway.

How would I know what it felt like to be gay? It could be hereditary. I had a chaotic crescendo of sex in my own body; I liked girls, thought about girls, but then again, at one point Mom had married a man.

Mom had seeded all sorts of other warnings and guidelines about sex over the years: Sex can ruin a relationship, don't have sex for two years, don't objectify women. When I was in tenth grade, she had broken up with Linda, so it seemed even the relationship she'd chosen over our own had been a mistake. I was a teenager when she told me she assumed her child would be a girl, her "little feminist." I may have been sitting on her lap as she told me this; even when I was fully grown, she never tired of jokingly calling me her little boy, pronounced in baby talk like "widow boy."

"Were you disappointed that I was a boy?" I asked.

"No, not at all," she said. "I just figured I'd raise a little boy feminist."

That was what I was trying to be, a widow boy feminist. It was easy to disagree with Dad about all of his strange choices; but I didn't have the perspective or the courage to disobey Mom's wishes, even though (or perhaps because) I didn't see her much. She had already lost me; I couldn't bear to disappoint her on top of that. From my side, she was already 95 percent gone. How could I give up the other 5 percent?

But being a boy feminist felt oxymoronic, especially a heterosexual teenage widow boy feminist. There was a fine line between attraction and objectification, if any line at all. I wouldn't dare tell Mom I thought a girl was hot. *Stunning* was the word she used for actresses and such—it sounded much less threatening—but I couldn't reasonably say to the Guitar Bandits, "Gee, guys, that Molly sure is stunning." And biting my lip up in the upstairs bathroom at home thinking about some girl in biology, that was practically sexual assault.

I was left to stake out some impossible middle ground that might have looked something like being gay. A self-hating straight, or an androgynous Christopher Robin. Boo told me later that the thought of my being gay had crossed his mind before I told him about Mom. In the world of South Dakota men like Boo's dad and the security guard at the capitol, I was queer in other ways: unathletic but not typically nerdy; poor in most every way that mattered to us as teenagers but also suspiciously well traveled (besides Oregon and most all of the American West, I'd been on the trip to Tanzania and spent the summer before that in Mexico with Mom); dead set on leaving (while most kids took only the ACT exam, I'd sat for the SAT alone in the school counselor's office using her watch as a timer); and cryptic and cerebral in writing lyrics for Stickman and His Trusty Steed (*Somewhere inside those sterile gray dwellings, there's a closet philosopher searching for more / You never know what's right up their alley if it's not on their front door*).

It seemed clear to me, too, that I was queer for my surroundings, that I didn't live where I belonged. The end, I thought, of the coming-going pendulum would be going (little did I know it never really stops swinging). When a Yankee fledgling woke up to find himself in an oppressive society with few prospects, the dictum was, of course, "Go west, young man!" But parts of my family had already come west at least twice—first after the Civil War and again in the 1970s—and here I was in the same bind. Against the ever-sparser wagon train of young men who'd needed escape of various kinds throughout American history, up to and including Dad, I decided to go east.

This again was queer, riding off into the sunrise.

Mom came for my graduation, her first visit to South Dakota since she'd left eight years earlier. Isaac told me that, although he had never told anybody else, he'd had to tell Mike that Mom was a lesbian that weekend after the second time Mike used *gay* as a synonym for *stupid* in front of her. So, including Pastor Jeff, that actually makes five guys who knew. There must be dozens of others: Dad's friends, anyone James might have told, plus the English teacher who read my college essay about it and the few people she might have told. In a small town, it's no sooner done than said.

FIVE

Other Selves

5.1

As I type this, I'm wearing a T-shirt subtly tie-dyed brown, with a herd of bison printed in a ring around my torso, something I got at a church thrift shop in Sheridan, Wyoming, for a dollar—kind of a redneck nature shirt. It's a little bit tongue in cheek, but not as much as you might think if you saw me on the street here in New York. Remember, this is the guy burning his neck red to sit and watch the bison at the Bronx Zoo.

(I should mention, better late than never, that I use *buffalo* and *bison* interchangeably, though purists insist on the latter. Technically, *buffalo* refers to water buffalo or Cape buffalo in Asia and Africa, and there are no buffalo, properly speaking, native to North America.)

I checked out a library book in New York—I couldn't believe they had it—an amateur history with a red marbled binding and gold embossment like a Gideon's Bible. It's titled *West from Fort Pierre: The Wild World of James (Scotty) Philip*, namesake of Philip, South Dakota, which my dad and I drove past every time we went to Rapid City. It's the type of Western history book I love and hate. It's a low-print-run, poorly edited book about an outsize rancher/huckster, "the man who saved the buffalo." It contains a biography of Scotty Philip, a memoir of working on Philip's ranch many years after he died, and a tour of West River South Dakota in the 1970s.[1] That's the part I love—the local history, the do-it-yourself-ness; it's almost punk rock. The part I hate is that it's the boring old story of the heroic white guy who founded our great state and made us the best folks on earth. The only history class I had in high school was taught by one "Video Volmer," who liked to show days-long documentaries in the dust-dry PBS style and who thought all we needed to know about the West was three varieties of barbed wire and two major cattle-drive trails. Video Volmer would have loved *West from Fort Pierre*.

But there was a photo in this book that jumped out at me as breathtakingly strange, something I could relate to in Scotty Philip's story as a typically atypical Plains founding father. It was a black-and-white picture of a bison and a longhorn bull facing off (sort of) in a bullring in Juárez, Mexico, in 1907. This scene was a couple of degrees more exotic than the Bronx Zoo bison: in a foreign country, and a hundred years old. The definitive account of this fight is an article that Scotty Philip's nephew wrote for the *South Dakota Historical Review* in 1937.[2] It's a story that epitomizes the sort of directionless ambition that grassland immigrants had, from French voyageurs to Prairie Dog Records, a champing at the bit to do something, whatever, in purportedly virgin land.

As a teenager, Scotty Philip was already independent, a new immigrant from Dallas, County Moray, in the Scottish High-lands, and now living in Victoria, west-central Kansas, USA, where he had followed his older brothers in alighting. He had a soft face, a gently dimpled chin, and dark downy hair, but was approaching two hundred pounds and was sure of himself and his future success. After he worked a few months as a farm- and ranch hand alongside his brothers, his restless optimism led him south to Dodge City. He was straining the gates of manhood like a young bull at a rodeo.[3]

The hundred miles between Victoria and Dodge City, a North Sea of grass like the rest of the Kansas prairies, were not purely flat at that time but pocked with stagecoach-size cankers in various stages of putrefaction. Many of the carcasses still had reeking meat attached; the wind was sickening, especially in summer. Others had been picked clean by coyotes, birds, and other scavengers and were just bleaching skeletons. White settlers took for granted that the buffalo would have to be extinguished to make room for civilization and its 160-acre homesteads. But of course this "inevitable" massacre was an ecological tragedy for American prairies, which would never be the same without the trampling and grazing of thirty million bearded beasts. The slaughter was also an offense, an act of war and of theft—attempted genocide, really—against the human inhabitants of the Plains whose societies relied on the animals. By the time of Scotty's arrival, the buffalo skinners were racing to see who could wolf down the biggest slice before the pie was gone. The best hunters could harvest seventy-five hides a day.[4]

Oddly, the shaggy and stoic bison, the symbols of American wildness, were not being shipped from the Dodge City rail yards mainly to make coats and rugs for rugged individualists. By the late nineteenth century, their hides largely went east to be stripped, tanned, and filleted into the belts for industrial machinery in the years before rubber belts existed.[5]

Scotty Philip didn't want to be a buffalo skinner or an

Indian fighter, but he accepted that both bison and Indians would have to vanish or make way in order for him to make his fortune on the Plains. At seventeen, in a landscape that offered only unsteady gains, Scotty moved west after a short stay in Dodge City to Cheyenne, Wyoming, and struck up a peripatetic series of ventures over the next several years. He twice joined parties of prospectors trespassing on the Great Sioux Reservation to dig for gold in the Black Hills. Both trips were unsuccessful. (July 22, 1876: "Still draining and no signs of pay." July 23: "Still draining and no signs of pay dirt." July 24: "Still nothing. The young fellow who works with me is going back disheartened, but I mean to stay yet. I have 100 lb of flour, and mean to work until that is done.")[6] The Sioux Reservation, as established by the Fort Laramie Treaty a few years earlier, included the entire western half of southern Dakota Territory. The U.S. Army, trying to hold back the stampede of miners scrambling after the late General Custer's gold-in-them-thar-hills, escorted Scotty off the reservation both times before his eleven-foot hand-dug holes yielded an ounce. Later prospectors would be luckier. The *New York Times* had predicted in 1875, "If the Black Hills prove rich in gold, the red man will be bought out or driven out, and the white man will take possession. This is not justice, but it is destiny."[7]

He became a wheeler and dealer, mowing the gold-bristled commons in northern Nebraska and selling the hay to the Army—and also running a few cattle of his own. Cattle were becoming the Plains' new beasts, gaunt shades of the bison. Once the government took the Black Hills, further reneging on the Fort Laramie Treaty after Custer's defeat at the Little Bighorn in 1876, Scotty hauled supplies through the diminished reservation to Indian agencies, forts, and mining camps.

He got along with his Indian neighbors, and wrote to his brother, "I can talk a deal of the Sioux language." Wherever business led him. "He was schooled," his nephew later wrote, "in an atmosphere where 'I'll bet you' was not an idle phrase."[8]

By the time Scotty was ready to settle down, around 1880, the buffalo were gone from the southern Plains, and only a fragment of the large herds had escaped north into Dakota Territory and Montana, still pursued by skinners. Scotty married a half-Sioux woman named Sally Larabee—whose sister was Crazy Horse's second wife, making Scotty Philip and Crazy Horse improbable brothers-in-law, if only after the latter's death. Scotty and Sally moved to a ranch west of Fort Pierre, Dakota Territory, on a remaining piece of the diminished Sioux Reservation. Sally was a quiet, private woman who never learned to write, "as faithful and self-sacrificing a helpmate as ever dedicated her life to a husband," wrote the nephew.[9] They were allowed to live there because she had Indian blood. Since the range had been cleared of buffalo and few Indians had taken up ranching, Scotty finally found success grazing cattle on the untouched grass, especially in years of abnormally high rainfall. Such were the advantages of being a "squaw man."

In the decade before South Dakota became a state in 1889, when Scotty was thirty-one, he got familiar with the country. He continued to dabble in other affairs: a freight business of wagons that looked like wooden fruit crates on wheels, running supplies from Fort Pierre, on the west bank of the Missouri River, west to Rapid City along a slippery gumbo road; artesian-well drilling; a county-seat fight; and real estate investment in Fort Pierre when it won that fight. But the base of his fortune was really the misfortune of the bison and the Indians, and the nearly decadelong head start he had over other white homesteaders on the Sioux Reservation. West of his ranch was founded that nondescript West River town Philip, which just over a century later would enjoy the scorn of a certain teenage punk who lived in Pierre, Fort Pierre's sister city across the Missouri.

Just a month before the Wounded Knee Massacre in 1890, the first governor of South Dakota wrote a letter to a U.S. Army major general, asking for guns and ammunition on the authority of a "reliable man of nerve, good judgment, and good character," Scotty Philip, who predicted an uprising based on the menacing behavior of Ghost Dancing Indians camped at his house. One Indian man had reportedly said he would soon "beat out the brains of children and drink women's blood."[10]

Scotty Philip's broader fame came as a result of a rich man's hobby, once he let his employees manage his cattle and moved into Fort Pierre. The Philip family (Scotty, Sally, the five of ten children who'd survived childhood, and the nephew) lived in a formidable and ornate house with dark Victorian carpets and a photograph of Scotty—mustached, in a tuxedo—displayed on the parlor wall. In 1901, he bought about ninety bison from another squaw man and rancher who lived northwest of Fort Pierre. Fred Dupree and his sons had saved five buffalo calves on a hunt in the early 1880s and built a herd over the next twenty years. Scotty's enthusiasm and ambition, undimmed in his forties, magnified this herd from a minor business venture to a spectacle. In 1904, he publicized a "last buffalo hunt" with the state governor, at which he and other gentlemen hunters culled the remaining unfenced stragglers roaming on the Dupree ranch. (Coincidentally, the French surname Dupree means "of the meadow" or "of the prairie.") Two years later, Scotty optioned a brand of cigars to promote his own fenced herd, marketed across the United States; the box was inscribed,

SCOTTY PHILIP, THE BUFFALO KING, NEW YORK, PIERRE, SAN FRANCISCO.[11]

Scotty's two-bit grandiosity was an enterprising counterpart to the bison preservation effort that was beginning to flourish around the Plains and especially back east. The same year Scotty bought his herd of bison, Theodore Roosevelt became president, bringing his love for nature preservation and for the Plains to the center of power. Roosevelt, exactly Scotty's age, had spent two years on a ranch in western North Dakota in the early 1880s, and in the course of displacing the bison (though he directly killed only a few trophies) he became enchanted with them. The beasts "most deeply imprest the imagination of all the old hunters and early settlers," T.R. noted, and concluded, "it would be a real misfortune to permit the species to become extinct."[12] Around the turn of the century, the New York Zoological Society and the American Bison Society both lobbied for the establishment of public herds. The Eastern advocates were moralistic and indignant about the wanton destruction of the bison, but like Roosevelt they didn't challenge the fundamental transformation of the Great Plains from Indian and bison territory to white states, from a landscape of motion to (at least in theory) a static grid of property. The buffalo herds would be tokens of nostalgia, not ecology.

In the fall of 1908, President Roosevelt's son Kermit went hunting on the Dupree ranch, where his Army escort had obtained permission to let the first son kill one of the last two or three "renegade" bison that Scotty Philip hadn't either moved to his ranch or bagged on his "last hunt." It was an extremely rare opportunity, one fit for a prince, as there were only known to be 1,917 of the animals left in the United States. Kermit quietly but firmly refused the offer, not wanting to "further deplete game that had been made almost extinct by the excess of hunters." Instead, he opted to take forty-eight grouse in one day.[13]

Scotty Philip, by contrast, was a classic Western bombastic booster. When his friend Bob Yokum told him about the wager he had made down in Juárez that an American buffalo could trounce a Mexican fighting bull in the *ruedo*, Scotty offered up two of his approximately one hundred bison. Yokum was a former Texan and a local saloon owner who had once harnessed two bison bulls and ridden behind them through downtown Pierre and Fort Pierre. Now that the last bison were essentially living artifacts, they could better serve as symbols of American virility.

"I'll bet you" was not an idle phrase. A fight or contest between men or between beasts or between man and beast has a thick gravity to it. An onlooker feels his own body clench, strike, and grapple as if he could see the match with his skin rather than his eyes. It's a story or novel stripped of words—down to the bones and vectors. Fear, pride, relief, and hope, all abstracted.

The Old West was similar. It was dry, empty, and dangerous. White "settlers," and their descendants who watched movies and read books about the settlement—male descendants, more often than not—saw the Plains like the ring before the gladiators enter: flat, pristine, and vibrating with the drama to come. For those watching and reading in easy chairs, the battles of conquest could stand in for the banal or irrational fears and struggles of modern life, incarnate in rattlers, pistols, mirages, villains, buffalo stampedes.

In January 1907, Scotty Philip and Bob Yokum modified a boxcar with two reinforced animal chambers and hay storage in between. Then they captured two bulls, a four-year-old and an eight-year-old, from Scotty's ranch north of Fort Pierre and dragged them, in crates mounted on sleds, across the frozen Missouri to the end of the Chicago and North Western railroad tracks in Pierre (the first bridge would open that fall). In the middle of a blizzard, they loaded the bison into their coach, and Scotty sent the animals south to Juárez escorted by Yokum and by his own nephew George Philip. The bison thrashed and kicked at the sides of the boxcar in terror as the train clanged over the gaps at the end of each rail, then stopped for oglers and changed direction in Sioux City, then got lost on a sidetrack in Omaha, then stampeded across the Dust Bowl (yet to be named) of southwestern Kansas and the Oklahoma and Texas panhandles, fueled by the quart of whiskey George gave the engineer, then halted at customs in El Paso, then finally pulled up beside the bullring in Ciudad Juárez. By the time they arrived, on the very Sunday of the match, the older bull had dislocated the fetlock joint just above his back left hoof.

As if he hadn't been harassed enough, the big buffalo with the dislocated ankle was then led through a chute into an enormous, roaring *ruedo* with Roman arches around the upper decks. He still wore his winter wool, even though it was much warmer in Juárez than in Fort Pierre. The capacity crowd had already watched four bulls killed by the matadors, and it cheered the novelty of a bison in the ring preparing to face a hometown bull.

The bison stood impassively in the center of the *ruedo* amid all the cheering until the gates opened and a rust-colored fighting bull with sharp horns entered the ring. The bison made no move. After a moment's hesitation, the *toro* charged. The bison cartwheeled around and lowered his head, which met his attacker's with a loud crack. The *toro* shook it off and charged again. Crack. The *toro* fell, his legs kicking, but he rose again, charged, cracked heads, and fell. Once more he charged, cracked, fell, but when he rose after the fourth impact, the *toro* ran toward the edge of the ring and tried in vain to climb over the wall into the safety of the *callejón* corridor.

The organizers sent in another bull, and then one more. Each headbanging match was a repeat of the last. The third bull retreated, and the bison lay down to rest in the center of the ring, from which he had not moved.

Then, after rebuffing (so to speak) a fourth bull, the buffalo was finally stirred to action. He raised his tail and charged, a bit slowly, favoring his injured fetlock, all four bulls hanging around the edge of the ring. Before he could catch one with a horn, the bulls were let out through the chute.

The next Sunday, after a series of four traditional bullfights, the younger bison was to face the matador El Cuco ("the sly one"). The Mexican organizers sent in the same four bulls from the previous match to face the matadors as warm-up acts, but each of them cowered to the sides of the ring, remembering that he had lost this territory to an American alpha the week before. Then, before El Cuco could enter the ring with the bison, the governor of Chihuahua called the event to an end. No victor was declared, the bet nullified. The Mexican organizers kept the injured buffalo, and Bob Yokum and George Philip sold the young one to an El Paso butcher for two hundred dollars. The proceeds of the first bullfight had paid for the trip, but otherwise it was a wash.

Four years later, at age fifty-three, "the man who saved the buffalo" died suddenly of a brain hemorrhage. By this time, American public and private bison herds had grown to 2,760 head and counting. The Chicago and North Western ran a special car for Scotty's South Dakotan fans free of charge out along the recently built spur from Fort Pierre to his ranch. In local lore, cowboys wept at the funeral, Stetsons in hand, and a few of his now four hundred buffalo on the pasture adjoining his family plot wandered over to pay silent respects to their savior.

I'm not altogether sure why, but that photograph of the fight, a footnote in the life of a B-list Plains hero, it stuns me. It's almost dreamlike—the bison in the *ruedo*. Here is an over-size four-legged orphan of the prairie, adopted or kidnapped into a Scotch-French-Sioux family as a bestial nephew of Crazy Horse, locked in a boxcar and hauled across the Rio Grande to prove the superiority of the nation that wiped out his species. The indiscernible throng ringed around him, cheering and chatting in Spanish and English in their Sunday finery. His beard nearly brushing the crushed rocks under his hooves. Nothing to graze, and blood from the slain *toros* in the air. His coat too hot for even January in Mexico. Being trapped in a perfect circle, no direction would be better to pursue or flee than any other, so he didn't move. This was lonelier than the Great Plains themselves. In the photo, he looks ill at ease, the essence of discomfort, his weight toward his front legs. Behind him, about halfway to the wall, a skinny *toro* stands at a right angle to the bison, regarding the regal profile of the gringo icon.

The echoing thunderclap of two bovine skulls clashing marked the lonely last stand of one bison against the animal that had replaced him.

5.2

After a summer driving Dad's old three-speed Dodge anti-Janklowmobile around to house-painting jobs, I left home.

Except for a week or a month here and there, I haven't come back. I had applied to a smattering of Eastern colleges, based on their brochures, the twenty-five-year-old information Dad gave me, and tours I took with my father's father (the Yale professor) and my aunt. I had also visited Reed College in Portland and really liked its ferny campus and edgy braininess, but some sense made me want to light out for new territory. I decided to go to Amherst College in western Massachusetts, a colonial campus in a hospitable small town—a school that had some cachet in the Northeast but that nobody at home had heard of. It was a continent away from Mom, and a part of the world Dad had rejected: pretty close to true independence, I thought. I had become self-conscious about leaving South Dakota and didn't want to seem uppity, so I was thrilled when a friend said *Amherst* sounded like a store brand of food.

One of my first decisions was to change my name, to readopt the hyphenated last name I hadn't used since I lived with Mom. For eight years I'd been Josh Davis, with Mom's last name, Garrett, hidden like my memories of Gay Pride marches. The change back to Garrett-Davis reminds me of a North Dakotan who rechristened himself when he left, Jay Gatsby. He had been born James Gatz to "shiftless and unsuccessful farm people" like so many on the Plains but became the Waspish West Egg hero of F. Scott Fitzgerald's American tragedy.[14] I suppose both of us felt we needed new monikers to realize whatever core selves we thought we fundamentally held or wished we did. Gatsby became moneyed and self-made; I wanted to claim a modernity and urbanity as a hyphenated child of the counterculture, and I also figured I would be free to unearth Mom's influence on me (also modern and urbane—what was cooler on a college campus in the diversity-craving '90s than a

lesbian mom in Portland?) now that I was free of the claustrophobic culture of the anticlaustrophobic Plains. No hayseed I.

But I wasn't free of the Plains, was neither modern nor
urbane. I'd never read *The Great Gatsby* or *The Scarlet Letter*, I'd
never seen a lacrosse stick or *Blue Velvet*, I didn't drink or take
drugs or use the Internet. Almost immediately my teenage
antipathy for home turned into an academic and storytelling
attraction. My freshman seminar was about Western memoirs,
and on my first day of class in a colonial chapel back east, I saw
on the syllabus an article my granddad, the Yale prof, had written in 1954 about the "cowboy myth." I had met him only a
handful of times — most recently on the college tours — and I'd
never thought about there being a cowboy myth. Though my
upbringing left me academically unprepared for and out of
place at this Eastern college, it seemed there was something of
value in hailing from a place that, if poor in sophistication, was
rich in myth and experience. Here was the familiar view out
the airplane window of grass, gullies, and cattle, and there was
plenty more to study.

There was also an allure to remaining as unique and out-
cast as I'd felt in South Dakota. I was so accustomed to being
out of place that I perhaps looked west to keep me familiarly
unsettled in the East; though maybe I didn't have a choice. "I
see now that this has been a story of the West, after all," Nick
Carraway observes near the end of *The Great Gatsby*, though
the whole story has taken place around New York City. He
notes that the main characters were all Westerners who "perhaps...possessed some deficiency in common which made us
subtly unadaptable to Eastern life."[15] Once the white settlement of the West was complete, there was nowhere for the
young to strike out for but back to the irresponsible, stuffy, and

dangerous East. But we couldn't really settle there. I began writing folk songs cribbing from my past, including my birth announcement: *I was born under sunny skies on the South Dakota prairie / I never told a lie, never even chopped a cherry tree.*

The next summer I went back to Pierre and worked for the State Historical Society in its granite-faced sod dugout. Back at school I took courses about California's history and mythology, Death Valley's geology, and Willa Cather's fiction—anything Western. There were strata of history, poetry, and, again, myth I'd not noticed in the arid world where I grew up. Senior year of college, I traveled home in what was to be the first of many trips to the Plains, explorations that would continue throughout my twenties and into the present. I suppose at their most unassuming these were "research trips," though I felt a deeper longing to pilgrimage: It was study lifted to reverent heights or lowered to gut hungers, hard to say which.

I made that first trip to gather information for a thesis in American studies: Picture a longhair paleface driving around the Yankton Sioux Reservation in January, interviewing whites and Natives who had been involved in an activist takeover five years before he was born. Local Red Power activists, loosely affiliated with the American Indian Movement, had occupied the Yankton Sioux Industries pork-processing plant, which had been built as a jobs project for the reservation. Tribal members felt the white Texan plant managers had made too little effort to ease Indian employees into the discipline of the white workaday world. Within a few months of the grand opening, the vast majority of the plant's employees were whites from nearby farms and reservation border towns, despite its receiving over a million dollars in federal grants and loans to provide economic development for Indians. Yankton Sioux activists took over the plant and occupied it for three days in March 1975 in an effort to force contract renegotiations between the tribe and the Texans.

A month and a half later, seven young men broke into the plant again, before dawn, taking two night workers hostage before releasing them and chaining the doors. The teenagers shot at the Texan plant manager's car when he arrived, and set up for an armed standoff with police and highway patrol outside. Tribal and state police cut off phone lines, the town of Wagner mandated a curfew, and students were sent home from school. About a hundred highway patrol officers surrounded the plant and waited for rash nineteen-year-olds with stolen firearms to give in.

The situation called for a superhero or a vigilante, and in swooped the new attorney general, thirty-five-year-old Bill Janklow, with some guns of his own and a yen to make his name as an Indian fighter, a defender against the outlaws of the American Indian Movement. The Yankton Seven, the boys in the plant, were basically delinquents, not AIM members, but no matter. The conflict was further complicated by the fact that the plant was on reservation land and therefore outside Janklow's jurisdiction (the Yankton Reservation is one of those "checkerboard" rezes of Indian and white land created by the Dawes Act of 1892, which divided tribal property into 160-acre homesteads and sold the "surplus" to white settlers). Again, no matter. After several hours, while an FBI SWAT team was en route to Wagner, a state patrolman "accidentally" fired a tear-gas canister onto the pork plant's air ducts and forced the young men out into handcuffs.

Janklow became a hero—this was his most effectual stand against "AIM." Three years later, he was governor. Changes in hiring and firing never occurred at the pork plant, and it shut down for good in the early '80s. Now it's a white cinder-block fossil on the Plains south of Wagner.[16]

I talked to a white lawyer who said politically incorrect and patronizing things about Indians through an electrolarynx microphone (presumably after throat cancer; he put chaw in his mouth as he talked and never spit it out). I visited a Native military veteran who served me some stir-fried beef and bell peppers and a half-pint carton of milk; I had been vegetarian for almost ten years already, but Mom warned me that it was deeply rude to refuse an offer of food on the rez. My first meat in a decade was "reservation Chinese cuisine." I interviewed the local police chief, who was white, in the local station house, and a Yankton Sioux activist in the state pen, where he was serving a long term for an unrelated homicide. As awkward and surreal as some of these interviews were, I felt a sense of accomplishment and distance when I returned to Amherst. Somehow, after my escape from South Dakota and my rechristening on the East Coast, I was able to return through investigation. It was less clinical than the word *investigation* suggests. I hadn't made peace with my own story—my superstition, in Willa Cather's terms. Instead I was digging up others' stories that reflected pieces of my alienation and distance from the place. The Yankton Sioux Industries story had plenty of division and alienation to gnaw on.

5.3

In spite of my other digging, for years I left unexcavated a crucial site of my own confused relationship to the Plains. My mom's move to Portland in 1990, when I was ten, and my parents' fierce fight over me that summer — the change in plans, from my point of view, and the competing pulls to stay in South Dakota or to move to Portland, the loss of my mother as a daily presence in my life — I didn't think much about it. Part of this was habitual fear and secrecy around her lesbianism, which was central to the fight. But there was also an echo of a roar in myself that frightened me. I left it underground.

The same summer, on August 12, 1990, a group of fossil hunters from the Black Hills Institute of Geological Research were about to finish a month of excavation in the Hell Creek Formation — two and a half hours northwest of Pierre, on the Cheyenne River Indian Reservation. They were on land owned by Maurice Williams, a sixty-six-year-old Cheyenne River Sioux tribal member. Though the skies out there are almost always wide open and blue, the prairie was covered in a thick fog that day. The team's beat-up Suburban had a flat tire, so while the boss drove on a weak spare into the town of Faith, Sue Hendrickson set out hiking in the fog with her golden retriever, Skywalker, toward a badlands cliff she'd been hoping to visit all month. After two hours in the fog, she wound up back where she started. She began to cry from frustration but set out again for the cliff, seven miles from the road.

Eight feet off the ground, coming out of the crumbly cliff, Sue found some enormous vertebrae and part of a four-and-a-half-foot femur. When she brought the team out to the cliff, they named the tyrannosaur after her.

Maurice Williams came by to visit sometimes as they excavated Sue. Peter Larson, the Black Hills Institute's founder, wrote Williams a check for $5,000 for the fossil. Everyone assumed it was Williams's to sell, and as the fossil market was completely unregulated anyway, a handshake agreement was the easiest way to go.

"You are going to mount her in Hill City?" Williams asked one day. Larson confirmed. "Good," he said. "And under that you'll write, 'Stolen from Maurice Williams.'" They laughed.[17]

Sue turned out to be the largest and most complete *Tyrannosaurus rex* fossil ever found, a multimillion-dollar artifact.

She had died in battle, in a landscape that, prior to drying up into the Great Plains, had been a Cretaceous tropical forest full of ferns and palmlike cycads near an inland sea. Peter Larson speculated that she, an aging *T. rex* with a number of broken and healed bones (leg, ribs) already, had been fatally bitten behind the left eye by a younger tyrannosaur in a battle for territory.[18]

After Sue was unearthed, another battle erupted among federal and tribal governments, Maurice Williams, and the Black Hills Institute. It turned out that the site where Sue was found was Indian "trust" land, which meant that any sale of land had to be approved by the Department of the Interior as being in Williams's best interest. Since the excavation sat within the borders of the reservation, the Cheyenne River Sioux Tribe asserted its own claim to the fossil under tribal laws and possibly antiquities laws. And, of course, the Black Hills Institute, a (white) family-owned company of paleontologists, fossil collectors, and dealers, believed they'd bought the greatest find of their careers—one of the greatest and most charismatic finds in the history of paleontology—fair and square.

By 1992, the case was going to court. On ABC's *Primetime Live*, Sam Donaldson called it "the custody battle of the century."[19]

Though usually she's a world-class junk-purger, Mom saved

a thick manila envelope labeled CUSTODY for me. Sixteen years after the fact, when I was long out of college, she gave me the envelope. As I was packing my suitcase to leave Portland after a visit, the envelope slipped out of my hands and its clasp sliced lengthwise into my left thumb. I calmly asked for a bandage, as a little surge of blood came out with each heartbeat. When I showed Mom how I'd cut myself, she said, "I hope that's not a metaphor."

Duly warned, I didn't open the envelope for almost a year.

I remembered shrieking that summer in Dad's tiny law-student house, my ten-year-old face hot and sticky with snot and tears, holding up the heavy black receiver of his rotary-dial phone and threatening to call Dr. Arbes, the psychologist who was rendering a professional opinion on my future, to say I'd changed my mind about having no preference between my parents. Dad stomped toward me across the living room, where in less complicated summers I'd sat on his knee following along as he read *Huck Finn* or *Kidnapped*. The knickknacks in his "knickknack cabinet" shuddered with each step. He pried the receiver out of my hand and pushed it into its cradle, his own rage only barely contained.

Over the next few years my increasingly tearless memory was that I had been confiscated, even stolen, from my lesbian mother by the provincial, conservative state that I found more and more socially oppressive as I reached my teens. I grew less prone to hysterical outbursts. Still, the history of being *taken* haunted me.

In 1992, after an investigation, the FBI seized Sue as evidence and locked her in crates in a university machine shop. The federal courts would decide whether dinosaur bones should be classified as land, antiquities, personal property, or something else entirely. According to that decision, they would rule whether Sue belonged to the Black Hills Institute, the government, the tribe, or Maurice Williams. In January 1993, a federal judge ruled that since Williams had sold it to the Black Hills Institute without federal approval, the transaction was null and void. The Eighth Circuit upheld that decision.

Meanwhile the case drew federal authorities' attention to the burgeoning international gray market for fossils, or perhaps it gave them a high-profile venue in which to tackle that market. In the fall of 1993 a U.S. attorney obtained an indictment against four staff members of the Black Hills Institute, and the institute itself, for unrelated cases of digging on public land without permits and for violating customs laws while taking fossils and money to and from international sales.

Most observers were primarily worried about Sue's fate. Would the federal government keep her or give her back to Williams? Would she stay in South Dakota or be sold away?

When I finally open the file Mom gave me, I walk around for a week in a pessimistic haze. I see the little ten-year-old Josh as an alter ego, an other self. I'm furious at the selfishness of the parents who yanked back and forth at him as if he were an artifact or trophy, who left him essentially transient, forever certain he ought to be elsewhere. Each of them had a fossilized philosophy of parenting, and the fight seemed as much about proving the other wrong as it was about the best interests of young Josh. Both had overcorrected from their own unhappy upbringings.

Not surprisingly, their divorce also hung over the custody

battle like the fog the day Sue was discovered. The worst blows—many to Josh—went unnoticed in the anger that clouded their relationship. Dad had always been trying to control Mom's plans, she thought; she imagined he was still following her around. He, meanwhile, wrote that she had abandoned her "moral obligation" to explain to him why she'd divorced him in the first place. (Dr. Arbes noted in his report, which he delivered about a week before Sue was discovered, "Interestingly, it did appear as if both Jay and Kathleen struggle to try and offer this evaluator clear reasons as to why they got a divorce.") As much as anything, I guess, it had been a power struggle between two people who'd once been desperate enough for independence that they'd left their respective coasts for the Plains.

"This whole custody issue is designed to allow Jay to exert some control over my life," Mom wrote to their former marriage counselor. "Jay offered to drop all his objections to me moving if I agreed to move less than 600 miles away from him. Jay would say that was because 600 miles would allow him more access to Josh. But 600 miles is a 12 hr drive. The flight from Portland is 4 hours. I can't think of any other argument, besides control, that makes sense in light of the fact that his mom is a millionaire." To Dad, a twelve-hour drive was almost routine, and he was stubbornly offended by the luxury of frequent flying. "It indicates to me," Mom judged, showing her own bones as a guidance counselor, "that he is still not meeting his own emotional needs and therefore cannot be a good role model for Josh. Jay's mom is still angry at Jay's dad for their divorce 20 years ago. Like mother, like son."

Dad had gone to law school after the divorce in part to recover, in part to escape the tyranny of having a wealthy

mother who would support him if asked—a source of shame
for a man who preferred to rent a poorly insulated, seven-
hundred-square-foot shack for $200 a month, $100 in the summer (years later, in 2007, it was on the market for $39,500), and
to use the black rotary phone he'd stolen from an apartment
he'd rented fifteen years earlier. There was revenge in his ruin-
ing her plans, but he was too legalistic and austere to allow
himself a purely emotional vengeance. He believed that living
with him was best for Josh. "What Arbes was most interested
in *wasn't* what he heard from you or me, but rather was what
Josh told him," he later wrote her, confirming my fear that I
was the cause of my own confiscation.

"When asked what he'd like to change about me," Dad
wrote, "Josh said that I worry too much. He's certainly not the
first person to tell me that, and I should take it to heart. When
asked what he'd change about you, Josh said you should quit
bad-mouthing me when you're around him. Not only did that
influence Arbes against you, it was a real eye-opener for me. I
talked to a friend of mine (who is also divorced) about this, and
he told me that 'women do that.' I refuse to believe that *all*
women run down their ex-husbands around their kids, though
my mother was terrible about it... and now I find out you were
guilty of the same thing." Clearly my grandparents' bitter
divorce, from which Dad's mother never really healed, also
clouded the fight.

Then there was this class struggle between my parents.
Mom had initially been attracted to Dad because he was an
educated intellectual, but she came to resent his privilege and
family money. He, meanwhile, transfused his own blue blood,
looked down his nose at any periodical with *New York* in its
title, resisted taking money from Grannie even when we were

on food stamps, even affected bad grammar—all probably to steer clear of his family misery and the *New York Review of Books*–contributor father who periodically disowned him for petty slights. Still, Dad wouldn't entirely forsake his roots. When I casually mentioned that if I moved to Portland, I would be attending an arts magnet school that fall, he consulted both of his parents, who disdained such a school as "trendy." I was far too young to abandon the liberal arts, they said. "Right now," he informed Mom, "when he doesn't talk of being a rock 'n' roll star or a pro skater, Josh says he wants to be an archaeologist."

Mom enumerated her "goals" for Josh, most of which could fall under the heading of "Don't end up like your dad." To wit: "That he learns how to meet his own emotional needs" and "that he learns that he is responsible for his feelings and his behavior (that he does *not* adopt blaming as a coping style)." She also included, "That he understands that experimentation with drugs or alcohol when he is underage is unacceptable and will not be allowed." Dad had stopped smoking marijuana for a while and even gone to counseling in a last-ditch attempt to save the marriage, and Mom's own sobriety was perhaps more aspirational than actual. In addition to both of my parents' once-prolific drug and alcohol use, Dad had a family history of alcoholism and his mother had quit drinking only five years earlier.

Then there was the most legally poisonous cloud. While denying that he was a "rabid homophobe" (he had a number of gay friends both in South Dakota and elsewhere), Dad was finally uneasy with his son being raised by lesbians. "I was haunted by the image of your bedroom door," he wrote Mom, referring to information I'd inadvertently told him or Dr. Arbes, "which was kept locked for obvious reasons, so you couldn't hear Josh in the night if he wet his bed or needed you for other reasons." Dad also listed the "social stigma" I might face having lesbian parents and my need for my father as a role model in my teenage years, and he noted with a shard of bitter sarcasm that Josh "didn't need to be in an all-wymyn environment, where the hostility to men might send him the other way and make him a misogynist." He didn't dare mention the opposite fear, that I'd turn out gay myself.

Mom's sexual orientation was a significant legal weapon to use against her. Over the next couple of years, two South Dakota Supreme Court rulings on the parental rights of lesbian mothers revealed some of the range of opinion on gay parenting. A case argued in 1991 involved a lesbian mother who had "a myriad of psychological problems" (an eating disorder, depression, suicidal threats, etc.). Her ex-husband had won custody, but the issue was whether the children could visit her overnight given that she and her lover lived together and "were affectionate toward each other in front of the children, caressing, kissing and saying 'I love you.'" She had twice taken her children into a gay bar in Sioux City, Iowa, while looking for her lover, and had allowed the children to sleep in bed with her and her lover while she was "unclothed." The court ruled that a lower court should have required a home study before allowing weekend visitation rights. The written opinion evinces a view of homosexuality as a mental illness, a perversion to be balanced against the need for children to have contact with their mother. Her lesbianism receives much more focus than her other inappropriate or disturbing behavior, and there was a serious concern about "adverse developmental messages in terms of [the children's] sexual preferences."[20] Never mind that she was a rash and immature decision maker. Would she turn them gay?

Alongside the majority's reasoned (if prejudiced) decision,

there was a "specially concurring" opinion by Justice Frank Henderson. Until the mother could prove, he wrote, "after years of therapy and demonstrated conduct, that she is no longer a lesbian living a life of abomination (*see* Leviticus 18:22), she should be totally estopped from contaminating these children." Along with Bible citations and archaic language (the decision was the "hour of judicial atonement"), Justice Henderson included a hopeful "Caveat" celebrating a newspaper article he'd found that said the activist group Queer Nation had disbanded over internal politics: "There is hope for our Nation," wrote the justice, who had been popularly elected. In this case, both Dad's lawyer and Dr. Arbes were on the losing side, arguing for the lesbian mother's right to visit her children.[21]

The other case came before the State Supreme Court in late 1994, more than four years after our own. In this case, the lesbian mother was clearly a good parent in a stable relationship, and she had won custody. The court clarified, "We are called upon to make a judicial review of the trial court's decision rather than a moral evaluation of the parties' conduct. As judicial officers, ruling on a legal controversy, we must be guided by principles of law. Personal conceptions of morality held by members of this Court have no place in the resolution of this controversy."[22] By this time Justice Henderson had retired, and with him the fears of "contamination." The cases were drastically different, but it seemed a certain shift had occurred, where lesbianism changed from a dangerous perversion to a moral judgment outside the law's purview. Of course, from retirement, Justice Henderson would have begged to dissent.

Sue's custody case was not exactly about Sue either.

The first fossil hunters had come to the Great Plains from

the East Coast in the 1870s, toward the end of the Indian wars. The federal government and the Sioux tribes had signed the Fort Laramie Treaty in 1868, which preserved all of what would be South Dakota west of the Missouri River—including where Sue was found—as the Great Sioux Reservation and forbade whites to even pass through without tribal permission. The United States unilaterally reneged on the treaty three years later to allow the Northern Pacific Railway to build across the reservation, and then in 1874 General Custer brought a thousand troops to investigate claims of gold in the Black Hills. Incursions by illegal gold rushers such as Scotty Philip ensued. That same year, Othniel C. Marsh, a pioneering paleontologist at Yale, first came to excavate on Indian land at the invitation of the U.S. Army. So Maurice Williams's joke during the excavation—that the Black Hills Institute should include a STOLEN FROM MAURICE WILLIAMS placard on the display of Sue—had more than a century's worth of acrimony in it.[23]

The owners of the Black Hills Institute, Peter Larson and his brother Neal, had grown up on a ranch on the Rosebud Sioux Indian Reservation southeast of where Sue was found. (Like the whites who lived within and around the Yankton Sioux Reservation, where Bill Janklow snagged the pork-plant protesters, the Larsons had benefited from the checkerboard effect of the 1892 Dawes Act.) Indian-white relations were most bitter in reservation border towns, and the Larsons went to college just as the bitterness peaked during the AIM years. I have no way of knowing the Larsons' personal opinions and feelings about race, but buying a multimillion-dollar natural resource from a Sioux man for less than a thousandth of its value continued a long tradition of race-based expropriation that might be read as theft.

Another issue hanging over Sue was western South Dakota's libertarian resentment of government intervention. Real and self-imagined cowboys and cowgirls had a paranoid sense that somebody in Washington was trying to control them and steal from them. (I think of my mom's sense that my dad was trying to control her movements.) Time was when you could just ask the landowner, or lessee of public land, and go out and dig. The image of the roadside rock and fossil shop inspired nostalgia and satisfaction with the way *our* world hadn't changed so much in the crazy twentieth century—the Plains were stable enough even over sixty-five million years that a colossal skeleton could rest intact.

In fact, fossils were becoming a big-money global business, and Sue epitomized how the stakes had risen. These weren't humble fossil hounds selling ammonite shells for five dollars. Fossils had become resources that were in some cases being shipped from the public domain to private collectors, many of them outside the United States, at extravagant prices. The Black Hills Institute sold to museums as much as possible and published papers on many of its fossils, but the Larsons were at times collecting under the table, not investigating too thoroughly if they were on federal, state, tribal, or private land, and taking suppliers at their word that samples were legally collected. In the absence of any clear code of law for fossils, when the Sue custody fight arose, the government made an example of the Institute in the criminal proceedings, and Peter Larson ultimately served two years in prison. As his lawyer complained, "What government can't get by directive, oftentimes it takes by indictment."[24]

As court hearing after court hearing went against the Black Hills Institute, a populist protest sprung up around South

Dakota and especially in the Institute's hometown, Hill City. The Institute covered its facade with a mural of a jailed tyrannosaur with tears falling from her eyes, with the legend FREE SUE. Locals held up cardboard signs reading, SEIZE DRUGS, NOT FOSSILS, YOUR TAX DOLLARS AT WORK, and FBI IS U.S. GESTAPO after the feds confiscated Sue's bones. The attorney for the Institute played the case to the press and the public by alluding to conspiracy-thriller novels and movies, describing the case as "paleontological McCarthyism," invoking the recent deaths at David Koresh's Branch Davidian compound, and comparing the prosecutor to Idi Amin.[25]

As in any lopsided battle, the losing side seethed over its powerlessness. The ivory tower paleontologists with PhDs and tenure wouldn't stick up for the nondegreed fossil hunters who collected the best specimens....My own mother cried and raged in frustration at my dad's access to financial and legal capital—she later told me he'd cynically hired the "top feminist lawyer in South Dakota" to accomplish the rare feat of winning custody from a competent mother. Of course, he'd also played the lesbian card in patent disregard for the ideals of Prairie Dog Records. But I think what was most maddening to her was his general savvy with systems, the same pitiless intellect he'd used to trump her feelings in countless little arguments. She included in her list of "goals for Josh" that I learn "that consideration of people's feelings in human relationships is more important than being 'right.'"

"It hurts me to think that you don't believe I care about Josh, and believe that I only wanted him to live with me as a kind of battle trophy," Dad wrote to Mom on New Year's Eve of 1990. I imagine him alone that night, sitting down at our dining room table with a can of "Milwaukee's Cheapest" (union brewed), maybe mixed with tomato juice, Western-style, and a legal pad he'd brought home from work. I was on my very first visit to Portland. Just in time for me to fly out alone and acquire my first UNACCOMPANIED MINOR pin, Mom had signed the new custody agreement: Christmas, spring break, and eight weeks in the summer. She could fly to South Dakota once a month if she wanted to or could afford to and hang out with me for the weekend (she never would). The case didn't ever go to court, where he would have won anyway.

Dad was still new in Hot Springs and didn't have anybody to kiss at midnight. Over a couple of hours, perhaps sipping his beer every paragraph or so, he wrote her a calm, nineteen-page history and analysis of the battle that stunned me when I read it, both with the facts it revealed (for example, that the deputy sheriff at his law school graduation-day party was his first inkling that we were moving to Portland in a few weeks) and for his reasonable tone. Hardly a word was crossed out or thought better of. "It would not be surprising that we have very different perspectives on what has happened this year," he wrote. "From your perspective, I stole your son away from you. From my perspective, it is more as though you abandoned him."

He was legalistic and rhetorically confident but also at times generous and vulnerable: "Without a doubt, I didn't give you enough credit for the job you did raising Josh while a single parent," or his admission that he'd "spent time obsessed over" things in their marriage he wished he "hadn't done, or hadn't said." I'd always found him to be unyielding and unwilling to admit mistakes, a brick wall to butt my head against in my efforts to have a somewhat normal adolescence. (Odd, considering that he worried that young Josh in Portland, "by arriving from South Dakota of all places, living in a lesbian household, and going to a strange art school across town, would have three strikes against him and would be tagged a weirdo.")

Mom continued to pull on me after the agreement was signed—she played to the press, so to speak. She told me, speciously, that Dr. Arbes had ruled in Dad's favor only because Dad had hired him, that my school wasn't good enough for me, that with child support she spent more money on me than he did. She refused to speak to him on the phone beyond "Josh, please" and often had me ask him to change dates on a planned visit. Another of her "goals for Josh" had naturally been "that he feels free to ask that he be allowed to live with his other parent and that his wish be granted without engendering court action or intervention."

I first learned about Sue's case my second year in Pierre, when I was thirteen and participating in a program called Odyssey of the Mind. My team's "odyssey" that year was to juxtapose a current event with a scene from *The Iliad*, so we attached the fight over Sue to a scene in which Achilles's "other self," Patroclus, is killed in battle and the Greeks and Trojans fight "in the likeness of fire" over his body. I remember that we built a mechanical Homer—a papier-mâché ladybug with a speaker in its belly—but of course I've forgotten all of his narration. I imagine, given the facts of the case and my own experience, that Homer ought to have concluded with a moral speech, a storyteller's reflection, something like:

"What did Sue want? What was best for her? She probably didn't have a terribly strong preference between the Black Hills Institute and the Cheyenne River Reservation, with their respective hypothetical museums founded around her, or between them and a big-city museum. It would have been easier—less disruptive—to just keep going on course with the folks who'd found her, to become the star of Hill City rather than just another attraction in some metropolis. But she did have a core of ambition, to be a real global rock star, as it were. Really, all of her options were pretty good, except going to some private mansion overseas—no one wanted that for her. She *did* resent the claims that this or that was in her interest, in the public's interest, when really most of the battle was about money and power and prestige. She resented the Black Hills Institute claiming, as a ploy to retrieve her from machine-shop limbo, that during the course of the trial the pyrite in her bones was turning to sulfuric acid that would destroy her.

"Hill City residents painted a mural of Sue in jail crying, but *they* were the ones crying. It wasn't *her* they seemed to want but the tourism that might augment their per capita annual income of $9,000. They wanted to air their resentment toward all of the snooty PhDs and meddlesome bureaucrats who made more money and got so much more respect for their privilege.

"Maurice Williams at least admitted that he only wanted the money. He'd been hustled so badly by accepting $5,000 for what turned out to be a multimillion-dollar fossil that it was criminal, and when he realized he could get a second chance—hey, who wouldn't take it?

"And the tribe was just like Hill City. They wanted visitors. Though fat chance of a dinosaur bringing that. As much as kids love dinosaurs, a tourist mecca on a forlorn reservation in the middle of the Great Plains was unlikely.

"It's a good thing all these parties didn't get a chance to physically pull on Sue's fragile bones like the Greeks and Trojans pulled on Patroclus. Sue actually came out pretty well. At

Sotheby's, she fetched over $8 million of McDonald's and Disney money—paid to Maurice Williams, to whom the Department of the Interior had returned Sue—and she went to the Field Museum in Chicago to become a big star."

Sue opened for exhibit on my twentieth birthday, in 2000, not a little traumatized. I was in Massachusetts, the conclusion of the takeoff, the flight that had begun with my own custody fight. Though I'm sure she enjoys her stardom at the Field, she stands there uneasily in its great hall, on her toes in a grappler's stance, facing the ghost of an enemy. Her last years in South Dakota were fraught and contentious and painful, but I'll bet she has a longing for that place where she spent her first sixty-five million years. All those places she could have ended up, where some argued she should have ended up, they haunt her.

PART TWO

My cousin Ruth Harris (top, center) in Montgomery, Alabama, in 1965, waiting for the Selma marchers.

(Photo archives of the General Board of Global Ministries of the United Methodist Church)

Six

The Pen and Plow

6.1

"The history of the West was made not by those who moved out but by those who stayed on."[1] That's a characteristic history-book line. Wheat from chaff, men from boys—it's easy to feel defensive as someone who hoofed it out of South Dakota as soon as I got my diploma, and especially as chaff who still cares about the Plains. In fact, though I was a bit quicker out of the gates, many of my most Plains-rooted classmates have moved to Minneapolis, Denver, Kansas City—even New York like me, or Los Angeles, or, for those who joined up, Basra or Kandahar. And if you include our own largest cities, Sioux Falls and Rapid City, as moves "away," it begins to seem the rest of the Plains is becoming one big ghost town. I imagine the Two Bit Saloon back there alone with its white steel ice cooler dripping out front, a big old F350 rusting into cracked asphalt where Dad and I once parked an overheated Dodge. Horses go feral. A synthesizer in the heavens plays something by Ennio Morricone. Out of nowhere, a spare tire rolls across the scene like a modern tumbleweed. And we youngsters with our old-fashioned work ethic sweat for the Man in urban office parks.

Still, any mention of the Dakota—Yoko Ono's and Lauren Bacall's Upper West Side apartment building—perks up my ears as if someone had just said my name, despite the fact that I've been on the East Coast for a decade. New York City is wonderful; the variety of people and places is grassland-vast, kinetic, and as democratic as anywhere on earth. New Yorkers walk the walk of "live and let live" more than most libertarian big talkers out west. I happily play in a loud, not-too-serious punk rock band with a guitarist from Maine and Texas and a drummer from the Basque Country in Spain, and I also play acoustic folk-rock troubadour music now and then.

But to senses that came to life in a land of (I'd now say *gorgeous*) monotony, monotony that trains you to look up for peripheral flutters and features, to study each human face, to smell a weeks-dead skunk or a bouquet of sage through dusty car vents, to hear the ringtone leitmotifs of two dozen birds you don't know the names of—to those senses, New York is overexposure. The elevated subway outside my windows shakes the building every four minutes, my rent keeps creeping up as much as the law allows, and every street crossing could be my last. Not to mention that my band can't attract more than a tiny roomful of audience members, but any concert I want to attend is sold out months in advance—here, tooting one's own horn is commonplace, in traffic or company. Often I'm saddled with longing for the old, open, imperfect Plains. So I go back to visit. Or I read Willa Cather novels, listen to Woody Guthrie sing "Ramblin' Round," or ride the subway to the Bronx Zoo on pay-what-you-wish day to see the penned bison. Or I look into genealogy.

6.2

A dozen members of the Brion family moved from western New York out to Nebraska beginning about fifteen years after the Civil War, but not all of them stuck it out. Many immigrants to the Plains were fleeing oppression and poverty in Europe or in the crowded East, but my family's "Western fever" was largely entrepreneurial, an attempt to benefit from the Homestead Act that had taken effect near the beginning of the war. They would find a place, prove up on a homestead, and maybe even get rich. The Brions had actually lived well back east, in a sizable house with a cellar full of frozen mince pies and sausage patties packed in lard that could be prepared at a moment's notice if a relative or neighbor dropped in at mealtime. They had a living room with cushioned rocking chairs, and a red-felted table that held a lamp and a stereograph with a box of pictures that miraculously popped out from the card stock like good stories. It's hard to see why they moved to such a trying place as Nebraska, other than through a congenital American restlessness.

They weren't aristocrats; it wasn't an easy life by any means. In her memoirs for the family history files, written in a fat, looping cursive, my great-great-grandmother Minnie Brion mixed nostalgic fondness with old gripes, and grippes. Her father nearly died of typhoid in Southern swamps as a drafted soldier in the Union Army; after being discharged, he soon enlisted again not out of heroism but because he heard a rumor (a false one, it turned out) that there was going to be another draft and volunteers received better assignments. He returned home in 1865 shivering with fever and ague, what we now call malaria. Soon Minnie's mother contracted spinal meningitis and barely survived. The family moved to a farm, then bought a general store. By the time she was eighteen, a soft-featured young woman with brown curls, Minnie had passed the New York State Regents Exam and begun teaching in a one-room school with thirty students ranging from toddlers to men and women older than herself.

Soon came the "glowing accounts" that the first family pioneers sent back from Nebraska, of "wonderfully furtile soils, of the tall corn they grew, with no stones, no hills &c. &c." Though Minnie had vivid memories of her neighbors lynching an effigy of *New York Tribune* editor Horace Greeley when he ran for president in 1872, the entire family ended up following his famous injunction to "Go west, young man, go forth into the Country." Farmers, cobblers, merchants, and elderly parents sold all of their belongings and bought train tickets to Nebraska. On an October morning in 1879, after she had quit her teaching job only a couple of months into the year, Minnie woke early to take a last walk through Woodhull, New York. The street was lined with mature maple trees in their yellow-and-red autumn splendor. She dragged her feet, swishing them through the leaves, then stooped to pick up a couple to press and save. She stood up again, then let the leaves drop. Her parents had already sold all of their books, and she decided she would have no way to press them.[2]

I notice, as I picture my ancestors going west to a "virgin" frontier newly scrubbed of Indians and bison (though the finality of Wounded Knee was still ten years away), that I'm somehow alongside them. Many early Americans—"Go west" Greeley among them—believed that westward expansion would provide a "safety valve" for the poor and jobless masses in Eastern cities. Even earlier, General Washington wrote to General Lafayette: "We have opened the fertile plains of the Ohio to the poor, the needy and the oppressed of the Earth; anyone therefore who is heavy laden or who wants land to cultivate, may repair thither & abound, as in the Land of promise, with milk and honey." Greeley considered the 1862 Homestead Act to be one of the nation's greatest achievements. Though the valve turned out not to work as designed (the truly needy and oppressed couldn't afford to get *to* the free land, and many pioneers ended up tenants on land given to the railroads), I have to admit I have made the Plains a fantasy safety valve of my own now that its population in parts has returned to the nineteenth-century statistical definition of *frontier*.[3] Perhaps that restless gene persists, and the Plains still capture the imagination as a blank slate. *When the East defeats me / And its feast exceeds me / When the newspaper shrieks and bleeds,* as I wrote in one of those troubadour songs in my midtwenties, I think, Wouldn't it be nice to take a train west with the Brions and start fresh?

Minnie Brion met Charley Davis in 1880, shortly after she and her parents arrived in Unadilla, Nebraska—a railroad town thirty miles west of the Iowa border named, like the neighboring towns Syracuse and Palmyra, for a place back in New York. Charley was nine years older than Minnie, a tall, bearded, square-headed man with a hawk nose—a nineteenth-century caricature of my dad, except for the height. He had been in Nebraska fifteen years, having also grown up in New York. As a child he had worked with his father, riding the horses that towed boats back and forth on the Erie Canal. His father, a town pioneer who had also moved west, had died in Unadilla seven years earlier. He'd been a drinker and cusser like most men on the canal crews, yet Charley had grown up attractively devout, a member of the Protestant sect simply called the Christian Church, the only church in town (the Brions were Methodists). Charley hated booze, tobacco, baseball, and fiction, held no fondness for Catholics but loved animals. He was a renowned breaker of wild horses in eastern Nebraska, with what Minnie called a "dashing span of dappled black ponies & a swell buggy." They courted and married, and the next spring, Minnie bore their first child.[4]

The newlyweds soon fixed up a small white cottage in Unadilla with a front porch, grape arbor, and cement sidewalk. Charley laughed good-naturedly when his young wife's first loaf of bread failed miserably. As she wiped her tears, he placed the leaden loaf on the top shelf of the pantry as a souvenir, and the next time he rode to Lincoln he bought her a cookbook. They studied it together, taught themselves to coax a homestead of yeast into proving up as an honest loaf. After a few months, once Minnie had mastered the knead, Charley took the old loaf from the pantry shelf to the yard and buried it under a miniature headstone with the epitaph, MINNIE'S FIRST ATTEMPT AT BREAD MAKING.

With the generational migrations in and out of the Plains, this attempt had to be made anew. My dad learned to bake bread from my mom when they were young South Dakota pioneers; in a spiral notebook she wrote the five-loaf recipe he uses to this day. He has never lowered himself to buying storebought bread, except for the first couple of years of our twoman homestead, when I demanded it for my lunch box, and even then we ate a slice of his homemade toasted each morning. Growing up I was as uninterested in learning to bake bread as I was in classic rock, drugs, or electoral politics. But a latter-day frontiersman and poet friend of ours gave me *The Tassajara*

Bread Book when I left home, and with its help, in college I learned not to kill the yeast with overhot water, not to break the elastic gluten of the dough, to leave plenty of time for rising. I was far from home, but bread baking went hand in hand with the books about the Dust Bowl I was reading and the Prairie Provinces punk of the Weakerthans, a band I came to love those first years away. My favorite part was making the "sponge," a sort of wheat soup that seemed to boil with the ferment of the flour, yeast, and warm water.

Together my great-great-grandparents planted cherry, apple, plum, and peach trees, Minnie holding each trunk straight while Charley packed the dirt around the root-ball. She was growing rooted herself in Unadilla, so it was against her wishes and judgment when she and Charley and their son moved west in 1884 to a homestead in Antelope County, Nebraska. (My great-grandfather described his father, Charley, as "a staunch advocate of woman suffrage, believing that women in politics not only would put crooked machine politicians to flight, but institute prohibition of tobacco as well as of intoxicating liquor. Yet I doubt if he ever asked my mother's opinion before issuing a family interdiction. She, poor woman, had read too many books to be taken seriously."[5])

Members of both Charley's and Minnie's families had already moved west into Nebraska's interior. Still, after lovely Unadilla, Minnie found Antelope County to be "lonesome country," with "no roads, no houses, not a tree. Nothing except occasionaly a baren sand hill." The desert soon enough bloomed with a nice four-room house, a second child (named Una, a hint at where Minnie would rather have been living), thirty head of horses, and a thousand sheep—but the country was tough. A rain cistern that Charley's brother was hand-digging caved in and suffocated him. Two $1,800 imported Clydesdales died from eating moldy bread the hired girl had thrown out for the pigs. Charley himself nearly died when a blizzard caught him and a wagonload of potatoes, flour, cornmeal, sugar, coffee, and kerosene on the way back from the county seat of Neligh. His horses navigated the trackless way home, but the potatoes had scattered across the prairie, and the flour, meal, and kerosene had formed a toxic dough in the wagon bed.

Like my mom, Minnie tried to stay comfortable and endure. She banished the hired sheepherder from her dinner table because he smelled so rotten. After her brother-in-law suffocated and they had to take up his homestead as well, she fixed up an alcove there with her sewing machine and rocking chair as a pleasant refuge in which to work. Though she emerged as a steely homesteader who worked hard and never got sick, it seemed any joy she had in Antelope County was in spite of the place.

After a few seasons of disappointment, in which horse and mutton prices fell but rain did not, Charley and Minnie's pioneer spirit wilted. They traded their homestead for a hardware store and house back in Unadilla. They were hamlet merchants like my folks, except they didn't sell bongs and their business prospered, expanding into furniture and undertaking supplies. Charley even bought a newspaper, the *Nebraska Advertiser*, where Minnie learned to set the type. She was the more literate of the two: She'd won a leather-bound Bible as a child in New York for reciting the most Scripture of anybody in her Sunday school class, and now she taught her children to read well before they started school despite Charley's distrust for almost any book *other* than Scripture. At some expense, they published pamphlets advocating the prohibition of alcohol for the Woman's Christian Temperance Union and the Anti-Saloon League.

In 1894 Minnie bore a third child, my great-grandfather Clyde Brion Davis. The next year, they gave up on Nebraska altogether—never proving up either legally or spiritually—and moved to Chillicothe, Missouri, southeast to the land of reliable rainfall. That's it for Nebraska for us.

6.3

Giving up on the Plains was the rule, staying the exception. My family was not unusual, but the more satisfying story would be the one where Charley and Minnie survive the blizzards and the dead horses and go on to become civic leaders in some bustling, white-clapboard farm town where the local library is named for them. But they left, just as Mom's father left Oklahoma for Los Angeles; his family had migrated to the southern Plains of Oklahoma from South Carolina by way of Indiana and Arkansas—a different, Dixie shift west but one that was equally transitory. They didn't leave me much of a breadcrumb trail to follow, just some census entries, so I can only connect the decennial dots. I joined a long tradition when I left South Dakota for the East after my parents had migrated there. When I was a kid in the 1980s, the trees that pioneers like my own forebears had planted were as big as the ones back east (Nebraska, not some forested Eastern state, is the home of Arbor Day), but their colors were relatively ashen with the poor moisture. Even before my parents' divorce, our home bore the fissures of dislocation—we had not grown naturally from the seeds of the previous generation.

Unadilla today bears only faint traces of its nineteenth-century past. It has 342 inhabitants (in 1880 it had about 200) planted on a single hill, an island between the Burlington Northern Santa Fe to the south and the Nebraska Highway (State Highway 2) to the north. The village calls itself the Groundhog Capital of Nebraska. Its one-sided Main Street still abuts the railroad as if that were the town's lifeline, with half a dozen attached brick buildings under historic preservation: the post office, the village office, The Bar, Classic Cuts by Tonya, the Countryside Bank, and a couple of empty storefronts. These curve northwest along the railroad so that, standing in front of the post office, you can't see the bank six doors down. These buildings were established beginning in 1908, thirteen years after the Davises left for Missouri, and most were rebuilt three years later after a fire destroyed Main Street. My relatives had lived there in the wood-frame fire-trap era.[6]

Unadilla's true orientation these days is to its north along the Nebraska Highway, where TR Unadilla Mart is the only business. Few houses in town look more than fifty years old, though one small white house on Seventh and H Streets I imagine might have been my family's. It has two Victorian ornamentations on its south eaves, one of which was broken and dangling perilously the day I visited. Charley's Christian Church, established in 1873, is still there, but it was rebuilt in 1964. This and the United Methodist Church are the only churches in town. Most Unadillans commute to Palmyra, Syracuse, Nebraska City, or Lincoln to work.

About a mile and a half southwest, across the Burlington Northern Santa Fe train tracks on gravel roads, I found the Henry Dieken Tallgrass Prairie, which abutted a field of fuzzy soybeans itching to be harvested. This is fertile farmland, so the remnant of even a doormat of virgin prairie was remarkable here. It was preserved by the Nebraska Environmental Trust and the Wachiska Audubon Society with funds from the Nebraska State Lottery; the funding sign had twenty-five bullet holes in it. I had to climb up about five feet from the road onto the prairie, a reminder of how much topsoil the surrounding corn and soybean fields have lost to erosion in the years since homesteaders like my great-great-greats plowed the rest of the land. The grasses turned copper in the afternoon light and vibrated in the wind like tuning forks just struck. In a little mailbox was a black spiral notebook in a plastic bag where visitors (nine that summer) had written "gorgeous day" and "nice sunny day." One note, in a shaky hand, read, "Seeking moments of awe." Serenaded by the electric hum of locusts, I added my own note in ballpoint: "My great-grandfather was born in Unadilla in 1894. Came by to check out what it looked like before."

Back in town I tried to drop by the village office, but men were pouring a new sidewalk in front. The alley door was unlocked and the lights on, but nobody was there. I walked back around to the post office to ask the postmaster where the village clerk was. "You just passed her," she said. Back around to the alley, I poked my head into the one-room village office and asked about local history. I said my great-grandfather was born here.

"Oh, what was his name?" she asked.

"Clyde Brion Davis."

"Is *that* right?" she said with a little chuckle. She seemed impressed. She said she once wondered if there were any of his descendants out there she might invite back for the local parade sometime. She directed me to the cemetery, where I could find the graves of Charley's father, my dad's namesake, Jeremiah Davis, and Charley's brother Byron. How about that? A little celebrity doesn't feel bad, and it's pretty rare that Clyde Brion Davis's name carries any weight in this century. Though he left town before he could talk, he's remembered in the three-ring binder of local history as a man who "immortalized" Unadilla and is still perhaps the town's most famous son.

As a child around the turn of the twentieth century, Clyde tagged along on business trips with Charley; the boy became a "confirmed tramp," as he later put it—a Midwestern slingshot-and-paper-route kid in Chillicothe.[7] He snuck dime novels past Charley underneath his shirt and read them in the hayloft of the barn; he went creek fishing with a friend named Sliver using pork liver as bait. For several years, Charley and Minnie owned a wooden-box factory where Clyde worked after school to pay for his "nickel-dime novel" habit. After losing everything in the Panic of 1907—which Charley, a loyal Democrat, called "Teddy Roosevelt's panic"—the family moved to Kansas City. Clyde had finished the eighth grade in Chillicothe, so he sought no further schooling and worked to support the family. Reacting against his father's righteousness, he sought out his first shot of bourbon at fifteen, as soon as he could pass for a man walking into a tavern. He would later describe one of his hobbies as spinning around members of the Woman's Christian Temperance Union (not his mother, one hopes) in revolving doors.[8]

After a stint in the Navy during World War I, Clyde moved to Denver and worked as, among other things, a furnace repairman, an electrician, a detective, a commercial artist, a printer's apprentice, and then a newspaper reporter. He married a German-American painter, Martha Wirt, who gave birth to their only child, David (my granddad), in 1927, a month before Charley died. Over the next decade, Clyde flitted from job to job, at newspapers in Denver, Albuquerque, Seattle, and Buffalo, chasing fortune even more restlessly than his parents had.

Minnie stayed with her youngest son Clyde's family through several cross-country moves during the Depression and the Second World War—a third parent to David, or sometimes, it seemed to him, an older sister. She attended Methodist church socials in each new town for many years, though her son was still irreverent (Clyde called himself "a Protestant in politics and a Democrat in religion"[9]). Once, the family took a Christmastime road trip from Denver to Los Angeles, driving straight south to New Mexico to avoid snowstorms in the Rockies, then west along the Mexican border. In Las Cruces, my granddad, aged about ten, and Minnie wandered around the adobe center while Clyde and Martha were sick with the flu. In the lobby of their pueblo inn, they puzzled over the Mexican relics and gewgaws, and Minnie embarrassingly mistook a picturesque Hispanic woman for a life-size doll.[10]

In middle age, despite his eighth-grade education, Clyde began to write novels. Charley was dead, along with his distaste for fiction. Clyde attributed his literary pursuits not to his father's demise but to an ulcer and a need to slow down. After his first book, *The Anointed*, became a Book of the Month Club selection in 1937, he quit reporting to write full-time. His second book, *"The Great American Novel,"* was even more successful. And it is his third that could perhaps snag me a parade-marshal gig in Unadilla. *Nebraska Coast* is a pioneer story that follows a Davis-like family from western New York (working on the Erie Canal and everything) to a Unadilla-like town during the Civil War years, told from the perspective of a boy who would have been about Charley's age.

I wonder if Clyde had the same wish I did, to own a stable and prosperous family history in Nebraska, because he imagined a town where his fictional grandfather was the founder, first postmaster, first banker, and first mayor of the fictional Unadilla, called Macdougall. In the end Jack Macdougall becomes a Democratic candidate for U.S. Congress. This is the myth of settlement, of *those who stayed on*. But *those who moved out*, our real family included, were inextricable from the history of this landscape of motion.

Nebraska Coast and Clyde Brion Davis's other books lack— self-consciously so—the dramatic and poetic grandeur of Willa Cather's pioneer novels. Young Clinton Macdougall, the narrator, grows up to a mundane fate, becoming a teller at Macdougall State Bank and giving a rather hagiographic account of his father's career. No mystic prairies here. In general Clyde fashioned an identity as an anti-intellectual intellect, a twentieth-century Mark Twain. He wrote a book defending modern American culture against the elitist attacks of "oolong-sipping esthetes" like T. S. Eliot (who, Clyde noted wryly, was also a Missourian despite his Continental pretensions).[11] He wrote three young-adult books for boys and edited an anthology of "good" writing for boys. He wrote twenty books in all, of gradually declining success. He returned to journalism briefly in World War II, trying to report from Europe; he got stranded in Portugal and sailed home after a couple of dyspeptic months. In 1945 *The Anointed* was adapted into a lesser Clark Gable movie called *Adventure*. Clyde, and apparently everybody else, hated the film. *Nebraska Coast* was not as well received or as successful as his first two books, but one week it was only five spots below another Plains novel, *The Grapes of Wrath*, on the bestseller list.[12]

Clyde may have immortalized Unadilla, but his restless touring severed any connection I might have to it. In the early 1940s, my granddad David attended five high schools in four years, including Beverly Hills High (a short-lived screenwriting gig for Clyde) and Bronx Science (when Clyde tried editing books in New York). He ultimately graduated from the YMCA's McBurney School in New York, alma mater of J. D. Salinger and, later, the Beastie Boys' King Ad-Rock. Granddad served as a post–World War II military policeman in Germany, then enrolled at Dartmouth on the GI Bill and later married my Connecticut WASP grannie, Frances Warner. He earned a PhD at Harvard and taught U.S. history at Cornell and Yale, ultimately picking up a Pulitzer Prize for his book *The Problem of Slavery in Western Culture* and a National Book Award for the sequel, *The Problem of Slavery in the Age of Revolution.*[13] Whew. How far we had come from Antelope County.

6.4

Beyond the fiction of *Nebraska Coast*, there is a true model for what *staying on* looked like in the nineteenth century, just as Dad's tenacious staying on was a foil for Mom's moving out in the twentieth. Minnie's older sister Clara migrated from New York State to Nebraska with her husband, the Reverend George F. Cole, a few months after Minnie came with Mother and Father Brion. Rather than settling in relative civilization like Minnie and her eventual husband, Charley, Clara and George Cole paused only briefly in grape-arbored Unadilla before migrating into the prairie wilderness to set about the evangelical work of "planting churches." They were the first of the family to move to Antelope County.

George was over six feet tall, with amused eyes and a bushy, graying Civil War goatee. His piety was steadfast; he would reliably bark, "Confound it!" rather than "Damn!" when he smacked his crown on the cellar doorjamb. Clara, twenty-one years his junior (they married when she was eighteen, he thirty-nine and back from the Civil War), stood barely five feet, with a soft voice, deep-set eyes, and a high forehead. In Antelope County, George began preaching at Oakdale and Buffalo Creek, and later Elm Grove on alternate Sundays. The editor of the Oakdale *Pen and Plow* teased "Reverend Father Cole" in his first Nebraska winter for foolishly or faithfully trekking ten miles into the country in temperatures 10 degrees below zero to perform a marriage. By the next spring, Reverend Father Cole was painting a new Methodist church building in Oakdale. "His progress however is quite slow," the *Pen and Plow* razzed, "on account of his having to stop every few minutes to give absolution to his profane carpenters."[14]

Beyond the hardships of climate, those sparsely settled plains were anarchic and amoral, a Janklovian frontier. Drunkard vigilantes competed for power with corrupt cattle barons, and fraud, violence, and vice abounded. "Sky pilots," that is, traveling missionaries like Reverend Cole, tried to reform the frontier society, but much of their morality never reached the subsoil—it blew dry in the unending wind or ran off from the plowed ground. At the Methodist church in Gordon, Nebraska, parishioners migrated straight from tent services to the saloon; a traveling sky pilot staying in a homesteader's dugout would put his missionary's Bible away and peel potatoes for his supper, and would partake in his host's homemade currant wine if he knew what was best for him.[15]

Reverend Cole was not so timid. Once, invited to preach south of Oakdale, he caught wind that some young rogues were fixing to disrupt his crusade. As he stepped to the front of the schoolhouse where he was to preach before the children's wooden desks, he brandished a pistol from the tail pocket of his Prince Albert coat, plonked it on the lectern, and said, "I have been invited to this school to preach the gospel and preach the gospel I shall do."[16]

Clara and George convinced pioneers in Oakdale to donate some of their meager spoils to build the one-room church and maybe even to pay the minister a pittance. Clara led the Ladies Aid Society, fund-raising to build a fifty-foot spire above the empty plain. Ladies Aid then hosted a twenty-five-cent supper, including sweet strawberries, ice cream, and lemonade, to buy an organ. The *Pen and Plow* celebrated the trappings of a permanent civilization in Oakdale and judged, "The church owes its existence to a few women who fussed and bothered about it."[17]

Fussing and bothering were to be lauded on the part of the sky pilot's family so long as they were confined to his "sacerdotal calling." In the summer of 1881, George F. Cole apparently cast his lot with one candidate for county office over another. The *Pen and Plow* reported rather gleefully that the clergyman was "bounced" by his congregation, and the paper reasoned, "It is dangerous to interest our missionaries in county seat matters very much. If any one of them should be so efficient in prayer as to call the Almighty down to this business *thoroughly* we believe that Oakdale and Neligh would suffer the fate of Sodom and Gomorrah, and that every mother's son of us would go to Hades."[18]

His civic sin was evidently soon absolved. The Oakdale Ladies Aid held another donation party in early 1882 to support the "temporal wants" of the Cole family, then expecting their third child—this rustled $30 cash and $31.25 in provisions for the penurious parson.[19] That winter ("Severe, snow and blow," George noted in a church logbook) the Methodist Episcopal bishop transferred the family east to the town of Allen, whose congregation planted a church ("We could not eat church") and bought the family a team of horses ("We could not eat horses") but did not pay George.[20] After just three months, he resigned from the Methodist conference and, with Clara and the three children, rejoined the extended family in Antelope County, just before Charley and Minnie made their short-lived homestead nearby.

George tried the lumber business in Ewing, preaching occasionally, but after three years, he towed his family west across sixty-five miles of absolutely treeless plains to a town called Brewster. There they tried running a grocery but soon moved, as if back in time, outside town to a sod homestead with newsprint and tomato-can labels as wallpaper. The family often subsisted on parched corn, an American Indian staple, and George resumed frontier sky-piloting, preaching in the Brewster schoolhouse every other Sunday afternoon. Clara ultimately bore six children between 1875 and 1898, and they raised an older foster daughter. In Brewster the children hunted and sold prairie chickens to pay their school tuition. After nine years, the family gave up and returned to Antelope County, then moved west along the Chicago and North Western line to a farm near O'Neill, where George F. Cole died in 1904 at age seventy-two. Here in the tiny town of Emmet, at last, the family settled.

The Coles were as restless as the Davises, except their moves were smaller and there was this end point. I wonder if the Cole children thought wistfully of the bountiful life their cousins Glen, Una, and Clyde lived in green Missouri the way I thought of the Dan Reed Network and my alternate self in

Portland. Perhaps not. The cycles of coming and going, staying on and moving out, have produced some conflicting chauvinisms regarding the region: the bemused *that must've sucked* pity I get when I tell people in New York or Oregon where I'm from, and the insistent *I couldn't live like that* disbelief when I tell Plains folk that I'm a New Yorker now. I sense insecurity on both sides, but it might be my own.

6.5

If *The Wonderful Wizard of Oz* is read as political allegory, the Cowardly Lion was William Jennings Bryan. Several historians have theorized that L. Frank Baum's 1900 fairy tale is an extended metaphor for the prairie politics of the late nineteenth century, and in particular for the debate over the gold standard and the Populists' support for free silver as shown by Dorothy's silver slippers (which the movie made ruby red) on the golden "road of yellow brick." In this formulation, Dorothy is the American Everygirl; the cyclone is the Populist movement; the Scarecrow, the farmer; the Tin Woodman, the industrial laborer; the Wicked Witch of the East is Grover Cleveland; the Wicked Witch of the West is the climatic harshness of the West, or perhaps William McKinley; the winged monkeys are American Indians (in 1890, as a newspaper editor in my birthplace, Aberdeen, South Dakota, L. Frank Baum had called for the "total annihilation" of the Indians, construing it as a mercy killing for a beaten-down race); the yellow Winkies are Filipinos subjugated by imperialism abroad; and the Wizard of Oz himself, the Republican strategist

Mark Hanna, the man behind the curtain.[21] Even reading the book with these emerald glasses on, the moments of correspondence are flash frames impossible to string together into a sensible reel. It's rather like watching the film version while listening to *Dark Side of the Moon:* If you want to believe they line up, the evidence will appear for a second at a time, intriguingly, but never quite beyond a reasonable doubt.

William Jennings Bryan took the pulpit in 1890 as the face of Populism. He was a Christian and a teetotaler (Toto?) like Clara and George, Charley and Minnie. Charley Davis once declared, "Only one greater and purer man ever lived on the face of this earth, and *He* never trod American soil."[22] As a Nebraska congressman, presidential candidate, and chautauqua circuit lecturer, Bryan spoke in a lion's roar of colorful absolutes, contrasting the "people to whom a ten-cent meal would be a luxury" with the Carnegies and other aristocrats in "stately palaces" who throw "banquets, which rival in magnificence the banquets of ancient times."[23] This mix of Presbyterian prairie morality and redistribution of wealth presaged my teenage punk song "Potluck Society"—they seem like strange bedfellows nowadays, but having grown up with an antiabortion, liberal Christian father I have seen a glimpse of it.[24]

A progressive reform spirit sprouted in this land where civic society had not yet furrowed its orderly rows. Free-market capitalism on the frontier, like the weather there—cold that cracked a cast-iron stove, hail that atomized a crop in minutes—was tyrannical and senseless, and strong settlers were weak in the face of panic and monopoly. Debt-triggered lunacy, suicide, fratricide, infanticide, were as common as freezing to death or suffocating in a hand-dug cistern. Before long, small farmers and merchants lost patience with the big-city robber barons and corporate trusts. Out on the Plains, the heartless corporations were primarily represented by the railroads, the octopuses that ran their tentacles across the people's land—subsidized by tax dollars—and then charged the people half their crop's market value to haul it only as far as Chicago. What's more, the monopolies that sold plows and barn planks to Plains farmers had lobbied for tariffs to shelter them from foreign competition, but the farmers' wheat and corn sold at grim prices on the open world market. Some farmers turned to burning their corn for heat, and others were strangled by their debt to the octopus. Before the turn of the twentieth century, a good share were ready, as Woody Guthrie would later wheeze, to "roll on into Congress on that Farmer-Labor Train"—to unite the Scarecrow and the Tin Woodman with Lion Bryan for the trip to Oz.

Whatever the silver-tongued "Boy Orator of the Platte" said floated across a hall on a voice so powerfully magnetic I can scarcely imagine it (a recording sounds to modern ears like a reedy deadpan, a didactic Woody Guthrie[25]). A Swiss immigrant who saw Bryan in western Nebraska in 1888 called his voice "a flood swift and clear as the Niobrara."[26] My great-grandfather Clyde called it "a magnificent voice, an *incredible* voice," a "star-gauge pipe organ."[27] Beyond the voice, some were less charitable—and in the end Clyde would agree with them—observing that like the Platte River, Bryan was six inches deep and a mile wide at the mouth. (The "cowardly" part is one of the many points where Oz-as-allegory scrapes bottom: Perhaps, a scholar speculates, Bryan didn't fight hard enough for silver in the 1896 presidential race?) Undaunted by criticism, he loomed from the stage, his round, worried face balanced on a six-foot columnar body, and paused every seven or eight words as if he had written his speeches out in psalm.

Willa Cather described Bryan as an embodiment of the paradox of the "entire Middle West; all of its newness and vigor, its magnitude and monotony, its richness and lack of variety, its inflammability and volubility, its strength and its crudeness, its high seriousness and self-confidence, its egotism and its nobility." He "buttered his toast with an epigram," she wrote—descriptions that display her own characteristic mix of skepticism and grandeur.[28]

My family was swept up in the rural wave of reform. In 1882 the *Pen and Plow* carried a list of twenty-five names prefaced, "We, the undersigned Ladies of Oakdale and vicinity, ask the voters of Antelope county to vote for woman suffrage." Clara M. Cole, my great-great-great aunt, was on the list.[29] Once the Coles moved east from Oakdale to plant another church in Dixon County, George wrote back to ask how the suffrage vote in Antelope County had gone; it failed statewide. (L. Frank Baum's mother-in-law was also a prominent suffragist, and Baum hosted Susan B. Anthony when she visited Aberdeen.) Clara's desire for enfranchisement fit within her Methodist commitment to making the world better, more moral. She and her brother-in-law Charley Davis also agreed on the alcohol question. Clara was known to barge into Nebraska saloons with the Woman's Christian Temperance Union to shame men off whiskey. In the throes of drought, their families did not have enough to eat and they were spending money on liquor; she begged them to go home. Charley, for his part, reasoned, "I think it's safe to say that for every drop of intoxicating beverage consumed by men in America, two tears have been shed by women and children."[30]

Charley Davis met William Jennings Bryan a year after the orator—another Plains carpetbagger—moved from Illinois to

Lincoln, Nebraska, with his wife, Mary. Charley and Minnie had recently abandoned their Antelope County homestead and returned to Unadilla and their Anti-Saloon League pamphlets. Democrats in Lincolnland, Davis and Bryan, two tall believers, worked together on a losing congressional campaign in 1888 — for J. Sterling Morton, originator of Arbor Day — and became hunting buddies. Charley was thirty-nine; Bryan, just twenty-eight. "I would have no idea," Charley's son Clyde later wrote, "what Bryan, who read both Greek and Latin fluently and who could quote Shakespeare and Milton by the rod, pole or perch, talked about to the horseman and hamlet merchant as they huddled behind a duck blind in a chill dawn."[31] The two became close enough that when Bryan was campaigning against McKinley in 1900, he pulled Charley and young Clyde up to the onstage VIP seating at one campaign stop and then visited their house after he spoke in Chillicothe.

Though Bryan was increasingly unsuccessful in his three campaigns for president, many of the reforms he fought for — to limit corporate power, to enforce antitrust laws, to enact income tax and child labor laws, to promote world peace — became hallmarks of the Progressive Era and beyond. In the run-up to World War I, Bryan resigned as Woodrow Wilson's secretary of state to protest the administration's bellicosity toward Germany. Yet, half a century later, one historian looked back and saw a "direct political bloodline" from Bryan to Wilson and on to Franklin D. Roosevelt and the New Deal. Bryan tirelessly stuck up for "people who live between the Alleghenies and the Golden Gate," the humble folk "whose rights have been violated and whose interests have been disregarded in order that somebody else may be enriched."[32] Later, his idealism became embarrassingly antimodern in fights against alcohol and Darwinism; that his ardent Plains piety was unbuffeted by rational argument was a tragic flaw as well as a virtue.

I don't know how valiantly my ancestors struggled against the trusts or against corporate patriarchy or war in the years of Populism's ascent. I want to believe they were protopacifist New Dealers. The Plains where I grew up bore only faint vestiges of its progressive past. Politics were increasingly dominated by reactionary figures such as Bill Janklow, and the Christian right kept up Bryanesque campaigns against evolution and legalized abortion (which Bryan, too, would certainly have abhorred) while dropping any trace of his antiwar passion or redistributive economics. I usually construed my parents' politics as nonnative, so tracing a "direct political bloodline" back through our real bloodline affords our beliefs a measure of legitimacy, of cred, that I never enjoyed growing up. Tendentious as it may be, it's reassuring to connect the fragments I have of these ancestors' lives into such a narrative.

SEVEN

Ruth Harris

7.1

Ruth Harris is my living bloodline to Nebraska, to the pioneer history of my Brion roots, and to the Christian radicalism of Populism and the Woman's Christian Temperance Union. For my forebears—Charley and Minnie, and then Clyde—Nebraska was just one stop in a restless pursuit of prosperity, and the next century of our history became a continual uprooting, taking off just when the arbor was starting to bear fruit. Ruth's grandparents, Clara and Reverend George F. Cole, once they landed in north-central Nebraska, stayed there. Plenty in ensuing generations scattered, but George and Clara had laid enough of a foundation that there was something to go back to. Minnie and Charley Davis's side of the family had no reunions (there was little unity to re-create), so we attended Clara and George's descendants' reunion in Nebraska every few years. On the painted family tree they displayed there, the Davis-Brion branch was actually a sapling beside the steady Cole-Brion trunk.

In part it was this symbolic rootedness that drew me to Ruth, my second cousin twice removed. It was also how her biography intersected with famous struggles for justice in the late twentieth century, with the civil rights movement in the 1950s and '60s and with its global echoes in ensuing decades. Mostly, though, it was that she appeared as an antidote to my loneliness, a parallel to the solitary line I'd drawn of my life as a now-expatriate South Dakotan: broken family, only child, contrarian interests, exiled, and now looking homeward. Identifying with Willa Cather or — why not? — Superman (only child in Kansas, outsider, with a changed name and a secret behind it...) is a way of glorifying one tiny existence inside such huge horizons, turning loneliness into singularity, anointment, promise. But finding a literal cousin who was also a kindred spirit was something new to hold on to. Ruth shone to me as a model for how to live outside as a product of the Plains, a paleoleftist, a commonsense intellectual (not as defensive as Clyde Brion Davis), a generous soul who wears the scars of childhood traumas and secrets with grace and doesn't cover them.

Ruth is the daughter of Clara and Reverend George Cole's youngest daughter, Esther. She was born in 1920 in O'Neill, Nebraska, sixteen years after George died. I'd met her at a couple of Nebraska reunions, and twice besides after I moved east, but it was at the 2005 reunion, when I was twenty-five and a reluctant and confused New Yorker, that she first struck me as a kindred spirit. We were in O'Neill, where she'd graduated from high school in 1937. On the surface, it was odd that I thought of her as my missing Plains link, because it was all too clear how far she and O'Neill had diverged. Ruth, eighty-five years old and never married, now lived in California. She had come to the reunion with her friend Patricia Patterson, whom she introduced in her childhood Methodist church, pulling herself up from her pew, as her "traveling companion" and as the author of a national United Methodist Women study guide that year. Ruth was visibly distraught over the Iraq War and was praying for peace. She had been praying and working for peace for sixty years.

The church, meanwhile, had acquired a new building since the days when Ruth sang in the choir there, not a wood-frame prairie church like the ones her grandparents planted but a modern, institutional brick affair. When the trim, mustached minister took the pulpit this Sunday, his sermon smugly implied, among other things, that Mahatma Gandhi, not a part of the body of Christ, was presently in hell. He derided the naive openness of a California church he'd visited that had hung a portrait of Gandhi in its narthex. Rural Nebraska today is dryly conservative country, not keen on redistribution of wealth, struggles for liberation, or freedom from exploitation, to use some of the Bryanesque "tions" with which I have been familiar since my *Reagan is a mean man* days, and which Ruth sees as fundamental to Christ's revolutionary teachings. Still, for me, Ruth belonged to that place—the church, the family, Nebraska—more than whatever parson the Methodist bishop had placed in O'Neill those few years. Dad and I gravitated toward Ruth and Pat at the Nebraska reunion as effortlessly as O'Neill's Elkhorn River flows east to the Platte and on to the Missouri across apparently flat and waterless land.

With summers in Portland and Amherst, I hadn't made it to a reunion in fifteen years, since the summer of my parents' custody fight. I was curious to see my fourth cousin Nicole, a spunky tomboy who'd been my best friend that week when I was ten (she was six months younger), out at Fort Robinson, just south of Hot Springs, where I had been about to move. This was the fort where Crazy Horse was sucker-punch bayoneted in

1877, where Scotty Philip worked as a messenger to various bands of Sioux and Cheyenne, and where he married Crazy Horse's sister-in-law Sally Larabee in 1879. On the broad porches of the old fort, Nicole introduced me to the Nintendo Game Boy and inspired an unsuccessful campaign to receive one of my own—sadly the addictive gray box was too similar to a TV. Yet, as if our two skateboards had different bearings, fifteen years later I was in New York playing in a punk rock band, while Nicole was an Air Force navigator stationed in Omaha and Qatar and the wife of a Marine.

After we'd all had breakfast one morning in a downtown O'Neill café, the Harris branch of the family—Ruth and Nicole's branch—held their catching-up session at the Holiday Inn. They sat in a circle and told one another what they'd been up to since the last reunion. Afterward, I saw Nicole rushing to her parents' minivan in the parking lot, her face red and tearstained, hair stuck to her cheeks. I looked quickly away. It turned out that Ruth, her grandmother's sister, had voiced stalwart opposition to the war and occupation in Iraq and had recounted her weekly protests against it in the name of Jesus Christ. This had been too much for a young woman who needed to believe she was risking her life for Iraqi freedom or Middle East stability. Ruth was sympathetic—her grandfather was a Civil War vet, her father a World War I vet, and she had helped her aunt Ethel in her efforts as a state champion scrap-metal-drive organizer during World War II—but she was finally unyielding in her morality.

Later I asked Ruth if she in fact believed there were *no* just wars. "*Yes,*" she said, "I'm there now. But I've come a long way, because I was born up in a country that—and I now have relatives that really absolutely, you know..." She paused ruefully, looking off and searching for the right words. "Their children are right in the middle of it. So sometimes in family reunions it gets tough, because I love 'em."[1]

7.2

Ruth makes me think of an unshelled almond: a fibrous, sunspotted exterior with a substantial and almost sweet heart. Not candied but powerfully, earthily sweet. Her manner is blunt. (The word *heart* is problematic, since she's more than a dozen years past a quadruple bypass that was supposed to last ten years.) She's a touch over five feet, stocky, and topped with boycut hair dyed the color of a penny — not a brand-new one but newer than she is. And her voice is "husky," as she puts it, thanks to a singing teacher at Morningside College, a Methodist school in Sioux City, Iowa, who "ruined more voices this side of the Mississippi than any other." Her whole range isn't gone, though. Standing next to her in church the first time, I got a surprise: She speaks gravel but still sings a vibrato soprano.

A couple of years after the O'Neill reunion, I flew from New York to Los Angeles, hoping to discover something about the country I passed over in between, feeling nearer to Ruth than second cousins twice removed. Ruth and Pat live in Claremont, California, in a Christian retirement community called Pilgrim Place. Their house is a single-level with river-stone pillars — a sign fastened to one proclaimed, WAR IS NOT THE ANSWER. When Ruth and I first sat down to talk beside the stone hearth, Pat told me to feel free to rein Ruth in and put her back on topic; she gets excited about a story and "says more than you need." Ruth lifted her large hands and said, "Guilty!"

before laughing almost soundlessly. Pat smiled. She is fifteen years younger than Ruth, several inches taller, and wears her silver curls short and natural. I stayed on their hide-a-bed couch in Pilgrim Place for a week, and for a few hours each day Ruth sat in her leather chair with her legs up on a matching hassock (for her circulation), following and drifting from a word-processed chronology of her life she'd prepared.

The first settled hometown of George and Clara Cole's descendants was Emmet, population eighty-eight, eight miles outside O'Neill and just twenty or thirty miles northwest of the old homesteads in Antelope County—toward the eastern side of the great empty room of the Plains. Topographic lines through Nebraska run north-south like the floorboards of a slouching pioneer house, tilting down ten feet per mile east. It looks more or less flat from the ground, but Rockies snowmelt and wetlands in the sand hills west of there will creep across the grassland like a glass of water spilled on the high side of the room.

Emmet sat nestled between the Chicago and North Western railroad tracks and the Elkhorn River. Ruth's mother, Esther Cole, was born thirty miles southeast, in Ewing, in 1898 and was just five years old when *her* father, George Cole, died. But there was still plenty of family around; two ponds nearby were called Grandma's Lake (after Clara) and Uncle Pat's Lake (after Esther's brother-in-law). In the center of town stood a four-thousand-ton-capacity hay barn part owned by George and Clara's youngest son, Guy. Five to twenty-five train cars of hay creaked east from Emmet each day in late summer; in the long-shadowed afternoons, after loading, hay farmers played cards in town until dark and headed home—there was no saloon. Thirty tough years in Nebraska, and the Cole family at last lived well.

In 1915, though, Clara up and left Emmet to take a new homestead near Sundance, Wyoming, where free land remained to prove up on. She was sixty-two and a widow ten years, but perhaps she'd grown so used to frontier poverty that her family's haying prosperity in Emmet made her nervous; perhaps, being Minnie's sister, she possessed that restless gene that wouldn't retire. She followed one of her older daughters west and lived in a one-room hut, sometimes with a dozen other former Nebraskans. Ruth's mother, Esther, was sixteen at the time and desperately wanted to finish high school, to become the first in her family with a diploma. She feared Wyoming would not furnish that chance, but Clara insisted that her daughter come homestead. Of two strong wills, Esther's won out: She stayed and attended first the Catholic boarding school in O'Neill, Nebraska (where the nuns mocked her for being a Methodist), and then a public school in nearby Atkinson.

When she graduated, she got a job teaching, just as her aunt Minnie (who also had a diploma) had done back in New York State. Esther soon met Ross Harris in O'Neill and fell in love. They married at Fort Leavenworth, Kansas, in 1918, just as Ross was to ship out for France. He sent her love letters from the trenches. After he returned the next year, they nested in Emmet, Nebraska, in a white frame house with a large front porch, a second floor with multiple rooms, and a broken Victrola that children might try to spin at 78 rpm. After a few years in Wyoming, Grandma Clara returned and moved in down the street to a white two-bedroom house with a chicken coop, and apple trees, corn, and potatoes abounding in her yard.

Like me, Ruth was born to a store-owning family and a fated marriage. When she was born in 1920, Esther and Ross owned the Emmet general store. Ross would hold Ruth sometimes in a cloud on his lap—she grew to love the smell of cigars—but he often worked late at the store and also perhaps tended to extra-marital interests he'd acquired during the war. Nonetheless, Esther was soon pregnant with a second child, busy, and ill. Ruth, then, wandered to Grandma Clara's house and followed around her apron strings.

Clara, by this time tinier than ever, bent by her voyages, had returned in part to shepherd her grandchildren. Despite her diminutiveness and her meek demeanor, she gave pious center to an increasingly dispersed and dissolute family. She still eschewed moonshine, and she kept the family Bible open in the center of her supper table. She taught her grandchildren how to squeeze weeks out of ten dollars and four good meals from a chicken—two days baked or broiled, then chicken à la king, then chicken patties. She paid Ruth pennies to read aloud or swat flies, and cured juvenile ailments by spiking honey or grape juice with kerosene.

"She was one of—my sister Betty does the same thing, they hum or sing or whisper kind of very softly while they work. I don't do that, but they do," Ruth told me. Clara sang "He Lead-eth Me," "Leaning on the Everlasting Arms," and "What a Friend We Have in Jesus" as she peeled potatoes or spun wool or knit. These were songs of comfort and stability in a life that had been anything but comfortable and stable. "Like I said," Ruth told me after rendering a sweet refrain of each hymn she recalled, chin lifted and soprano intact—*Leaning, leaning, leaning, on the everlasting arms*—"when I was in China and the going really got tough, I found myself, under my breath, sing-ing the same hymns."

In 1926 Ross sold the Emmet store to Esther's sister and bought a bigger one in O'Neill, the Holt County seat, home to two thousand customers. Esther had had a third child the year before and was about to become pregnant again. All of hers were hard pregnancies, but she helped Ross establish the new store whenever she wasn't sick or tending the children. He worked late a lot, and she and the children would sit around the table waiting for him as their supper got cold.

Ruth wonders if it was the shell shock from trench warfare that led her father to liquor, if he acquired his taste for philandering in the chaos of world war as well. He was certainly drinking and almost certainly running around before the Depression hit, but after the stock market crashed in 1929, he lost his wits. He suddenly abandoned his wife with five children (one a newborn and two chronically ill) and left O'Neill with another woman. The grocery closed without him that winter, and the family had no money, only a root cellar stocked with the frozen potatoes and beans that cashless customers had tendered.

7.3

Despite her tough exterior, Ruth is what an ecologist might call a bioindicator, a hypersensitive species that can serve as a bellwether for pollution or climate shifts, like a prairie lichen that begins to disappear when sulfur-dioxide levels get too high. This became clear to me right away. The first night I stayed in Claremont, Ruth and Pat took me out for Italian at the Harvard Square Café. It was late spring, when a "marine layer" of fog grows threadbare and wisps away each noon, uncovering a rainbow of flowers until the dark and desert-cool evening. A mounted fan on the restaurant patio blew directly down Ruth's neck; we asked the waitress to turn it off. Ruth had nearly died of pneumonia a few summers back and was now vigilant to avoid the chill or bug or fall that could stop her fragile body.

Before our pasta came, Pat ordered a cabernet sauvignon and offered Ruth a taste. Ruth smiled, patient and eager both. "I think I will," she said in a hoarse whisper, nodding and raising her eyebrows. She lifted the glass bulb, her hand shaking, and let a splash of the crimson wash into her mouth. She smiled again and savored the last drops from her lips. From that one warm sip, the daughter of teetotalers and alcoholics took a great joy.

When we pulled up beside the stone pillars back home, it was dark, and Pat strolled toward their little lane and gazed skyward. "Would you look at that?"

Ruth eased out of the passenger seat and scooted through the twilight, aluminum cane in hand, toward Pat.

"It's just a little fingernail of moon," Pat said. It was accompanied by a twinkling Venus. Ruth grinned at me and raised her eyebrows again as if to say, *Did you see that? Wow* — as awed as I would have been if we'd all just seen a moon-size shooting star. The evening prepared me for a week of heightened emphasis and sensitivity.

A few nights later, during our nightly routine of watching the BBC News from five to five thirty, Ruth became frantically agitated by reports of gang rapes by Tutsi warlords in Congo and Israeli air strikes on money-changing shops in Gaza. We turned off the TV and she went to start making guacamole, hushing Pat and me: "I just want some quiet and to make this." Her doctor had advised her to fast from the news, and salt, for the sake of her heart, but she disobeyed every day for the *BBC World Report* and Amy Goodman's *Democracy Now!* On this day she couldn't even watch *Amy*, as she calls it. Perhaps her wonder and empathy are in part generational — I think of crowds swooning for William Jennings Bryan compared with my jaded reaction to MP3s of his wax-cylinder recordings. Yet much of it is Ruth's temperament, simply: The world and its problems stir her tremendously, and she does not shield herself from them but seeks them out.

Bryan himself once explained, his silver tongue nowhere near his cheek:

> I am fond of radishes; my good wife knows it and keeps me supplied with them when she can. I eat radishes in the morning; I eat radishes at noon; I eat radishes at night; I eat radishes between meals; I like radishes. I plant radish seed—put the little seed into the ground, and go out in a few days and find a full grown radish. The top is green, the body of the root is white and almost transparent, and around it I sometimes find a delicate pink or red. Whose hand caught the hues of a summer sunset and wrapped them around the radish's root down there in the darkness in the ground? I cannot understand a radish; can you? If one refused to eat anything until he could understand the mystery of its growth, he would die of starvation; but mystery does not bother us in the dining-room—it is only in the church that mystery seems to give us trouble.[2]

One evening when Ruth was eight or nine and her mother, Esther, couldn't watch her and her brother Bink (Ross Jr.), Ross Sr. drove the children to a farm outside O'Neill where he and the farmer were to slaughter the beef to be sold the next day (refrigeration had not yet come to the Plains). Ross got out of the car, told Ruth and Bink he would return in a minute, and slammed the door. They climbed into the back to wait, stand-ing on the seat and gazing out the window, their small, soft arms propped on the dash. They couldn't see the barn in the fading light, but soon they heard a shrieking animal. Terrified, they pounded on the window, but Ross couldn't hear them. The shrieking went on. After eighty years, Ruth can still hear it.

"All of the experience that my life brought me after China was, I became—I'll have to tell you that later, but my job was world traveling," she said to me one day, losing track of the chronological list of topics on her lap and jumping ahead to her late twenties as a Methodist missionary in China during Mao's revolution and the Korean War. "Traveling all over and seeing people everywhere in terrible situations in the third world. And I mean, I really, I couldn't possibly be a Republican, and I just thought Reagan was *terrible*, and when he died last year or whenever it was, I thought, *My God, we still worship that guy because he was a Hollywood star. What* is *this?*" Her voice began to crescendo, and she batoned the air with her pencil like a choir conductor approaching a frenzied peak. "Aren't we ever going to grow up? Didn't we learn *any*thing from the Vietnam War? You know, I hired Pat, I virtually hired her to come and work on the *peace* emphasis of a job that I had in the World Division, and we worked our *tail* off in terms of opposition—that was Board of Missions work, it's missionary work. That's *part* of the Church's work." She was insistent, and her raspy voice climbed into tune. "And it didn't take—we could see all the time, and then this war, I mean, *preemptive war?!*"

Finally she caught herself, let her arm rest, and laid her clipboard in her lap. I myself was a bit shaken by this. Though Ruth's orientation is dramatically more activist and outward than mine, I, too, felt keenly the depressing truth that a woman who spent decades of her adult life working toward peace and civil rights would spend her last good years watching a preemptive war and a reactionary era on the news. Perhaps a family breakup at a formative age heightens one's sensitivity.

"You know," she said quietly, "I mean, it's just so painful. And then I go out, and Nicole, and to have her cry all night at the family reunion because I overspeak and let some of my pain hurt. That's part of the story."

7.4

After Ross left, Esther Cole Harris got a job. She had her diploma and experience as a teacher and a teller at Emmet State Bank. Her brother lent his car, and she began taking the 1930 census, accounting for a portion of the 16,509 people in the 2,393 square miles of Holt County, a boiling cloud of dust, and no doubt gossip, trailing behind her. Esther's mother, Clara, came from Emmet to care for Ruth and her brothers and sisters, and Esther's brothers invited her family to Emmet for suppers. She moved her children to a smaller house on the north side of O'Neill, which had no running water, only a pump in the kitchen, despite being right next to the town standpipe. After the census, Esther considered her options. She did not want to get married again; Ross was the only man she would ever love. She did not want to be a nurse or a teacher. In another brave move, she decided to run for public office.

In 1931, Holt County had an open seat for its register of deeds, and despite the fact that Franklin Roosevelt would carry Nebraska with 63 percent of the vote the next year, briefly upsetting the Republican majority of the state that named its capital Lincoln—despite this momentary *whoa* once the Populists' soothsaying about unbridled capitalism came to pass with the Depression—and despite sexism and the disgrace she felt at her husband leaving her, Esther thought she might win as a Republican woman.

She had already canvassed the county as census taker, and pitying whispers had surely preceded her. She was also sure to run as Esther *Cole* Harris, hitching her wagon to a now-established Holt County pedigree. If a woman was going to be elected even to local office in 1931—universal suffrage was only eleven years old, the same as Ruth—it was probably going to be in the West. Of the Plains states, Wyoming, the "Equality State," had given women the right to vote back in 1869, when it was still a territory, and elected a woman governor in 1924; Colorado granted women suffrage in 1893, and Kansas allowed women to vote in school elections from statehood in 1861, in municipal elections after 1887, and generally in 1912; Montana followed in 1914 and two years later elected the first woman to Congress (the pacifist Republican Jeannette Rankin, the only member of Congress to vote against entering both World Wars).[3]

The West shaped its culture—the austere terrain forced its new white denizens, men and women alike, to become citizens, to work together in communities while simultaneously distrusting organization. The little Methodist church Grandma Clara helped build in Emmet, Ruth's first church, had a female minister, an unmarried woman who preached even though the Methodist denomination wouldn't ordain her. Lest I romanticize Plains feminism too much, I should note that women were initially quite rare in much of the white West—a nineteenth-century writer for *Harper's Weekly* noted that "Wyoming gave women the right to vote in much the same spirit that New York or Pennsylvania might vote to enfranchise angels or Martians."[4] Nevertheless, Plains women like Esther often took on traditionally male roles, not out of idealism but out of necessity. Victorian gentility dried up and blew away.

Esther won. Of all the factors pulling for and against her, Ruth attributes much of her mother's victory to a sympathy vote. Be that as it may, Esther could soon support her children as a politician–single mother, a seemingly modern and cosmopolitan combination. They were poor—her salary was $125 per month—but she tried not to let her children know. "She was just quiet about whatever kind of grief was going on," Ruth told me. "Whoever's shoulder she was crying on, she wasn't crying on her children's shoulder." Ruth and Bink rode on the running boards of the local milk truck each night, pulling bottles out of the back and leaving them on stoops, collecting the empties. The dairy farmer paid them a few cents but also paid Ruth unwanted attention, stationing her young body within his reach on the driver's side running board—"a very unfortunate thing…he was one of those guys." The children collected their earnings in a sugar bowl in the kitchen cabinet for treats and movie tickets at the Royal Theater.

Over the first couple of years after Ross left, he drifted into town erratically to tell Esther he'd made a mistake or tell his children he loved them. Sometimes he let himself into the house and frightened his ex-wife like a sour-breathed ghost sitting there in a wooden chair. After one of his visits, Ruth looked in the cabinet and the sugar bowl of coins was empty. "What kind of a guy is this?" she pleads, slowly shaking her head even three-quarters of a century later. "He may have been desperate—better left unsaid, I don't know."

Soon the prodigal father drifted off for good. Esther bought a new stucco house, a "castle" with a basement and a furnace around whose register the family gathered in winter. They still lacked a car, but Esther filled a glass-fronted bookcase with a World Book set and a Book of the Month Club subscription (the most memorable month would be when *The Anointed*, by Esther's cousin Clyde Brion Davis, arrived in 1937, when Ruth was in high school). If Ruth and Bink ran home delighted after the first screening at the Royal, Esther would join them for the replay. The children galloped through dirt streets astride tree branches, imitating the Western movies.

Perhaps because Ruth had grown up marshaling her younger siblings to clean the house while Esther worked Saturday mornings, or because she'd once been mothered by Grandma Clara, Ruth felt somewhat like a younger sister to Esther. The two of them traveled by train to take Ruth's sister Esther Mary to the Mayo Clinic when it seemed clear she wasn't developing right. Esther Mary died when Ruth was fifteen, and later Bink, who was always weak after contracting scarlet fever as a child, would die while she was in China—leaving just three Harris children.

Ruth found that her closest friends turned out to be girls from St. Mary's Academy rather than her public schoolmates. Irish and Bohemian Catholics made up the professional, educated class of O'Neill and usually kept a polite distance from Protestants. Ruth's friends had more money than she did, even access to a family car. Grandma Cole may have frowned on Ruth's ecumenism—though her own children had strained the Sabbath rules, playing outside with Catholics on Sundays—but low populations forced a certain amount of interfaith mixing. (Charley Davis thought of Catholic children as "imps from hell" sent to corrupt his own Protestant cherubs, but Clyde played with them undaunted.[5]) In this sorority, Ruth was particularly fond of Mary Janet Kubicek, a Bohemian Catholic whose name the girls merged into Merj. Ruth and Merj mooned away afternoons speculating about their futures; neither seemed content with housewife.

When they hung around boys the air changed. Some guy would bring a little wine or hooch to get a girl tipsy enough to jump in the backseat. From her father to the dairy farmer and these teenage guys, the predominant masculinity of O'Neill was aggressive and heedless. "It never went through with me," Ruth told me. The counterexample, her grandfather Reverend Cole, had died before even Esther could get to know him, and that type of pious and sober guy was scarce among Ruth's peers in those Depression years.

"I think it had to do with the land," Ruth said. The coarse land seemed to have conquered the settlers as much as the other way around. Within five years in Nebraska, a European immigrant who had once played the violin would become maladroit, hands good only for working. My own dad's youthful affectations of prairie *where at?*s and double negatives hardened into grammatical calluses I always associated with his suspicion of new technologies and ideas: computers, compact discs, the transgendered. The same hostile land that demanded its women take on male roles, land whose gentle, womanly shape disguised its sometimes vulgar and violent underpinnings—that land brought out vulgarity, violence, hardened thinking, and hard drinking in its citizens within a generation or two. In Mari Sandoz's Nebraska sand hills history *Old Jules*, a knowing homesteader observes, "One can go into a wild country and make it tame, but, like a coat and cap and mittens that he can never take off, he must always carry the look of the land as it was."[6]

The Plains are a paradoxical place, where the by-turns

soothing and terrifying landscape begets polite civilities like Arbor Day and can-do reforms like women's suffrage alongside violent heroes like Bill Janklow or the brutal murders of Matthew Shepard in 1998 and the Clutter family in 1959 (the subject of Truman Capote's *In Cold Blood*). "And Americana," Ruth continued, "oh, no, the Westerns, those Western movies, we grew up on those, too." She loved them in O'Neill but now believes Americana left out a vast variety of the men and women who populated and still populate the Plains. The Hollywood Westerns projected a myth that real cowpokes thought they ought to live up to, imitating the imitation of their forebears rather than learning directly from men like Reverend Cole. This may be a side effect of the land's endemic nomadism: One thing that never moves away is the myth, and without multigenerational traditions the myth takes the place of ancestors or a strong culture.

Religion, Esther and Ruth both came to feel, was the community's only defense against the booze and vice that ran rampant just under O'Neill's conservative surface. "Ruth, Ruth, what would we *do* if we didn't have the church?" Esther would say. "Look where we'd be if we didn't have that plumb line."

Ruth's friend Merj decided to attend Duchesne College, a Sacred Heart School in Omaha, and to become a nun. Ruth became the first in her family to go to college, enrolling in the music conservatory at Morningside College in Sioux City and training to become a choral music teacher.

7.5

"I never became a musician. I was always a cheerleader in a kind of way," Ruth told me one day, insisting she could never find middle C reliably. In high school Ruth loved cheerleading for the O'Neill Eagles, drawing out the crowd's effulgence while avoiding the spotlight herself. At Morningside College, whatever she says about her abilities, she toured the country singing Bach double motets with a sixty-voice choir and a few numbers with a swing trio called Two Keys and a Chord. After graduating, she began teaching music, first at a school in Iowa and then in western Nebraska. I couldn't tell if she was being overly modest, but it's true that for most of us music is a medium for other impulses. For me, from shortly after my parents' divorce to now, it's been a way to write, to hammer ideas into intuitive, beautiful, or goofball shapes I can memorize and sing a hundred times. I can perform confident that I won't slip and reveal too much or put my foot in my mouth, even if I sometimes find new significance in old lines. (To describe "Potluck Society" now as quasi-Christian, indigenous Plains radicalism—*Everyone's given a gift to give to contribute to their community*—is to take a bird's-eye view on my original intent, which was earnest political entreaty.)

For Ruth, music's main purpose was social coalescence: The music she knew was choral music, in which the conductor, like a cheerleader, herds a half dozen or a hundred voices together into unison and even harmony. This collectivist impulse would become her life's work even after she largely left music behind. After World War II its scope expanded from a class of music students to essentially all humankind.

Pearl Harbor came six months after she graduated from Morningside; during the war, with other Nebraska women, she gathered scrap metal for the war effort. After Jesus instructed, *Love thy neighbor*, a lawyer asked, "Who is my neighbor?" Christ answered with the parable of the Good Samaritan, who tended to a beaten stranger lying by the road. In her midtwenties,

Ruth began to wonder if the war's casualties all over the world were not her neighbors. At the suggestion of her adult Sunday school leader in Gering, Nebraska—where she'd gotten her second job after college—she applied to teach music through the Methodist Board of Missions at a school somewhere across an ocean. She was accepted just before the bombs dropped on Hiroshima and Nagasaki.

A year and a half later, in February 1947, she arrived by taxi at Pier 44 in San Francisco to embark on the S.S. *Marine Lynx* for Shanghai. She had no idea what a pier would look like. To her it resembled the long exhibit hall at the Holt County Fair, where farmers and 4-H-ers showed off prize plants and livestock. Indeed it had a carnival atmosphere, and after she and the rest of the passengers (most of them missionaries) had boarded, the pier filled with well-wishers and jazz gospel tunes and confetti. "Jesus, Jesus, Jesus," the band wailed, "Sweetest name I know!"[7]

Ruth didn't care for these tunes ("It sounded like something out of a fox-trot album," she wrote her family), and she avoided most of the frivolous numbers in the Army and Navy hymnal aboard the *Lynx*. Once the ship had left the wharf, she led group singing of *serious* hymns and listened to Brahms's First Symphony on a friend's windup Victrola in the ship lounge as she began her two-week voyage across the rolling grassland of Pacific brine. But her provincial perspective and conservative tastes could not last long in the face of her drive to meet new people and her sensitivity to others' pain. Her letters home fairly overflowed with enthusiasm for the wide world, even as she was confined to a berth on a swords-to-plowshares World War II Navy ship. Her long rows of exclamation points— formed with an apostrophe typed over a period—nearly perforated the tissue-thin airmail paper she folded and sent to

Nebraska. While almost everyone on board was laid low with seasickness, Ruth bounded around on her sea legs, climbing stairs and ladders and eating in the near-empty cafeteria with the Amerasian child she babysat for a seasick Filipina woman who was also traveling in emergency class. "The thin get thinner and the fat get fatter," she wrote home. "Guess I'll have to wait 'til I get to China to lose those pounds. Me, who eats Chinese food by the pound!"

The Sunday before the *Lynx* reached Shanghai, a young missionary on board gave a sermon from Ephesians that emphasized the love and unity for which Christians must strive. The whole body of Christ, St. Paul wrote, "joined and held together by every supporting ligament, grows and builds itself up in love, as each part does its work."[8] As she sat in the ship's chapel, Ruth was struck by these words, awestruck by the twenty-eight denominations of Christians on board, by the French-speaking nuns in a sheeted-off berth, the Seventh-day Adventists who didn't eat meat and worshiped on Saturday, the "old Britisher" with the "cutest cockney accent" and strange Cuban-heel shoes. She also thrilled in trying out her Chinese on the ship's crew, most of whom were not Christian, and learned that some conservative missionaries were praying for the souls of mainstream Protestants on board. There was always this sectarian counterpoint within the ecumenical choir, the shooting pain in the body of Christ, that shocked Ruth and dismayed her.

At 4:45 a.m. the next Tuesday, she woke in her bunk, unable to sleep any longer knowing China must be in sight. She clambered to the steel deck in the faint predawn light. "I will not soon forget the sight that greeted my eyes as I walked out onto deck," she wrote her family. Sixty years later she hadn't forgotten. In the misty distance she could make out the gray silhouettes of her first Chinese junk boats, with their scalloped fan sails. In the mouth of the Yangtze, red and green port and starboard lights of other big ships reflected on the black water. "It was really a China picture, I mean my gosh, you just about can't *believe* this," she told me, thinking back. "Just a perfect scene, like a scroll."

Soon the scroll was ripped by reality. The *Lynx* dropped anchor, and immediately junks and rowboats swarmed the ship. The boatmen shouted up at the missionaries, begging for scraps of food. At first, passengers tossed down crusts and orange peels, which the beggars raced to fish out of the river with nets. Then the *Lynx* crew started spraying any boat that came near with a fire hose. Ruth wrote, "It was so cold that it just seemed downright pitiful, yet I guess it was for their own good in the long run." I can't imagine such an *oh well* from Ruth now. In coming weeks she would see men like oxen pulling massive carts, fifteenfold inflation in a few months, small bundles left out as trash that turned out to be dead infants. This would all add up to a different conclusion, one she could state bluntly as an octogenarian: "China had to have a revolution!"[9]

"Every single day," Ruth wrote in a letter home, "new things happen to make me overflow with thankfulness that I AM IN CHINA!" The country had been decimated by World War II, and the current political situation was "hopeless": It had become a civil war between the Maoists and Chiang Kai-shek, with the Communists advancing from Manchuria down the coast toward Beijing, where Ruth was staying. But she felt hope. Her first Christmas she led a choir at the ecumenical English-language Union Church, hymns helping to ease tensions between government and business agents and missionaries: "Another witness to my often-sung song that music is a wonderful barrier-breaker-downer," she wrote. Here again was her impulse, her life's *mission*, toward reunion. It was almost as if she could heal the family of God in lieu of her own.

Above the sofa bed where I slept in Claremont, Ruth had hung a framed silk embroidery of a fluffy-headed bird resembling a brown phoenix. After almost a year in training in Beijing, she moved to Shanghai, farther from the fighting, to teach music in Chinese at the McTyeire girls' school. One of her favorite students gave her the embroidery her first year there, in 1948. McTyeire had shards of glass cemented to its ramparts to separate the mayors' and executives' daughters within from the desperate masses without, but even among these rich students nationalistic folk songs overtook Christian hymns as the Communist forces advanced. In 1949 the student who had given Ruth the silk embroidery denounced her at a Communist rally as an envoy of Western imperialism, "the iron fist in a velvet glove."

When the Communists finally took Shanghai, McTyeire students and teachers watched the "fireworks" from the roof. Afterward, the Party allowed the school to continue operating, without religious education. But the climate grew more nationalistic, and it became dangerous for any student to be openly friendly with Ruth. In 1950 the Korean War broke out as a proxy war between the Soviet Union and China on one side, and the United Nations and the United States on the other. Through global events around her, Ruth became a representative of the enemy. Now she says she had "seen how desperate the need" in China was and that "God used people power" in the revolution, but the rift with her students grieved her horribly at the time. It was in those years that she found herself singing Clara's favorite hymns, such as "Leaning on the Everlasting Arms," under her breath.

In 1951, Ruth finally had to leave China, where she'd once

thought she might spend her whole adult life. With two friends she traveled home the long way, through Southeast Asia, India, and newly occupied Palestine. By chance, they took a taxi tour with a Palestinian driver who pointed to a horizon and said, "You see way over there? You see that place? That's the home of my family for five hundred years." Ruth's voice strained as she recalled his pain and fury (an American Indian guide in her childhood could have given a similar tour in Nebraska or South Dakota). "I have a question for you," the Palestinian man said. "Why didn't you give them Texas?"

The last stop on their world tour was Europe, and Ruth ended up in Geneva at the brand-new United Nations. By coincidence, Eleanor Roosevelt was also there, drafting the Universal Declaration of Human Rights. Ruth went to watch from the observers' gallery one day and stayed for a week. Here a strong, pious American woman was assembling a choir with men and women from all over the world. "My soul was hungry for their words," she recalled.[10] Eleanor Roosevelt hadn't been popular in Nebraska as first lady; Ruth had heard her criticized as a nosy do-gooder. But, she told me, "I really always felt that my grandmother and my mother had both lived that kind of life, that they *were* activists in a certain kind of way, too. I had a sense of pride about it, because I really loved them and admired them." When I visited Ruth's house, the old glass-fronted bookshelf that once held my great-grandfather's Book of the Month Club selection alongside the encyclopedia set now held at least a half dozen biographies of Eleanor Roosevelt.

The United Nations was a global choir, modulating toward some form of universal harmony. After China, and even the brief visit to Israel and Palestine, Ruth told me, "I just had a vision of, somehow or another, how could we ever get back together?"

7.6

At Pilgrim Place, Ruth and Pat's community in California, twice a week before lunch, a dozen Pilgrims gathered for a twenty-minute silent vigil around the flagpole, as they had each week since the war in Iraq started in 2003. It wasn't for outsiders, like the demonstrations they frequently staged on an island in a busy Claremont intersection (Ruth and Pat stored everybody's picket signs in their garage). It was just between the Pilgrims and God. When the three of us went together, the marine layer fog was gone, the late morning heating up, and the white-crested flock of doves already assembled. In a loose ring about the pole were a plaid-trousered husband resting a hand on his wheelchair-bound wife's shoulder; a woman in an electric cart wearing big dark cataract sunglasses; the late-fifties couple who looked ready to hit the driving range after the vigil; an Austrian friend of Ruth and Pat's, half Catholic and half Jewish, whose parents had sent her to England as a child to escape the Nazis; blue cardigans, slumping backs. Their faith inspired a refusal to accept the violence and division in the world—no *Alas* or *I guess it was for their own good in the long run*—or to stoop to the slightest Machiavellian wiles. It was just geriatric soldiers of Christ straining osteoporotic joints in surging heat and praying beneath Old Glory and Ruth's beloved light blue flag with a white globe wreathed in olive branches.

In further pursuit of communion, Ruth and Pat lined up two cafeteria lunches for me with Pilgrims who had grown up in Plains states, skimming the bios of all the residents to find six Nebraskans and Kansans. At the first, we ate with a quiet

Lutheran couple from Nebraska who had served as missionaries in Japan for many years. The Dales looked much like the older people I went to church with as a child: Ken had almost transparent Swedish skin, and his wife, Eloise, had short brown hair and wore a pink Chanel-style skirt suit. They hardly spoke a word, but it came out that Ken had organized a large e-mail newsletter against the Iraq War. Our other lunch companion was a younger woman, Linda Vogel, a Methodist theologian from Topeka who had recently retired from a seminary professorship in Chicago. At one point she mentioned her fellow Topekan, the Reverend Fred Phelps of the infamous "God Hates Fags" church. "God can't take him soon enough as far as I'm concerned," Linda said. "And I have a feeling he's in for a surprise."

"We all are, I suppose," Eloise added wryly.

Both Ken and Linda lent me copies of their family histories to bolster my Plains research, fragments of an archive of homesteading history scattered in local libraries, museums, and family genealogies like the stories passed to me about Charley and Minnie Davis and George and Clara Cole.... A prairie dugout wall caved in on Albert, Theodore, and Frank Andersen's shared bed while they were sleeping, and their father had to pull them out by the legs.... Hilda Gustafson brought a trunkful of fine clothes and trinkets from Stockholm to Nebraska and gradually gave them all away to young brides when she realized she didn't need them.... The Reverend C. F. Erffmeyer heard the call to move from Wisconsin to Kansas in 1878, and he served in the Methodist itinerancy as a "preacher-on-trial" and a sky pilot planting churches....[11]

At a second lunch, we ate with two more Kansans, both

women from the Wichita area. Laura Fukada was another missionary, who had married a Japanese-American man and then worked in Japan. Elise Gorges was eighty and so beautiful I kept gazing at her placid blue eyes, silver-blond hair, and Santa Fe jewelry. In her twenties, Elise had taken a vacation from an office job to visit a friend at the Grail, a Catholic women's center in Ohio; she mailed her resignation letter back to Wichita. The third plainswoman at the table that day was Ruth Thomson, a Nebraskan. Born in 1913, the year Willa Cather published *O Pioneers!*, she made Ruth Harris a veritable spring chicken, and her blunt declarations made Ruth Harris seem demure.

"I'm kind of a rebel here," Ruth Thomson said loudly over her chicken and rice. She was hard of hearing and had to keep reminding me to speak up. Before retiring to Pilgrim Place, she was not a minister or missionary but a YWCA social worker. Way back, shortly after national suffrage, when she was in fourth or fifth grade, she had complained to her country-school teacher about the exclusively male pronouns for God. Hers was a strict Methodist household, no drinking or dancing—"no *playing* cards until I was in high school!" But her parents were egalitarian: Her mother had studied for two years at a teacher's college and her father was a socialist doctor who voted for Norman Thomas, a Presbyterian minister and perennial presidential candidate, even against Franklin Roosevelt. After graduating from the University of Nebraska and teaching in rural schools for fifty-four dollars per month, Ruth moved back to Lincoln and took a job with the YWCA.

Around that time a new Walgreens opened in downtown Lincoln. The first time she walked into the soda fountain, on a warm day in 1941, she saw two friends from the Y sitting uneasily in a booth. They were black. When Ruth joined them they told her they had not been served in an hour.

Ruth promptly demanded the waitress's attention: "Listen, we haven't been served." She ordered ice creams all around. When the waitress delivered, without a word, their order, the black women's scoops were crusted with salt and pepper—a bitter symbol of desegregation. Ruth fired off a complaint letter to Walgreens headquarters, and her friends apparently never had trouble there again. (Another Plains precedent to the lunch counter sit-in movement occurred in 1958 at Dockum Drug Store in Wichita, Kansas. Black students occupied the lunch counter every day for three weeks before the manager relented and served them.)

I should interrogate the appeal these fierce prairie women hold for me. Their fierceness takes various forms, from the delicate, just-so assuredness of licking an envelope and sending a resignation letter back to Wichita, to the fightin' instincts of Ruth Thomson—in the 1990s she was the first person to petition to move to Pilgrim Place with a same-sex partner—to the sensitive communitarian enthusiasm of Ruth Harris. (The two Nebraskan Ruths are quite opposite women despite their political affinities; Ruth Thomson a warrior and my Ruth a peacemaker.) But they're all straight-spined, and brave. This is one of the great tropes of the Plains: Alexandra Bergson in *O Pioneers!*, Laura Ingalls Wilder, Ma Joad, Dorothea Lange's *Migrant Mother*, or the ruddy-faced mother looking to the horizon as she cuts wildflowers in the South Dakota painter Harvey Dunn's work *The Prairie Is My Garden*.[12] In a tough land she is an unwavering alto beside the erratic bass of the high-heeled cowboy, a stable force like Esther Cole Harris when the man vanishes.

In my own case, it was my mother who vanished. After a promising start as a forceful South Dakota woman, the decisive business manager at Prairie Dog Records ultimately decided that *life is not meant to be tolerated with an attitude of "I'll just get through this."* The stoicism she refused is ultimately an essential stance if one is to stay in the Plains. All the women at Pilgrim Place also left the region, as did Laura Ingalls Wilder, Willa Cather, the migrant mother, and Ma Joad. Mom kept a little prairie grit, but she wasn't with me all year. In the absence of a full-time mother, it seems I've adopted myself to freelancers an hour or a week at a time.

So Ruth Harris, in addition to being a sort of sister, was a mother figure as well. Our temperaments diverge, choir leader versus songwriter, but we share a desire to build communities, to *get us back together.*

7.7

It happened that the world in the 1950s was in dire need of community, and that an impulse derived from Ruth's personal pain was of great use to others.

When she returned to the United States from China and Europe, she docked in New York City, trying straight off to land a job at the United Nations. Instead, she was hired by the Methodist Church to introduce congregations from around the country *to* the UN. She would work in various Methodist and ecumenical positions over the next forty years, most of them in the "God Box," the blocky limestone Interchurch Center in Morningside Heights, Manhattan—far, far from her alma mater, Morningside College, but only a few blocks from a walk-up apartment where I would live for three years. She would no longer be a literal choir director, but her ardent efforts to achieve harmony continued.

Ruth began working with Christian college students in 1954 and soon expressed concern about the "establishment of stereotype personalities" among them.[13] Her time amid the Chinese revolution gave her experience to guide students through the political and spiritual unease many of them felt. "Nuclear fallout, trials in Cuba, the status of Berlin, Sputnik and Lunik, Apartheid, Little Rock, Cyprus, Mao Tse Tung—what does it all mean?" asked the United Student Christian Council's newsletter, *Communique*, in March 1959. "It cannot be that God is, and that he is not active" in this troubled time.[14] Ruth helped organize the quadrennial Ecumenical Student Conference on the Christian World Mission in 1955 and 1959 as an opportunity to make sense of all this.

The Reverend Martin Luther King Jr. spoke at the 1959 conference in Athens, Ohio, at ten o'clock on Wednesday morning, December 30; *Communique* mentioned his visit only in the last sentence of the conference announcement. I don't know what he said, but the conference theme was "Frontiers of Mission," and he gave a "Frontier Address." Undoubtedly he recommended civil rights as a frontier of Christian mission; a backdrop of Jesus on the Cross displayed behind him reminded students that "as men have created barriers between races they have crucified Christ anew."[15] It's hard to imagine this demigod just shy of his thirty-first birthday—halfway in age between Ruth, who was almost forty, and the students she advised—pounding the pavement like William Jennings Bryan at little chautauquas and speaking to a thousand people at a time. Two days later King would be at the Virginia capitol protesting a school district's all-out closure to avoid a federal desegregation order. "Never underestimate what you are doing today," he'd tell 2,700 black protesters in Richmond. "I can assure you that it will have far-reaching effects."[16] As a young minister, he was coming to Athens to ask Christian students from all races, from seventy-eight countries, to join the struggle.

Together with the rest of the Athens conference, his speech flipped the students' calendars from the '50s to the '60s. Ruth was delighted as she walked the hallways managing logistics to see clusters of students gathered around Jim Lawson, a black seminary student who had studied Gandhi's nonviolent strategies as a Methodist missionary in India. Within a month or two, in early 1960, student civil rights activism took off, beginning with sit-ins at whites-only lunch counters across the South. Two thousand students, most of them black, were arrested in the first half of that year. According to Ruth, almost every sit-in included at least one student who had been at the Athens conference.

It's not difficult to trace the branches of the Cole-Brion family tree to Ruth's frontiers of mission. Her grandparents had traveled to a hostile, amoral frontier to plant churches and thereby civility. Her mother was an elected official. Ruth, at least third in a line of strong, pious women, has worked to extend the frontier of civility across the globe. The word *frontier* suggests a particularly energetic sort of border, a landscape of motion: It's a French word that sounds terribly American, and it sports that industrious final "eer" sound like *engineer, pamphleteer, pioneer.* One young culture forges itself as it overruns an older one along a frontier, and almost a century later a nearly grown-up nation reinterprets its past, its constitution, to include blacks and Indians and others as equal members on a legal and cultural frontier. Skin itself—the surface of civil rights—is a sort of frontier between a self and the world; it changes and moves in response to movement both inside and out. I'm thinking of my cousin Nikki's red, tearstained cheeks after Ruth's sermon on Iraq, or the multicolor, bruised, and bloodied skin of the Freedom Riders. On the scarred skin of prairie earth I can make out a line from Clara's Ladies Aid suppers to the March on Washington.

August 27, 1963, found Ruth standing beside her Methodist student leaders as one by one they phoned their parents to announce they would be busing to Washington, DC, the next day for that very march. When moms and dads panicked at the turn Bible study had taken, Ruth took the receiver as a Methodist authority and reassured them that this was an excellent reinforcement of leadership training. "I thought, *For heaven's sakes, the students should have that experience*," she told me. The March on Washington turned out peaceful, the multitudes listening to King's dream and, Ruth recalled, "sharing their sandwiches in a Sunday school picnic atmosphere."[17] Potluck society, indeed.

Two years later she joined King's Selma-to-Montgomery march, crossed the Edmund Pettus Bridge on King's second try, then drove ahead to prepare accommodations for the marchers in Montgomery. No picnic: To avoid being lynched for ferrying blacks into Montgomery, she had them crouch on the floor of her car's backseat.

After 1965, Ruth's work at the God Box became more international. As a church executive, she traveled to dozens of third-world frontiers to support Methodist involvement in the global student Christian movement and to boost political and economic solidarity in the Christian mission at large—often in countries revolting against colonial rule. In 1971, she hired Pat, who had been a missionary teacher in Japan and worked with Christian groups in Korea, to work with her at the Methodist Board of Global Ministries. A few years later the two of them started a mission intern program to train a new generation of missionary activists with a sense of solidarity, of listening rather than preaching—as far as can be from the old picture of missionaries harvesting heathen souls and throwing them in the thresher of Western capitalism, *the iron fist in a velvet glove.*

The '80s brought liberation theology, which in a sense codified what Ruth had believed for decades: that Christianity must always align itself with the economically and socially oppressed rather than with their oppressors. This was another iteration of a ghost dance, enlisting supernatural help for liberation, but instead of Apocalypse and afterlife it worked for revolution and equality in *this* world. Through this theology Ruth supported the antiapartheid struggle in South Africa, as well as resistance to the Marcos regime in the Philippines. In 1987, when she was already eligible for Social Security, she flew to Manila with a committee on agricultural missions to discuss opportunities for helping rural peasants. As it happened, the Peasant Movement of the Philippines was negotiating for agrarian reforms at the same time and held a protest outside the presidential palace, now occupied by the ostensible reformer Corazon Aquino. Ruth brought her American colleagues out to see the stakes of their work on the ground. A mass of ten thousand protesters crept toward the military line on Mendiola Bridge, and suddenly the police and military began teargassing and then shooting at the crowd.

"I was scared to death," Ruth recalled. "I had all these church women there, and [the soldiers] were shooting." One member of her group was injured in the stampede, more solidarity than she'd bargained for. Thirteen Filipino farmers had been killed; here was a modern incarnation of the Wounded Knee massacre, of power overreacting to protect itself against a liberation theology.

Once she retired and eventually moved to Pilgrim Place, Ruth began to reflect on theology in an abstract sense and became interested in a school of thought called "process theology," which envisioned God luring us all forward toward harmony like a choir director or a cheerleader. God isn't omnipotent but exerts a positive pull on all people in moving toward a— as Ruth and Pat put it in their Christmas card one year— "radically inclusive and justice-centered commonwealth of God."

7.8

Ruth, Pat, and I pulled up to the Claremont United Methodist Church on the seventh Sunday of Easter, the Sunday after the Ascension—also known at this particular church as Reconciling Sunday. This was the week when the congregation celebrated and reaffirmed its 1993 decision to become a "reconciling congregation," to break from Methodist doctrine by welcoming gays and lesbians. As we walked slowly from Ruth and Pat's little white Toyota to the angular, modern church building, we passed seven flags, one of each color of the rainbow, sunk into empty Costco laundry detergent buckets. In the narthex hung a political display—not a picture of Gandhi but close enough: a galaxy of silver stars, each one representing a coalition soldier killed in Iraq. Around a small altar, a pile of pebbles represented the tens of thousands of Iraqi victims of the war.

Ruth and Pat looked the part of elderly church ladies, Ruth in a brown polyester suit and SAS walking shoes, Pat in navy polyester. An earringed, middle-aged man held a basket of rainbow ribbons for us to pin to our shirts, and his partner led us to our pew. "They're a gay couple," Ruth whispered to me. When a woman with a flattop hairdo and denim shirt read the scripture, Ruth leaned over to me and whispered again, "She's a lesbian." She raised her eyebrows expectantly, and I raised mine in response and nodded as if she were telling me something I hadn't surmised or even suspected. Behind the pulpit, giant windows looked out on green spring foliage—glorious, unstained glass.

In her sermon, the minister recalled crying angrily after one of the many Methodist conventions at which the worldwide denomination reaffirmed *its* nonreconciling policy of rejecting gay and lesbian clergy. Though she herself was straight, she had thought of leaving the church until it changed its policy but then realized, "If God waited to love us until we were perfect, well…" The congregation chuckled appreciatively.

After affirming officially that we sought "a world where all people are welcomed, and where silenced voices are heard," we placed our bulletins on the pews and shook hands with those around us with the two-handed clasp of diplomats, saying, "The peace of the Lord be always with you," or just, "Peace." Though Claremont United Methodist Church didn't slant quite as old as Pilgrim Place, I was still something of a novelty as a young guest of Ruth and Pat. They were honored and active members of the church, and Pat had again written a national study guide for Methodist women, this one called *Shalom, Salaam, Peace*, to help build a culture of peace among Judaism, Islam, and Christianity. The whole scene had a surreal perfection that sparked skepticism in me, the same way I came to feel about Portland and Amherst as I grew older, like I could find alienation in the most agreeable environment.

The second hymn of the service was "Rise Up Shining," new lyrics set to the cascading arpeggios of a traditional hymn. Ruth didn't need sheet music for the tune: It was "Come, Thou Long-Expected Jesus," written by Charles Wesley in 1745, the kind of foundational Methodist hymn Clara had sung softly while Ruth hovered around her, back in Emmet. *Come, thou long-expected Jesus, / born to set thy people free*, Wesley's ode began; *from our fears and sins release us, / let us find our rest in thee.* This was the message of hope and deliverance that had comforted Clara through the frontier years in Nebraska and then Ruth during the Chinese revolution. Now, the three of us stood up and followed the new words in our bulletins, Ruth's warbling voice jumping up the register: *Rise up shining, sons and daughters, summoned as the light of earth! / All created in Love's image, manifest creation's worth. / Gay and lesbian, straight or searching, bi, transgendered: called by name. / Blessed uniqueness, sacred bodies each enkindled by God's flame.*

By the middle of that first verse, I was having trouble following along without giggling at the incongruousness of the kind of tune that I knew from my own childhood churchgoing, a major-key melody that unfolds unchallenged by the slightest dissonance, paired with fantastically unhymnlike words such as *bi*—not to mention that I'd never heard a hymn with anything as steamy as bodies "enkindled by God's flame." At the same time I felt the poignancy there, looking out at the green through the unstained glass and wishing I could summon William Jennings Bryan's reverence for the sunset's colors wrapped around a radish.

The wide-eyed welcome of Reconciling Sunday was a diorama-scale achievement of what Ruth had been working toward across sixty years, a momentary harmony. These congregants weren't innocents; they had probably suffered more than I, and had come to embrace the silly and the sacred of God's green earth. "This one speaks prophetic challenge, that one hears a priestly call," we sang. "Singer, healer, counselor, teacher: of Christ's body members all."

PART THREE

Native wheatgrass (crossbred to the variety trademarked "Kernza") and annual wheat, in summer, grown by the Land Institute, Salina, Kansas.

(© 2010 The Land Institute — Steve Renich)

A Buffalo Commonplace

8.1

In his 1949 essay *Here Is New York*, E. B. White divided the city's population into the "natives," the "commuters," and the "settlers." The third group, those with ambition and talent who come here from other countries and other parts of the United States, are the greatest, he wrote, because they give the city its artistic and mercantile energy.[1] By the time I read the essay, in the early twenty-first century, it felt as if the settlers were displacing the natives. I lived along the L train in Williamsburg, Brooklyn, where ambitious young artists and musicians like me were moving ever farther from Manhattan as land values and rents bloomed in formerly working-class and poor neighborhoods, in shuttered warehouses converted first into art studios, then makeshift loft apartments, and finally into condominiums as investors proved up on their properties.

Perhaps out of longing for home, I was starting to see everything in the city with Oz-like goggles (in the book, the Emerald City is green only because the Wizard's minions make you put on tinted goggles at the gate)—in my case everything appeared in terms of Western history. White's categories, especially "natives" and "settlers," had an eerie ring to them. The process of gentrification had a feeling of inevitability, like Manifest Destiny, and the subway stops on the L appeared like meridians of longitude going west on the frontier. The first and second stops on the L (perhaps like Ohio or Indiana in the mid-nineteenth century) were reliably safe for settlers, but beyond the third stop the natives were reputedly dangerous and unwelcoming. There were rumors of rapes and muggings. Within a few years (I was living "back east" in Manhattan for some of this time), the third, fourth, and fifth stops had been tamed, and real pioneers were living in Bushwick and in Ridgewood, Queens, the next neighborhoods out.

It wasn't an all-bad process, this "revitalization," but I didn't like being part of it. I felt ashamed to be a settler pushing out the natives, or confining them, through high rents, to sad reservations called projects. I was also embarrassed to be part of White's settler category at all, because in the intervening half century it had become a cliché to come to New York to be an artist or to "make it." There were scads of smug talents from the suburbs coming to be Gatsby or F. Scott Fitzgerald, Bob Dylan or Jackson Pollock, or to write the next *Rent*. I was here by chance, mainly because my college sweetheart, Marina, had graduated a year ahead of me and moved to New York, and I couldn't convince her to move anywhere else.

But I was undeniably part of the scene. I played open mics as the acoustic troubadour, played bass in a punk band, went to performance art and dance-theater shows with Marina, lived well on less than twenty thousand a year, with permanent and temporary jobs, with and without health insurance, wearing plastic-frame eyeglasses all the while. In short, I am indistinguishable from the hipster cliché. As the real estate market grew out of control in the mid-aughts, I began to look ahead and worry that I would never be able to afford to own a house, in New York or even in another "cool" city like Portland or Minneapolis. That made me look back toward home and wonder if there was any way the Plains could be "gentrified," made livable for my generation and later ones now that the agricultural, homesteader society was in its depopulated dotage.

This would require a reimagining of the Plains somewhat akin to what New York artists in the '60s did in empty factories in SoHo. As the SoHo model spread into Brooklyn and other cities around the country, it became aesthetically more sterile (viz: "loft condominiums") and morally more problematic when poor people and artists were pushed out of their neighborhoods. These would not be concerns on the rural Plains, which have never lacked for space and whose small towns are becoming empty. But the task on the Great Plains has its own problems, chiefly a stubborn geography: a hard climate and massive distances that challenge the idea that anybody should live there permanently, ever. The shadow of Manifest Destiny would haunt the enterprise as well.

Personally, I also needed to reimagine the Plains' culture and history, to highlight characters and episodes from its history that spoke to me, that reminded me that I'm *from* there and that I *belonged* there. I needed to prove up before I could consider it home again. Some of these episodes and people, such as Wounded Knee and Willa Cather, are part of the canonical history of the region. Others, like the bison-bullfight and Ruth Harris, are not. My investigations led me to the present-day Plains, to research trips that were ultimately part of a personal effort to come to terms with where and how I grew up.

8.2

Droves of my Plains cohorts and I, the descendants of white homesteaders, keep on leaving as soon as we reach the age of majority. South Dakota farms have consolidated into open-air, monoculture warehouses that support a minuscule fraction of the population they once did. The job options for the college-educated are limited, and many of us want to live some-where a famous band might tour or where we could see a pro basketball game. More than a century after whites crowded most of the Great Plains, towns there now give newcomers free home lots or down-payment grants to buy existing ones. In 2006, a Montreal man made a series of fifteen trades on the Internet, starting with a red paper clip. He exchanged that for a fish-shaped pen, then traded up for a Budweiser "instant party," a Kiss snow globe, and a credited role in a movie, among other items, and eventually acquired an entire house in Kipling, Saskatchewan, a struggling Plains town hoping to keep itself alive with the publicity the event briefly generated.[2] Behind such desperate giveaways is a slow but phenomenal exodus over the past century from a huge swath of North America. Many rural Plains counties have lost a third or half of the popula-tion they had in 1900; some are "unsettled," demographically speaking.

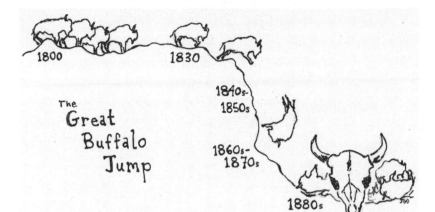

Year	Numbers	Notes
1800	Estimated between 30–75 million bison.	Introduction of the horse to most Plains Indian tribes by around 1700 completely altered ways of life, creating year-round bison-based societies.[3]
1830	1,500 head killed by Yanktonai Sioux in one day near Pierre; ~150,000 hides per year shipped east.	Tribes' personal use more or less sustainable; profligate hunting for trade with fur companies that paid cynical prices (1 hide for a pint of sugar and a few bullets; 5 hides for a gallon of watered-down whiskey).[4]

(continued)

Year	Numbers	Notes
1840s–1850s	75,000 hides from Fort Pierre in 1849; Oregon Trail, Santa Fe Trail destroy winter forage.	Bison began to disappear on the Missouri; tribes (hungry and decimated by smallpox, cholera, etc.) and white hunters followed them west; 1 million cattle and sheep crossed Plains with California gold rushers and West Coast settlers, grazing river valleys.[5]
1860s–1870s	Southern herd 15 million in 1860; 3,158,730 (est.) killed by hide hunters 1872–1874 alone.[6]	With post–Civil War railroad/mining incursion and broken treaties, Indian wars began; eradication of bison by white civilians seen as an effective weapon; fire, drought, cattle-borne diseases; heyday of buffalo skinners.
1880s	Southern herd gone by 1880; large herds in Montana, Wyoming, Dakota Territory reduced to ~1,000 by 1884; just 300 hides shipped that year.[7]	Railroad to Montana completed 1880 after tribes were starved into peace; Glendive was briefly the "Dodge City of the North;" bison bones supplemented the earnings of poor homesteaders; National Zoo (Washington, DC) founded in 1889 primarily for the preservation of the bison.[8]

In 1987, New Jersey geographers Frank and Deborah Popper mapped out three major boom-and-bust cycles of white Plains settlement since the Homestead Act of 1862. The booms came on free land and federal subsidies and spates of rain: first in the nineteenth century, then around the turn of the twentieth, and finally from the 1940s through the 1970s. The ensuing busts and Dust Bowls and ghost towns came simply from the reality of the semiarid Great Plains climate setting in — the tight checkerboard of farms between Appalachia and Iowa could not abide on the Plains. This empty region, full as it is of anything, is now full of "austere monument[s] to American self-delusion": mothballed grain elevators, sagging gray homesteads, or the National Grasslands, bought back from farmers during the Dust Bowl. The Poppers proposed another, unfathomably vast buyback of Plains land, a "deprivatization" of virtually all of the rural Plains by the government. "The federal government's commanding task on the Plains for the next century will be to recreate the nineteenth century," they wrote. This would involve restoring prairie grasses and restocking wildlife, and reimagining the region using the metaphor of the "Buffalo Commons."[9]

Looking at a 2010 county-by-county census map that shows population loss in tan, and growth in varying shades of blue, one can almost describe the boundaries of the Great Plains by the cloud of tan (with a few aberrant speckles of light blue) heedless of state lines. In some counties the population has plummeted consistently for several decades, while in others the decline has begun to level off—if only because there wasn't much lower to go. There are exceptions, where energy booms in Montana, North Dakota, and Wyoming have drawn in growth, probably temporarily. The Black Hills region of South Dakota is a geologic island in the middle of the Plains, and it's become a demographic island of growth, a low-budget Colorado. But otherwise it's a steady decline, decline, decline.[10] In those numbers, and the very real desolation they reflect, lies the appeal of the Buffalo Commons.

How soothing that a place so rent and overturned—not just a place but an entire *world*—might be restored! If I can't truly escape the Plains and can't live there as it is now, imagine this vision of rich rolling textures, fur and grass knitted back together with the grainy sheen of an old color photograph: The burgeoning herd of woolly fugitives from the Bronx Zoo would enter the Buffalo Commons and range as freely as its thirty-million-strong antecedent once did across a fenceless patchwork of public prairie. As the seasons changed, as drought blew across one state or another, the bison and elk would follow the richest grasses, grazing around the ruins of boomtowns in a long north-south Commons corridor. And hardy folk would live, land-hewn and upstanding, in pockets throughout...

The other main exceptions to the current Plains decline are American Indians. White populations in Plains states barely nudged up in the first decade of the twenty-first century, and dropped in most rural places. Native populations, by contrast, grew by about 20 percent in the 1990s and another 15 percent in the 2000s, with high birthrates and cultural ties that draw young tribal members back from cities to a degree that homesick whites don't begin to match.[11] (This is to speak nothing of the astonishing growth of Latino populations—many of whose members have indigenous ancestry—who have flocked to meatpacking towns like Liberal, Kansas, and Dakota City, Nebraska, in recent years and who may soon outnumber those American Indians whose forebears lived north of the present U.S.-Mexico border.[12]) In his 1969 Red Power manifesto *Custer Died for Your Sins*, the late Sioux scholar Vine Deloria Jr. joked that American Indians supported urban renewal programs, and presumably gentrification, in coastal cities far from present-day Indian country because "after the cities are rebuilt and everyone is settled there, we are going to fence them off and run our buffalo all over the country again."[13] The whites will be the ones on reservations, in loft condominiums.

Bison populations are also growing—the animals now number half a million. During the great nineteenth-century buffalo kill, remnant herds survived on a few ranches and in places like the Northwest Territories, Antelope Island in the Great Salt Lake, and the mountains around Yellowstone National Park. After cultivating seed herds in Montana, South Dakota (Scotty Philip's), Texas, and back east in New Hampshire, Massachusetts, and the Bronx Zoo, preservationists shipped grown bison in custom railroad crates to new Plains refuges. Though not self-consciously so, this was the pioneering moment of "rewilding" the Plains, laying out at least some fragments of its land use with a nod to the region's fundamental nature as a landscape of motion.

The American Bison Society, formed in 1905 at the New York Zoological Society, began shipping bearded bovines west from the Bronx Zoo. The bison from the traveling advertisements proving the strength of Page Woven Wire Fences were descendants of two animals originally captured in Oklahoma and donated to a city park in Keokuk, Iowa, then sold to Page and finally donated to the zoo. In 1907, these bison were among those shipped from the Bronx back "home" to Oklahoma to start the Wichita Mountains Wildlife Refuge. In 1913, seven males and seven females from the zoo traveled west to Wind Cave National Park, six miles north of Hot Springs, South Dakota, to parent a herd now maintained at about 350 head—one of the healthiest, most genetically pure herds in the country (many bison on private ranches have some cattle genes from past breeding) and the first one I remember seeing.[14] Is this rewilding a slow-motion fulfillment of Wovoka's Ghost Dance prophecy? Are Indians and bison coming back as whites return to where they came from?

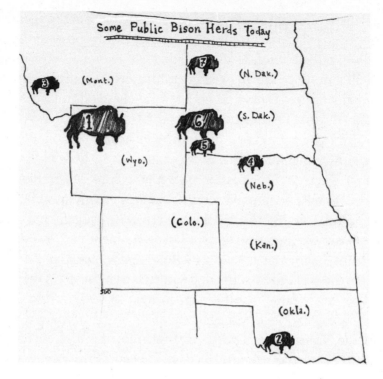

	Name	Bison	Herd Estd.	Notes
1	Yellow-stone National Park	3,000+	1872	Poachers continued to diminish the herd of refugee bison even after the Army came to protect them in 1886; in 1902 only 23 remained, 21 more brought from ranches in Montana and Texas; present-day controversy over hunts to prevent spread of brucellosis (an Old World disease) from bison to neighboring cattle.[15]

	Name	Bison	Herd Estd.	Notes
2	Wichita Mountains Wildlife Refuge	550	1905	Established by President T. Roosevelt in response to Wild West Show, attended by 65,000 and featuring Geronimo in a "last buffalo hunt"; T.R.: a "disgraceful exhibition"; refuge on "surplus" land after Kiowa-Comanche Reservation was divided into 160-acre homesteads allotted to tribal members.[16]
3	National Bison Range	350–450	1908	Established by Congress on "surplus" Flathead tribal land; money for 36 bison donated by philanthropists including Andrew Carnegie; tourist attraction on the Northern Pacific line.[17]
4	Fort Niobrara National Wildlife Refuge	350	1912	Created by executive order, stocked with 6 females from a private herd in Friend, Nebraska, and 2 bulls from Yellowstone.[18]

(*continued*)

	Name	Bison	Herd Estd.	Notes
5	Wind Cave National Park	350	1913	14 bison from the Bronx Zoo donated by the American Bison Society; three years later, they were joined by 6 more from Yellowstone; since 1994, all bison have microchips planted behind their right ears for identification.[19]
6	Custer State Park	1,500	1914	36 head from Scotty Philip ranch taken by rail west to Hermosa, then by horse-drawn wagons into the park named for the Indian-killing hero of the 19th-century Plains.[20]
7	Theodore Roosevelt National Park	350–700	1956	Including the ranch in which T.R. invested after he fell in love with the West; established as a national memorial park in 1947 and later stocked with bison from Nebraska's Fort Niobrara NWR.[21]

It would be naive to cast modern-day reservation life—epidemic diabetes, alcoholism, and paperboard government housing—as an earthly paradise or a magical return to pre-reservation times, or to compare ranch-raised bison to the endless herds of the early nineteenth century. Given another century, though, some imperfect restoration may take root.

The Buffalo Commons has become an elastic idea, a guiding metaphor for a more uneven, parcel-by-parcel shift. As it has evolved, the Commons now includes new economies for a less populous Plains based on ranching, wildlife, and tourism, and the change, sure enough, has begun to occur (in part thanks to the Commons metaphor itself): Federal, state, and tribal governments and private land trusts have restored or protected more and more pieces of prairie. Both the Poppers and the Plains folk who violently resisted their idea have given ground in the ensuing two decades. The Poppers no longer support (if they ever really did) a wholesale federal sweep of the region, and the former Kansas governor who initially attacked them as socialist outsiders publicly apologized in 2004. Once vilified, the Buffalo Commons (in the form of a national park proposed for western Kansas) received its first newspaper endorsement in 2009, from the *Kansas City Star*, after a U.S. Senate candidate endorsed it.[22] Bison herds continue to amass one animal at a time, more and more of them escaping from the tiny Bronx herd I saw peering out at the scrap of mainland America it seemed they were grazing just hours earlier.

I'm not sure what I hope to restore by assembling my own patchwork of public and private Plains, traveling from the Bronx's jailed buffalo to some gravel road out west where I can't see anything but the boundless smorgasbord of grasses they might eat and the cloudless tank of sky they might breathe. It's an impulse much like Ruth's, to make a choir coalesce in the midst of dissension and hurt. I suppose all history is a sort of ghost dance, a stab at building a future home out of the debris from the old times. After our brief six years all together, my family always felt like the clouds that stampede over that blue firmament, three shape-shifting and recombining ghosts up there. It would be nice for them to reconverge—or would the meeting of fronts only produce twisters?

8.3

A golf course, with its sharply delineated sections, clipped grass, and sprinklered greens, is hardly the Wild West. It's more a parody of the prairie landscape in which buffalo grass, sagebrush, and bison have been replaced with nonnative species like Kentucky bluegrass, elms, and Toro riding mowers. Come to think of it, most grassland agriculture is a less extreme parody of the natural ecology in that region: animals (once bison, prairie dogs, pronghorn, and the rest of the food chain; now cattle or humans) alchemizing grass (blue grama and buffalo grass; now crested wheatgrass and wheat) into protein and muscle.

Reversing the process of parody that created the golf course could stand, in miniature, for the creeping effort to restore grasslands in general, reseeding native species on patches of Great Plains from the Prairie Provinces to Texas and New Mexico. In fact, this has been done, just once that I know of, at Scotts Bluff National Monument in western Nebraska. Curious to see how this tricky reverse engineering has turned out, I visit the monument and take a tour with Bob Manasek, a federal park ranger who led the effort.[23]

We jump into Bob's white National Park Service truck, and he pilots us in and out of a steep gully on a dusty access road. His tires are probably smuggling some exotic, nonnative seeds sunk into the rubber—maybe goathead or redroot pigweed. On the park side of the road, the Gering–Fort Laramie Canal meanders down from the North Platte River, flowing in the opposite direction as Bob's truck and lined with thick brows of kochia and foxtail barley, also exotic. Beyond the canal, the dramatic view of Scotts Bluff is interrupted by a row of two-legged power lines, a cortege of giant pterodactyl skeletons followed by a caged-in radio tower striped red and white. A new bike path, parallel to the access road, pipes in more rubber-trundled weed seeds along the park boundary up to Country Club Road, which dead-ends at the park's edge, at a green steel gate.

"And then, please excuse the broken gate," Bob says, stopping the truck, "but somebody ran into this about ten days ago. Sort of totaled the gate out—Oh!" He interrupts himself. "There's a couple of prairie dogs." He points through the windshield toward some nervous tan sentries watching us from a little dirt mound. "We'll just go up here and see how the guys are doing." He chuckles, killing the ignition and climbing unhurriedly out of the truck. I follow, stepping over the mangled iron gate, not mentioning Prairie Dog Records. "Then," he says, "I'll show you the real difference between the native prairie and the *not*-so-native prairie."

Bob is in his fifties. I realize as he's telling me about prairies that he bears some resemblance to his former governor and senator (and a 1992 presidential candidate), Bob Kerrey: Middle Western, mild-featured, blue-eyed. His job at Scotts Bluff National Monument is to manage the resources—animal, vegetable, mineral, historical, fossil—on the four-hundred-foot Scotts Bluff protrusion, a huge monolith bursting out of the plain, and on the skirt of prairie around it. If prairie metaphors must hinge on the sea, as they so often do, Bob Manasek has the confusing job of maintaining an island of sea in a sea of developed land, buffeting back waves of exotic weeds that wash in on tires and boots and irrigation currents, not to mention cars crashing the dikes.

Complicating this task is the fact that most of the native prairie around the bluff is reclaimed land—or sea?—formerly cropland, hog farm, cattle range, feedlot, and, on these forty-two acres, nine holes of the Scotts Bluff Country Club.

I would have thought that putting a prairie back together again would be like assembling a Miocene rhinoceros skeleton dug from a Plains excavation, scraping out the right bones and mortaring them all together, casting artificial bridge bones where a rib was packed off by a coyote or washed away by a stream. But in fact a prairie is alive: You can't just jigsaw its dry grasses like in the bison and pronghorn diorama at the Museum of Natural History on Central Park West and Eighty-first Street. Prairie restoration is rather like reassembling the skeleton and bringing the menoceras back to life Frankenstein-style; prairies aren't extinct like menoceras, but resurrection is not much simpler in Scotts Bluff National Monument than in Jurassic Park.

I sympathize with Bob's task as I try to restore some sort of imagined Plains preserve in spite of time's introductions and erasures in the landscape of motion. I think of those "commonplace books" of wisdom, details, quotes, and notes that writers and scientists used to keep like scatterbrained grasslands of words. As I research and travel the Plains, I'm assembling a Buffalo Commonplace from memories, books, visits, and souvenirs, and hoping they add up to a psychic blueprint for my version of the Buffalo Commons.

Here in the Nebraska panhandle, about twenty miles from Wyoming and three hours south of my onetime hometown Hot Springs, Scotts Bluff once stood as a landmark on the Oregon Trail. Covered-wagon ruts still scar Mitchell Pass, where westward migrants filed out of the North Platte River valley and circumnavigated the bluff like a parade of ants looping around a brick. Scotts Bluff was the last in a series of geologic cairns the wagon trains met along the North Platte; coming from the flat east, they spotted Courthouse and Jail Rocks, Chimney Rock, and Castle Rock—then finally the great Scotts Bluff. Under a roof of calcite-cemented limestone, each outcrop preserves ten million years of historical record in chalky layers up its sides. The rest of the history has eroded away like the source text of a quote in a commonplace book. In 1919, Woodrow Wilson authorized Scotts Bluff National Monument as a relic of America's pioneer heritage; he enlisted the National Park Service to maintain the site the way the migrants found it. (Perhaps it was a Nebraska nod to William Jennings Bryan, who'd resigned as Wilson's secretary of state four years earlier.) Initially, the monument included only the bluff itself; the skirt around it was private agricultural and recreational land. Over time, the government bought several hundred acres of grassland around the outcrop.

On what turns out to be another baking August day, just a couple of weeks after I communed with the displaced bison in New York, Bob and I walk up a path that until about 1999 was the continuation of Country Club Road. The Scotts Bluff Country Club moved north across the North Platte in the mid-'70s, but a second course, the Gering municipal golf course (called Monument Shadows), maintained two old fairways, a putting green, and a tee box on about five acres of leased Park Service land for another twenty-five years. After Monument Shadows finally pulled out, Bob hired a contractor to tear out the asphalt, but we can still easily follow its gravelly underbed. At our approach, the prairie dogs bark frantically, then vanish.

With seven years of severe drought (Nebraska's biggest reservoir, just downstream on the North Platte, withers at

20 percent of its capacity), all of the prairie is bare and brittle. The greenest patch is a recently converted fairway, blossoming with a rash of kochia, a Eurasian tumbleweed. A week ago, the Plains sky dropped an inch of rain in forty minutes; most of it ran off the crusted ground, but the kochia soaked up the rest and shot up like magic beanstalks. Vital as it looks today, it will soon dry out, break off, and roll away. Strangely, in the middle of the green kochia lies a brown perfect circle of native prairie sandreed.

"And guess what was right there?" Bob asks me, pointing out the sandreed and its prairie dog town. Maybe it was the bunker, I suggest. "Not a sand trap," he says. "This was the location of the golf green." Under the velvet putting green, the course's designers had deposited a base of sand for stability and drainage; once the fine grass was gone, plants that typically thrive in the sand hills east of Scotts Bluff took over. Now, instead of just one hole, the brown green is pocked with somewhere between nine and eighteen prairie dog dens.

Outside these three or four acres of fairway kochia, the former country club has successfully reverted to native prairie. It shows little trace of the road graders, the broadcast herbicides, the grass fires and brush fires, the greenhouse transplants, or the hundred thousand dollars that brought it back.

Bob describes the country club land as having looked "altered" in the 1990s, before the restoration began. Walking through the grass, he would come upon the asphalt ring of a golf cart trail or a concrete sidewalk—though the pavement was mostly obscured by grasses from ground level, visitors would puzzle over the vestiges of pavement from the top of the bluff. Four hundred dead, gray Siberian elms lined the former fairways (victims of disease or halted irrigation), and exotic grasses such as smooth brome, cheatgrass, and crested wheatgrass carpeted scattered patches.

In 1996, the monument undertook the prairie resurrection with grant money from the Nebraska State Lottery. Once the land managers scratched the surface they discovered more alterations. After a prescribed grass fire to uncover the trails and any other debris, sinkholes appeared in the scorched ground as if there were caves underneath: In the '70s, park managers had collapsed the clubhouse and a golf course outbuilding into the buildings' own basements and covered them with dirt. Smaller dump sites the country club had buried sank after the fire as well, and Bob discovered a canal system that had probably once fed the Siberian elms. A larger sinkhole turned out to be an intact swimming pool. The history that had haunted the grassland with skeleton trees and cryptic winding trails turned out to have extensive foundations.

Once, Plains Indian tribes followed bison herds to the North Platte near the "hill that is hard to go around," or Me-a-pa-te in Lakota; once, a fur trader named Hiram Scott perished near the bluff and unwittingly renamed it; once, Oregon-bound covered wagons — prairie schooners, they were called — navigated around this "Nebraska Gibraltar"; once, local businessmen teed off and their children dog-paddled at the Scotts Bluff Country Club. Standing at the edge of the kochia and the native prairie, I start to wish some of this hadn't happened, to wish I were standing in a thick golden prairie unmarred by wagon ruts or crop furrows or pitching-wedge divots. But history is what it is in this land of boom and bust, coming and going. The layers of sandstone and limestone in Scotts Bluff hold extinct species and ash from an annihilating volcano, and now even after the Park Service has jackhammered out the foundations, the paths, and the swimming pool, and carted them off with the Siberian elm trunks, the land around the bluff will retain small concrete, glass, and metal fragments.

Bob stoops and picks up a black, mushroom-shaped piece of plastic beside his boot. "Looks like the end of a champagne bottle or something," he says, holding it up, "or maybe it's something to do with golf." It is indeed the plug from the end of a golf club's "reminder grip," the kind with a ridge underneath the rubber tape to remind you where to line up your hands. Its metal screw is corroded and the plastic worse for wear, but the patent number is still legible.

"This park will never be totally clean," Bob says, his eyes nearly closing as he speaks. "That history of private ownership will…" He trails off.

After the grass fire, a bonfire of smaller elm branches, and the debris removal, road graders smoothed over the canals and sinkholes—"We wanted to make that area more natural-looking," Bob says. He and his colleagues then sprayed the whole area with Roundup, a kill-all herbicide that left the soil colorless and clean. With a blank canvas to work on, they set out to create an ideal landscape, based on a healthy piece of virgin prairie on the opposite side of the bluff. The palette of grasses, forbs, sedges, and other plants always varies from one patch of prairie to the next, depending on water flow and soil minerals—it's impossible to know which plants grew where in this land's pre–golf course past. The myth of a stable ecosystem omits ancient volcanoes, more recent wildfires, and the hooves and chips from a few hundred thousand migrating bison—not to mention indigenous people and immigrants. Prairie restoration must therefore take a shotgun approach, scattering seeds like Jackson Pollock (who was born a couple of mountain ranges northwest of here in Wyoming), and letting them sort out their own patterns.

Needle-and-thread, blue grama, and threadleaf sedge make up most of the native prairie around Scotts Bluff. Needle-and-thread is a bunchgrass about a foot and a half tall with a long, sharp seed and a sheath, or awn, that hangs away from the seed like thread. Blue grama is shorter with a crescent head. Threadleaf sedge looks like overgrown lawn grass and grows in a leafy tuft. Native-plant catalogs sell needle-and-thread and blue grama seeds, but nobody had ever successfully harvested and germinated threadleaf sedge seeds. With the lottery money, rangers tried transplanting plugs of sod from across the monument, but the plugging machine took only four inches of roots, and the sedges died. Finally, they enlisted prairie botanists from the University of Nebraska to dig blocks of sedge sod from healthy prairie, truck it six hours east to Lincoln, juice it with nitrogen-phosphorous-potassium in a greenhouse for six months, and replant the bulked-up blocks in the new prairie. The process cost a fortune but largely worked: 82 percent of the plants survived the first year.[24]

As we start back toward his white truck, Bob spots a tall prairie sandreed that the prairie dogs haven't yet nibbled. He rolls the seed head in his fingers to scatter the seeds, but they aren't yet ripe. When he sees a puncture vine sprouting, he bends down to pull it up and toss it aside, grinning at himself. "See? I want to come out here and weed it by hand," he says. I laugh sympathetically. "Which," he continues, "would take a while."

Just outside the broken gate, suburban-style developments with names like Monument Heights and The Preserve provide bluff-view habitat for Gering's pickup-truck gentry around the relocated Monument Shadows course. Mini-mansions on Lariat Loop and Saddle Drive sport brick facades and three-car garages standard—one even has a Chimney Rock–shaped cupola—and they continue to sprout almost as fast as kochia in former agricultural land: yet another geologic layer, but here the fossils will be vinyl siding and Tyvek insulation. One lone cornfield endures like a bluff surrounded by fairways, driveways, and driving ranges. Gering also bears the traces of Ruth Harris; it was where she lived and taught when her adult Sunday school leader convinced her to become a missionary.

"You ask your average guy on the street, and he doesn't give a darn about native prairie," Bob tells me. He's right. Progress toward the Buffalo Commons notwithstanding, America's only prairie national parks are, like Scotts Bluff, incidental—pieces of grassland preserved for their proximity to other historical or geologic wonders: Wind Cave and the Badlands in South Dakota, Theodore Roosevelt's ranch in North Dakota, a bit of Yellowstone. Almost nobody sets foot in the National Grasslands, and there is no designated grassland wilderness.[25] Government preservation and ecology-minded organizations have tended to focus on sexier landscapes such as sequoias, sierras, or canyons. Besides, prairies make good farm- and ranch land.

Grasslands may be the most decimated ecosystem in the world: Since three-fourths of a prairie's biomass and stored carbon hide in the root systems, plowing it destroys a thick underground world as well as terrestrial habitat. Prairie ecologists compare sodbusting to clear-cutting redwoods. Some early settlers first planted corn by axing a crack in the overturned sod and dropping in a seed, because the roots were so thick. With technological advances, sodbusters could overturn the whole prairie more efficiently. The tallgrass prairies, where head-high grasses grew in the rich and well-watered soils of the Midwest (Minnesota, Iowa, Missouri, Illinois), are for all intents and purposes gone. Mixed- and short-grass prairies continue to fall under the plow or the Roundup herbicide as dryland farming techniques improve and Americans continue to demand corn-fed beef, high-fructose corn syrup, and ethanol gasoline. Because it is many times cheaper to preserve than restore these lands, in the Plains environmentalists have focused on placing conservation easements on existing native prairie. This struggling island of prairie at Scotts Bluff is, like the Henry Dieken prairie outside Unadilla, lucky to win the losses of Nebraska gamblers.

In the years since I left home, along with research trips for the Yankton Sioux Industries project or other journalistic projects, I've burned tank upon tank of ethanol-enhanced gas traveling to prairie preserves from the Canadian Prairie Provinces (Saskatchewan's Grasslands National Park, the only pure prairie national park in North America) to the New Mexico Dust Bowl (around Capulin Volcano National Monument) and the Kansas Flint Hills (Tallgrass Prairie National Preserve). None of them quite fulfills my tabula rasa fantasy. There's always a farmhouse or a paved road on the horizon to break the spell. Only the expanses of the National Grasslands system begin to suggest what a great American Serengeti park or a Buffalo Commons might look like, minus the tourists. After leaving Scotts Bluff, I will drive north past drought-scourged ranches grazed short as gray putting greens, on up to the Oglala National Grassland, which covers the Nebraska-Wyoming-South Dakota borderland. North of the Pine Ridge I will stop the car and climb out where two spaniel-size jackrabbits hound each other, surrounded by just grass and sky and the sounds of my dust settling back to the road and a light wind washing over my ear cartilage. It can be soothing land, apparently unhaunted by outcrops or the protruding bones of the past.

Bob's is a more prosaic prairie. He must monitor grasses

and weeds and prairie dog populations—even with a number of badgers and rattlesnakes, the monument may not support enough predators to keep them in check.

"It's just to get a handle on, where are we going with our little patch of heaven right here?" He laughs. "Whether we'll ever be successful, I don't know. We can't put a bubble over Scotts Bluff National Monument and keep everybody out and shut off the canals and tell the railroad they can't come through anymore. That's never going to happen. So it's going to be sort of a constant management program to try to maintain the native prairie, and to try to restore it where it isn't so good."

He's become frustrated with those four acres of kochia, where every year he scatters seven hundred dollars in native seed he might as well be throwing across the Monument Shadows parking lot. But such trial and error, and such vigilance, is what rewilding requires and what my own rewilding of the Plains will require: scattering seeds of Willa Cather's Superstition and Investigation on the gravestone of Minnie's first attempt at bread making in another ghost dance to bring back a Plains that I would be right at home in. Then tending this Buffalo Commonplace ecologically, historically, and imaginatively.

"Only seven years," I tell him. "You've got some—you've got a lot of time."

"Yeah," he allows, shaking his head. "Yeah. It feels like I'm running out of time, and I'm running out of patience." We approach his white truck, and a train whistle blows to the north of us, near the river. "I'm just not seeing the success, and I don't know if it's drought, I don't know if there's chemicals in the soil that keep the natives from growing." He regards the four acres of kochia. "We don't come out and spray all this, but I am going to have to mow it."

NINE

Leaves of Grass

9.1

The Buffalo Commons would not be complete without its predators. As their populations rebound due to hunting limits and other conservation measures, mountain lions and wolves are already expanding their ranges, returning to the Plains from mountain preserves in the Rockies and Black Hills. Then there are the fires that periodically scour the grasslands. Oz wouldn't be Oz without its Wicked Witches and its Kalidahs, beasts with bodies like bears and heads like tigers. And a Buffalo Commonplace isn't just a prairie punk Eden, a potluck society without villains. There's Bill Janklow, of course, but in the Plains of my mind no villain looms as starkly as the venomous visionary Fred Phelps, the Topekan Moses of hate speech.

The "God Hates Fags" website says the regular weekly service time at Westboro Baptist Church is 11:30 a.m.[1] I've got on my Sunday best, but my East Coast plastic-frame glasses and the IMPEACH BUSH bumper sticker on the car I borrowed from my dad will give me away as one of the "modern day Sadducees," like those privileged and skeptical Jews in Biblical times to whom Westboro Baptist's website compares "bleeding heart liberals."[2] I also worry I've forgotten deodorant this summer morning; it's going to be 105. I'm running a little early, as if I were attending church in a foreign country and wanted in my bleeding heart only to sit in the back and not offend local custom.

Southwest 12th is a shady, leafy way of mature trees and houses running from downtown Topeka out past another Baptist church and a Methodist church, domestic cars herringboned into their parking lots for services. Westboro's website says, "Feel free to attend one of our weekly church meetings," so I've decided to stop by. Suddenly I spot a white van with REPENT OR BURN IN HELL written on its side, waiting at a stop sign. I've almost missed the twenty-foot WWW.GODHATESAMERICA .COM banner, red letters on white below the eaves of a fenced-in, not-quite-churchlike building. I park my car and its bumper sticker three blocks away and walk.

The Westboro church compound looks like the deck of a battleship in distress. A two-layer gunwale—a hedge outside a wooden fence—protects the property, and three flagpole masts rise from the front yard inside. The largest pole, closest to the street, flies a tattered Canadian flag above a tattered American one. Closer to the side of the property where the entrance is, two more poles fly the humble Kansas and Topeka flags. All four flags are upside down. Westboro's astonishingly long-winded SOS, abbreviated as "God Hates Fags," seems quite appropriate to the Plains—native, even, though like so many of the region's key figures Reverend Phelps is an import. Demagogues, from Bill Janklow to William Jennings Bryan— even to a small degree George and Clara Cole and Charley and Minnie Davis—do well among the sons of homesteaders. But

Phelps's poetry goes beyond any of these settlers' words; it's like wildfire, horrific but emotionally irresistible.

Walking up to the east side of the property near the Topeka flag (a faded green, gold, and white banner with a seal for the "Golden City"), I see a preadolescent boy scurry from an emerald minivan to the building and back. The van's sliding door is still open when I reach the padlocked gate. The boy sits in back, and two women sit up front. Both women are plain in a way anachronistic Christians often are—stocky, old country, antiglamorous. The younger woman in the passenger seat wears a head scarf that reminds me of Hutterite uniforms in other parts of the Plains. The boy is noticeably uncool for his age.

"Do you, um, know where the entrance is?" I ask, peering into the van through my Sadducee specs.

"The entrance is usually here, but it's locked now," the driver replies helpfully. "Sorry." I back away to wait for the church elders to arrive and unlock the door. I'm still ten minutes early.

I stand shifting my weight in the half shade of their trees, little Jacob's ladders of light dropping between the leaves. It must be 90 already. I have left a reporter's notebook sticking out of my back pocket to be aboveboard about the fact that I'm a writer without actually saying so.

The distressed ship is actually a brilliant publicity machine, a behemoth nuclear battleship helmed by an aging captain and powered by a mustard seed of uranium. With a few dozen members and at that time only a fax machine, Reverend Phelps and his church began making national headlines in the early 1990s, picketing the funerals of gay AIDS victims with messages like AIDS IS GOD'S CURSE and FAGS DIE, GOD LAUGHS. In

1994, a dozen Westboro members lasted about thirty seconds outside the San Francisco funeral of gay journalist Randy Shilts (author of *And the Band Played On*) before being escorted away by police in a hail of eggs and fruit.[3] Their language, in innumerable press releases, memos, and picket signs, has a radioactive wrath that, sincere as their hatred is, is not unself-consciously funny. It's hard not to be drawn in by their language, either as shocking, stifled-laugh comedy or as fight-picking. Or both:

WBC to picket Elizabeth Taylor's funeral, in religious protest to her sinful enabling of fags

This evil woman is drawing ever closer to the end of her wicked, Christ-rejecting, Satan-worshipping life....Having fornicated her adulterous life away, she capped her sins by becoming a fag pimp....In her moral cesspool, she thrashes—her brain long fried in lust's fires....

Hell from beneath will soon move, to meet Liz Taylor at her coming.

...For all eternity, Liz Taylor will be tormented with fire and brimstone, everlasting fire, eternal punishment.... She will see the myriads of souls she has trapped into sodomy by her influence, and they will curse each other, gnawing their tongues for pain and blaspheming God forever.

(August 11, 2000)[4]

Or observe the elegant Calvinist antimetabole of "God does not hate them because they are homosexuals; they are homosexuals because God hates them."[5] Their invective reminds me of the Wizard of Oz's booming, alliterative insults (in the movie version) to scare the Tin Man—"You clinking, clanking collection of caliginous junk!"—and the Scarecrow—"You billowing bale of bovine fodder!"

Fred Phelps is Walt Whitman's evil twin, generating an overflowing word count, a commonplace book of hate-filled, exclusionary, overwrought, antique, hyperbolic, unedited provocation.

In 1998—in a triumph of First Amendment over Sixth Commandment—the church upped the ante by celebrating the lynching of the gay college student Matthew Shepard at his funeral in Laramie, Wyoming. Soon, with the advent of the Internet's arms race of outrageousness, in which visitors link and flock to the bizarre, Westboro assembled one of the most fearsome fleets: God Hates Fags, God Hates America, God Hates Canada, God Hates the World, Priests Rape Boys, Signs of the Times, and Smell the Brimstone. Dot-com.[6]

The antigay antics seemed like so much alluringly distasteful *Inside Edition* content to most Americans. Not content to be a freak show, and facing a protracted drought of gay AIDS funerals, the church changed course and, through a leap of logic comprehensible only in the distorted gravity of publicity making, began in 2005 a campaign picketing the funerals of soldiers killed in the Iraq War. They now aimed to disgrace some of the last sacred ground in America, proclaiming, THANK GOD FOR IEDS (improvised explosive devices, or roadside bombs), THANK GOD FOR SEPT. 11, and THANK GOD FOR DEAD SOLDIERS. The soldiers are dying in retribution for our modern Sodom's tolerance of gays ("They turned America / Over to fags; / They're coming home / In body bags"[7]), and for its intolerance of God's "anointed" and His "prophets" at Westboro Baptist. (Their prophecy of Liz Taylor's death was 3,876 days premature; when she died in 2011 they promised to picket her funeral but didn't show up.) In May 2006, Congress passed and the president signed the Respect for America's Fallen Heroes Act, prohibiting demonstrations within an hour of a funeral at a national cemetery. Some states passed similar laws. In October 2007, a federal jury in Baltimore awarded $10.9 million in damages to the father of a Marine whose funeral Phelps and crew had picketed. In March 2011, by an 8-to-1 majority, the U.S. Supreme Court upheld an appellate court judgment overturning this award. The courts ruled that Westboro's funeral protests are constitutionally protected speech.[8] A small Topeka church had elbowed its way into the mainstream of United States rhetorical history.

American *art brut* poet Fred Phelps grew up Methodist in Meridian, Mississippi. He graduated from high school at sixteen and secured a place at West Point but wasn't yet old enough to attend. During his year off, he heard the Call at a tent revival. Within six months, in early 1947, the honor student, Eagle Scout, and Golden Gloves boxer had traded West Point for Bob Jones University and Methodism for Baptism. On a mission trip to Vernal, Utah, after his first semester, Phelps was ordained as a Southern Baptist minister and baptized in a mountain stream. In Vernal, he was trying, at times in physical danger, to convert small-town Mormons to Baptism.[9] Before long he tasted media publicity as an evangelical tool. In 1951, at age twenty-one, Phelps (described as "a tall [6 ft. 3 in.], craggy-faced engineering student") appeared in *Time* magazine after drawing large crowds—and ultimately the police—outside a college in Pasadena, California, by protesting students' "promiscuous petting" and "teachers' filthy jokes in classrooms."[10]

Phelps, his wife, and the first of their thirteen children moved from Pasadena to Topeka in 1954 and soon set up Westboro as a Primitive Baptist church.[11] Ten years later, still preaching every Sunday and on the radio besides, Phelps earned a law degree and became a righteous nuisance to the Kansas capital—"City of Bastards," "City of Whores." (The *Topeka Capital-Journal* published the fullest biography of Phelps in a weeklong series in 1994.[12])

Before he was disbarred, his legal career was simultaneously quixotic and petty—in some ways nobly so. He had a vicious, intelligent courtroom manner and was inclined to take on cases for poor clients against the government or institutions. Indeed, he says he went to law school to fight against the kind of racial injustice he saw growing up in Mississippi. Westboro's short monograph on the God Hates Fags site emphasizes how Phelps represented "longsuffering" Kansas blacks in civil rights cases in the years after Topeka's famous 1954 *Brown v. Board of Education* case. He won a $19,500 settlement against the Topeka school board in 1978 for providing an inferior education to a black student and thus failing to honor the *Brown* ruling. The next year he represented several victims of a police raid on a black American Legion hall, in which more than fifty women were strip-searched for drugs and weapons. He received civil rights awards into the 1980s, including one from a small-town Kansas chapter of the NAACP that noted his "steely determination for justice."[13]

He later showed himself willing to use racist rhetoric in other fights; a number of subsequent Westboro faxes referred to miscellaneous Phelps enemies as "black trash," "black thug," and "incompetent black whore."[14] In February 2009, the church wrote, in an open letter to President Barack Obama, "You are a

Muslim. Your mother was a promiscuous white female tramp, and your father was a run-of-the-mill, black, deadbeat dad who abandoned you and your mother and fled to more fertile breeding grounds in Africa."[15] Westboro concurs with those who believe Obama is the literal Antichrist.

In 1973, two of Fred Phelps's teenage sons began purchasing a $184.59, twelve-inch color television set on layaway from the local Sears. When they made their final payment after two months, Sears had sold the TV to another customer and had to order another. Phelps promptly filed a $50 million class-action suit against Sears Holdings Corporation, claiming to represent a million layaway customers, litigating for almost six years and ultimately receiving a settlement of $126.34. Later he sued the local Washburn University when some of his children were denied admission to the law school there: First, he sued on the grounds that they should be admitted as minorities under affirmative action because the Phelps family law firm (eleven of the thirteen children ultimately became lawyers) represented black clients in civil rights cases. When that argument failed, he sued for reverse discrimination, claiming that less-qualified black students had been admitted before his white children. Phelps also sued President Ronald Reagan for breaching the wall between church and state by appointing an ambassador to the Vatican.[16] (His respect for this wall goes only so far: The God Hates Fags website demands that "All nations must immediately outlaw sodomy" and, according to Mosaic law in Leviticus, "impose the death penalty," presumably by stoning.[17]) In 1974 a county court reporter in Topeka failed to deliver a trial transcript to him on time. Phelps sued her for $22,000, declared her a hostile witness, and grilled her on the witness stand for three days.[18]

As a result of this last case, and a pattern of witch-hunt courtroom behavior leading up to it, he was disbarred from Kansas state court in 1979. Ten years later, in response to a disciplinary complaint from nine federal judges, he agreed to stop practicing in federal court. He promptly ran for governor of Kansas in 1990, receiving 6 percent of the vote in the Democratic primary, and ran for U.S. Senate in 1992 and governor again in 1994 and 1998.[19] Not long after his law career ended, in 1991, Westboro members first picketed against gays trysting in Topeka's Gage Park, and they haven't let a week go by since without displaying their GOD HATES FAGS signs there.

How did a civil rights lawyer come to advocate mass executions of a small minority group? Poking the eyes of the powers that be in the name of justice was not an unthinkable prelude to Phelps's God Hates Fags work. He embodied and still embodies the fearlessness and righteousness and self-righteousness that characterize many political activists, both right and left wing. His is an iconoclastic and, as the NAACP award put it, *steely* Christianity. Bill Janklow's brazen behavior was not religious, but it derived from the same steely determination for his version of justice. To a lesser extent, my dad's combative bumper stickers—IMPEACH BUSH, or HE'S STILL A JERK—are part of the same lively democratic determination. Phelps exhibits certain traits of radicals in their purest form, distilled beyond practical use to the point of being either ridiculous or poetic.

My own history flows in the opposite direction, but parallel. I started out in the Plains, a long day's drive north of Topeka, and was more outspoken as a tyke than now. I learned about the existence and controversy of homosexuality in the late '80s, probably around the same time Phelps did; but instead of inspiring obnoxious displays of righteous plumage, the issue eventually drove me underground like that three-fourths of prairie biomass retained in the roots. Grassland plants produce tiny flowers, invisible from any distance, like little *Geum triflorum*, prairie smoke. They endure droughts, blizzards, wildfires, and trampling hooves by maintaining a foundation safely underground.

I was also raised with Protestant faith but was in part driven away when a theology like Phelps's seemed more consistent with the brutality of the Bible, and the world, than the "maudlin, kissy-pooh, feel-good, touchy-feely preachers of today's society," as Westboro puts it.[20] A dark cynicism courses through my root system, prepared for the worst. I want to believe in something like Ruth Harris's exactly opposite but equally revolutionary theology—as appropriate to the Plains as Westboro Baptist's, and as poetic and visionary—but I retreat underground, or skyward to that view from the oval airplane window, that scientific distance.

9.2

The green minivan's door slides shut, and inexplicably my hatemonger friends speed away. I'm left waiting in the heat, well past 11:30, ringing the doorbell a few times and hearing occasional phantom noises inside. Westboro's building is a conjoined parsonage and church (the parsonage outshines the sanctuary by a fair margin), a new white stucco villa with brown stripes, chalet-style. Disharmoniously, the church sign is the same modest brick marquee that would greet visitors at any church in town. Such signs invariably include the word WELCOME in white movable letters, but Westboro's sign is blank.

Out on Southwest 12th, a white quarter-ton pickup truck slows, and I notice a stack of colorful signs in the bed. FAGS DOOM NATIONS. GOD IS YOUR ENEMY. The teenage driver looks toward me, and the church, shakes his head, and drives on. Shortly after, I see a couple walking across the far side of the churchyard, having entered through a tiny entrance in the opposite corner of the fence; a woman and a teenage boy follow a minute later.

"Excuse me!" I call out. "Excuse me!" They don't turn their heads. Finally, fully sweaty at 12:15 p.m., I give up and walk back to the car.

"It's not a campaign, hon, we're just preaching the truth. Listen, have you looked at signmovies.com? Have you looked at godhatesfags.com? You're taking too many words to ask your question. Get to the point." I have called Westboro two days later to ask why there was no regular service on Sunday.[21] Church was held earlier in the morning, it seems. A number of church members had traveled that day to Wolf Creek, Montana, to celebrate divine retribution against Senator Max Baucus. ("Sen. Baucus voted twice recently to condemn WBC's funeral pickets. 'Vengeance is mine; I will repay, saith the Lord.' Romans 12:19.") Marine Corporal Phillip E. Baucus, the senator's nephew, had died in combat in Iraq a week earlier, and his funeral in Montana coincided with my visit to Topeka.[22]

The woman on the phone does not identify herself, but I assume she is Shirley Phelps-Roper, Fred's daughter, who in her father's advanced age has taken the cockpit as spokesperson for the S.S. *God Hates Your Tears*. "You need to be there when the service is happening," she tells me. "We're not going to go to extraordinary lengths to help someone who is just curious.

That's not our job." (Westboro is a tax-exempt organization, and its incorporation papers state that "all persons whatsoever are wanted, welcome and invited."[23])

Not one to confront a stranger, I move on, inquiring if Ms. Phelps-Roper can suggest some books, background on the Phelps theology, for a curious outsider to read. She names a 1919 work by Arthur Pink called *The Sovereignty of God*—described by its current publisher as "a prime book to give to anyone who defends the free will of man."[24] She also suggests a couple of older titles: *Absolute Predestination* by Jerome Zanchius (1516–1590) and *The Bondage of the Will* by Martin Luther (1483–1546). Westboro Baptist is not a modern evangelical church where someone who is *just curious* can walk in, kneel at the altar, condemn some fags, and be saved. Westboro's theology is essentially sixteenth-century Calvinism with an obsessive homophobic bent and a strain of Branch Davidian cultism. Virtually God's entire predestined "elect" worldwide just happen to be the seventy-five or so members of Westboro Baptist Church, almost all of whom happen to be Phelps's family members.[25] Mainstream members of the religious right are "lukewarm cowards" and "Pharisees."[26]

Fred Phelps's personal volatility is not what one would expect from the leader of God's elect, unless one expects that God is a terribly wrathful God. When his children were young, Phelps would beat them in Old Testament–like furies, with a belt or with the handle of a mattock (the type of grub ax the Joad family used to dig Grampa's grave in the hard Dust Bowl ground beside the highway in *The Grapes of Wrath*). One Christmas, according to two of his sons who later defected, Phelps beat them with the mattock for two or three hours. "Mark was about to pass out a couple of times, and my mom would take him over to the bathtub to wipe his face off," Nate Phelps told the *Topeka Capital-Journal* in 1994. The boys' crime had been unscrewing Christmas lights from a neighbor's house (the Phelpses don't celebrate Christmas) and tossing them to pop on the street.[27]

Nate and Mark Phelps described their father becoming possessed by anger—"It wasn't the same human"—and smashing dishes and jars of ketchup, mustard, and mayonnaise across the kitchen, pushing their mother down the stairs, dislocating her arm, or beating her with the mattock stick because he "wasn't happy about her weight."[28] Phelps would fly into a rage if one of the children peeled an apple the wrong way.[29] After the *Capital-Journal* printed Mark and Nate Phelps's accusations, five siblings still loyal to the church publicly refuted the abuse charges, though they acknowledged that they were spanked with a belt and a hairbrush.[30] Court records, however, seemed to substantiate Nate Phelps's story that he was appointed a guardian *ad litem* and referred to child welfare officers after refusing to change into a T-shirt and shorts in middle school gym class for fear of showing his bruises.[31] In their statements to the *Capital-Journal* about their upbringing, the two apostate sons seemed more scarred by their father's coldness than his beatings. "His goal was to annihilate you if you had any human need," Mark said.[32]

A 2006 Associated Press story described Phelps's contradictory nature as one of abrupt changes: "He laughs, then looks sullen. Calls a granddaughter 'love bug,' but is then set off in a brief tirade on Jews." Though God's true list of the chosen never changes, Phelps's divining of that list may; in 2005, a fifty-two-year-old man (not a relative) was voted out of the elect and permanently cut off from his wife and children.[33] After Mark Phelps left the church of his own free will (so to speak) in 1973, he ran into his father at the Topeka YMCA, where Fred Phelps said to his second child, "I hope God kills you."[34]

Though weakened with age, Phelps leads the church still; as I listen to the MP3 recording of the sermon I somehow missed, I am surprised at his measured speech. He has the professional tone of an old-time radio newsman, with only a trace of his Mississippi drawl remaining. But he works himself into a quiet froth addressing his flock—*ye seed of Israel, his servants... ye children of Jacob, his chosen ones.* He winds through an encyclopedic recall of Scripture and his own nearly biblical language in slow, serpentine sentences.

> We're not just whistling Dixie when we say to these people that jump on us that they're playing with fire, and that they are in fact pouring gasoline on the flaming fires of God's wrath that's presently being poured out on this evil nation, and is guaranteed to get worse and worse *soon* and with each passing *day*. We have a *message* for this evil country, and at their peril do they continue to not only *ignore* it but to retaliate against *us* for even daring to preach it.

Sharp declarations punctuate this speech: "They shall fall. They're going to hell. They're going to reap destruction. They're going to reap nothing but misery." Finally, his voice becomes grandfatherly and gentle, and he says, "And everybody will know that it's for *thy* sake, it's for the sake of Westboro Baptist Church, that those guys keep getting slaughtered and sent home in little pieces from Iraq."[35]

I imagine myself in a pew, hypnotized by the queered tent-revival clichés. This is the Eagle Scout's integrity and self-regard, the American bard's gluttonous, unedited style, and the visionary firebrand's jaw-dropping rhetoric, all taken to the violent frontier of sanity. I hope Phelps's oeuvre can be anthologized someday, or put in a museum, so the timber in his eye can reveal the splinters in our own. I don't mean our homophobia per se—more our hunger for publicity, our bipolar furies, political righteousness, and contradictions.

So far, Topeka's response over the years to Westboro's actions has been an uncharacteristic acceptance of homosexuality. The *Capital-Journal* observed, "Most people in northeast Kansas—generally tolerant, gentle people whose roots are in farming and operating small businesses—have accepted the hateful pickets and faxes the way they accept tornadoes and violent thunderstorms that march across the state each spring."[36] A local woman told the *New York Times* in 2005, "Topeka is a much more tolerant community because of Fred. . . . People are so outraged you could be so mean to people."[37] But many would hate a Phelps anthology or museum, would prefer to ignore him; a telling reader response to the 1994 *Capital-Journal* series about Phelps concluded, "I, for one, would be far more interested in the life story of Grant Cushinberry, an exemplary member of our community."[38]

In September 2004, in what appeared to be a direct response to Westboro's activities, the Topeka City Council appointed Tiffany Muller, a lesbian, to fill a vacant seat. The next March, Fred Phelps's granddaughter Jael ran against Muller and a third candidate, Richard Harmon, in the primary. Harmon received 1,935 votes; Muller, 1,329; Jael Phelps, 202. On the same ballot, Topeka voters upheld the council's decision, sponsored by Muller, to add sexual orientation to the city's antidiscrimination statute.[39] The community remains conservative and religious, but its polite temperament cannot fathom how Westboro could be *so mean*. (On a subsequent visit to Topeka, I will see a red graffiti scrawl on the church's antiwelcome sign: GOD HATES THE PHELPS.) Muller's modest gay rights achievements in Topeka unfolded just before the Phelpses began picketing soldiers' funerals.

In an open letter to Topekans, Mark Phelps once advised the community on how to "confine" his father's "destructive behaviors and...limit his influence." He counseled them not to fear the "foul language" and "booming voice," and drew on a little Kansas mythology, observing that ultimately "when Toto pulls the curtain back, instead of this big powerful individual, it's only a small, pathetic old man."[40]

On the phone, Shirley Phelps-Roper—if indeed it is her—becomes ruder with each second of hers that I waste trying to formulate a question. Gingerly, in a Midwestern roundabout, I begin to ask about violations of Mosaic code that straight people might commit: adultery, fornication, sex during menstruation, other abominations. If these are more common and accepted than homosexuality, then why—"Don't ask impudent, stupid questions. Go find His word in Hebrews," she interrupts. "I don't care if you're married, and she's your wife of sacred covenant, and you're serving God, and if you want to swing from your lamp shade or whatever, don't ask me about it. Don't ask me any more stupid questions about your sex acts." Then she hangs up without saying good-bye.

9.3

I reckon it was long about '96, the summer that thieves swiped my trove of phonograms and my digital gramophone, that Ma and I took a ride down to Oaxaca, in Old Mexico. Spent seven weeks there in all, the first month mastering Espanyol and touring the old Zapotecan Indian ruins in the dry mountains of inland Oaxaca. We saw present-day Mexican Indian folks making and selling pottery as black and shiny as a prairie night, and rugs so purty they'd stop a bison stampede on a buffalo nickel. Ma wanted to lasso me out of my familiar neck of the woods, give me a taste of a different world. Mexico was that indeed.

Four weeks of book-learning Spanish, and our native tongue was good and thirsty. We lit out for a little coastal town, Puerto Angel. It was reputed to be something of an outpost for wanderer-type gringos—knapsackers, saddlebaggers, restless spirits. I was feeling by this point a *derned* sharp yearning for home. I missed my old chums. I missed peanut butter and jelly. Looking at Puerto Angel Bay one day, I sketched out in colored chalk a picture of the horseshoe of hills surrounding a sapphire Pacific inlet with rolling waves like Dakota grasslands. In the sky over the sea, no joke, I drew a pair of ruby slippers. Then I added the legend, *No hay un lugar como el hogar.* That's Spanish for "Ain't no place like home."

Well, we didn't find too many gringos around there, but we found some of their scat: In a Main Street shop, there was a little shelf or maybe a basket with a dozen or so used English paperbacks. I wasn't interested in any namby-pamby romances or vampire tales, so that left me with a book of true stories by a British animal doc, and a few Louis L'Amour Westerns. L'Amour was practically a neighbor, being a son of Jamestown, North Dakota, just a couple hundred miles to the northeast of Pierre. Both of us would've been citizens of Dakota Territory back in frontier days. Funny, he changed the spelling of his family name from "LaMoore" when he left home. Not sure what that says about a man.

Truth be told, I hadn't read a L'Amour Western before, and I ain't read one since. Nickel-dime Westerns always seemed a bit put-on, by my lights. But I pronked through these Sackett stories there in a hammock in Puerto Angel like a pronghorn that heard a gunshot. Did I ever. Give a half-starved boy some hardtack and blackstrap, and he'll gobble it up like it was warm chocolate cake with butter frosting. I can still smell the smoke of a noble Indian's mesquite fire drifting out of some arroyo. My palms still sweat thinking of a pony's hoof slipping on a rock over a *halloooo* precipice. Louis L'Amour brought me right through those last days away from home with a frontier that warn't exactly *real*— excepting in my mind and imagination, where it was a good deal realer than the lizards crawling up a Mexican hotel wall.

9.4

It was not long ago that I stumbled upon an intriguing book, a small-run Western perhaps even more pulpish than a Louis L'Amour paperback. Its typefaces and design were elementary, its proofreading imperfect, its cover art cheesy and hopelessly dated to the early 1990s: an acrylic portrait of Dakota Taylor gazing seductively at the reader, the collar of his denim jacket turned up and faded almost white, a handkerchief tied like a cravat around his neck, his mustache and sideburns a disco hangover beneath his brown Stetson. Dakota Taylor is the gay gunslinger, and three volumes of his exploits were published by Alyson Publications between 1992 and 1995. They are, in order, *Arson!*, *Silver Saddles*, and *Rattler!*

Dakota Taylor is the only hero who can really face off against the mad Reverend Phelps. Lawyers have tried with suits, patriotic Harley-Davidson hogs have tried with unbaffled exhaust rumbles, idealistic students have tried with love, and Phelps has only grown in power. But Phelps's weapon is not merely hate but a literary oeuvre, and it's only with equally potent words that he can be beaten back. Not eliminated, mind you, because the shadowy villain never dies—that would be the end of the saga, and we're not ready for that. So let us imagine high noon in the Buffalo Commonplace, where the snaky old preacher meets his sexy young match.

Cap Iversen, Dakota's author, masters the Western genre right up to the precipice of parody. Dakota is a stereotypical gay-male fantasy: slender but tough; wise but not "word smart"[41]; more manly than most of the straight male characters, and willing to fight with fists and brains as well as Colts; occasionally prone to reflection and sensitivity. Dakota exhibits a rough breed of valor. His weaknesses for poker, whiskey, and good-looking men are downright charming, especially when he pains over them. He also sympathizes with the plight of Indians and honors their cultures and environments to a degree that shows his cards as a creation of the 1990s, published in Boston.

In fact, the palpability of his having been *created* as a character for use in late-twentieth-century gay readers' lives is what makes the Dakota Taylor books compelling for me now. There's a tacit dramatic irony that gives these books a frisson that many other Western novels and histories lack—similar to the motives underlying my own assemblage of history and myth in this commonplace book. It would be as if there were a constant raised eyebrow in a L'Amour novel that hinted, *Hey, dude, you and I both know we're just allaying our fears about our ticky-tacky lives crumbling in nuclear war or civil rights uprisings, about our lack of rugged American authenticity in this push-button era. Giddyap!* Even better-written "new" Westerns lack Iversen's particular spark. Cormac McCarthy, Ivan Doig, and Annie Proulx atone for L'Amour's stylistic sins by being more true to life, gritty, or vulgarly poetic, not by reckoning with the appeal of using the Plains and West as ore from which to forge American stories in the first place. Proulx's story "Brokeback Mountain" famously roped gay men into the Western (five years after Iversen did), but great as it is, it doesn't really grapple or take issue with the Western genre in general, just its conventions. Maybe the Western's appeal is a nonissue at this point, like quoting the Bible. But it's worth wondering why writers keep returning to the genre.

I may be giving Cap Iversen a bit more credit than he's due. The Dakota Taylor books don't exactly *grapple* with the Western either. They make out with the Western and make off with its Colt revolvers. Dakota was born, as he relates it to a lover who doesn't quite believe him (should *we?*), in the Black Hills in the back of a buckboard about to be attacked by Dakota Sioux. It was sometime in the middle of the nineteenth century. The Sioux took mercy on a white woman in labor and spared the whole Taylor family; Rose Taylor christened her only child Dakota in gratitude. He left home at about the age of twelve, or fifteen, or whatever. He did a stint in the Union Army to impress a handsome free Negro in Kansas. After the war, he became a buffalo runner until it made him vomit with disgust and shame; then he killed his fellow hunters to save a Hopi shaman's life.

By the time we meet him, Dakota is around thirty but

doesn't know his precise age. He hasn't spoken with his parents in five years. His father, Temple Taylor, is or was a mountebank preacher — *Oh, so there's an oedipal angle to this battle with Phelps, too* — who used to perform stunts like pulling a pig liver out from under young Dakota's shirt before a Wichita throng and declaring it to be an exorcised sickness. Rose Taylor has disowned her son for being a gunslinger, and one who "hankers after other men" to boot.[42] His parents live in lawless San Francisco ("Tombstone is a nunnery in comparison," he says[43]), or is it that his father has died of consumption and his mother has moved to Snake Eye, on the California-Nevada line? Never mind. As in Superman comics, the details of time and place are not well fixed, and it only raises awkward questions of history and geography to piece together Dakota's bio from a bunch of plot-driven flashbacks scattered through the three books. The upshot: He's a loner, a wanderer, a gun for hire.

In *Arson!* we meet his true love, Benjamin Colsen Jr., a London-born student from Harvard Law, son of an exiled Spanish princess and an English tea importer who moved out west to raise sheep. While Bennie was off at school, Ben Colsen Sr. and the rest of the family were murdered by a mob, their ranch burned to the ground, for mysterious reasons that turn out to involve a Hopi legend of an Eternal Spring in the middle of their desert ranch, water politics in drought, cattlemen's hatred for sheep, and xenophobia toward the cultured Europeans. Bennie returns to bury his family and hires the renowned Dakota Taylor to carry out his vengeance. One of the story lines of *Arson!* follows Dakota's growing conscience and hesitation about murder as he gets on in years and gets sweet on Bennie. In fact, though he recounts many cool-hand executions of the past, he never actually kills anybody in this first volume. In the end, he burns down Turnpike, Arizona, to avenge the original mob arson (in which the whole town was complicit), but it seems nobody dies in the fires. The last scene has Dakota confronting the mob leader, who is haunted by guilt. As James T. Anderson walks out of the room, "His back was as wide open as the Great Plains. His shoulders slightly stiffened as he waited for the hot sting of a bullet to enter his flesh."[44] But Dakota can't pull the trigger.

In *Silver Saddles*, we catch up with Dakota and Bennie after two years of nonlegally wedded bliss in the remote Sierra Nevada. After receiving word that his mother has died, Dakota is shot in the back and chest on page twenty-seven, before he can read her last letter to him. He spends months in a fevered bed rest two hundred miles from Bennie under the care of a pale, deaf-mute boy he calls Angel (nothing kinky, pure nursing, and magical-realist nursing at that). It turns out that Temple Taylor wasn't Dakota's real father after all and that a Charles Buckridge left his gunslinger son one of the biggest ranches and silver mines in Nevada. The only problem is that Dakota's long-lost brother, Caleb, has put a dead-or-alive price on his head to avoid giving up the bequest. This time Dakota has to kill at least nine gunslingers to save his own neck before he can reason with Caleb. He negotiates to give the better part of the land back to the Paiutes, whose ancestors are buried there, and to stop Caleb's "raping" of the land for more silver.[45] After nine months and half a dozen bullet wounds, Dakota returns home to Bennie and their humble cabin.

The final book, *Rattler!*, begins with the remarkable premise that Dakota and Bennie are headed east by stagecoach to Camden, New Jersey, to meet Walt Whitman for tea. This is not Whitman's first appearance in the series. When Bennie initially comes out to Dakota in *Arson!*, he describes his "affectional proclivities" as "a Whitmanish sort of thing." Dakota looks blankly at his lover-to-be, and so Bennie fetches a dog-eared copy of *Leaves of Grass* from his saddlebag and reads one of the Calamus poems in which "his arm lay lightly around my breast."[46] Lonely for the intellectual ferment of Harvard, Bennie has struck up correspondence with a few Eastern writers: Whitman, Herman Melville, and, somehow, though there were only a handful of people who knew she was a poet at the time, Emily Dickinson.[47] Whitman writes to say he has read Bennie's poems "in the garden with the moon as my light" and invites him east for tea.[48] In the coach, Dakota chafes at the ruffled collar Bennie has dressed him in—chafes at the very idea of tea—and he's almost overjoyed after the coach is hijacked by the Juan Caballe gang, which springs loose a prisoner who's been riding with them toward his hanging in the town of Broken Wagon Wheel, somewhere east of El Paso. Dakota finds himself volunteering to be deputy marshal of Broken Wagon Wheel, chiefly to retrieve his ivory-inlaid Colts from the Caballe cabal and to avoid a ruffle-collared tea in New Jersey. Unfortunately, when all is said and done, Bennie writes an apology to Walt Whitman, and the couple heads back to California. I would have loved to read Dakota Taylor's account of a tea with the Bard of Brooklyn. He might have come to regard Whitman, "one of the roughs," as not so much of a ninny as he imagines.[49]

Like all good dime Westerns, these books gallop swiftly and suspensefully, with a quasi-mystery of a plot. The names of the characters are spot-on, from Riker Sims and Clayton Moorly to Judd Brooks and Caramel Edellton (a rare woman). Dakota's voice is put-on, like a Louis L'Amour character's. It's riddled with clichés: "It was hard to tell where the horse ended and I began"; small Hopi children with "round chocolate eyes" peer out from behind their mothers' skirts, and Swift Running Deer, a Hopi lover, smells of "willow, sand, river. Of the earth"; when he almost dies, Dakota recounts, "My journey took me into the fiery depths of hell, where I fought the devil, wrestled him to the ground, and eventually won"; or, as he declares at one point, "I had an unholy fire burning in me."[50] These passages often make me laugh out loud with delight, because it seems Cap Iversen is in on the joke in a way that Louis L'Amour is not. He's laughing as he's writing it, but it's not mere parody.

There are some fresher images that are even funnier: an adobe house that is "baby-shit yellow," for instance, or Western stars "as thick as red ants on molasses."[51] A gay banker's face is "as gray and wrinkled as an old petticoat."[52] And how about this sunset: "The sun was gone, melted into the desert like butter on hot flapjacks, but its leftovers splashed deep scarlets and purples across the sky."[53]

Dakota Taylor's sexual orientation swirls smoothly into the boilerplate adventures like a streak of lavender in a maple syrup sunset. There are an astounding number of gay men, and a few lesbians, in Cap Iversen's Old West. *Take that, Phelps.* Dakota walks up to a telegraph office and, in the course of a tense exchange with the corrupt agent, notices that the man is "effeminate as all hell" and starts flirting.[54] His doppelgänger gunslinger, Ryder McCloud, is also a onetime lover. Swift Running Deer, the grandson of the shaman Dakota once saved, steams up a kiva with Dakota in a peyote stupor. Dakota's brother, Caleb Buckridge, of course shares his affectional proclivities, and Caleb and Dakota even share a lover, Willie Blue

Eyes. A duo of child deputies in *Rattler!* consists of a girl who chews tobacco and imagines marrying a woman someday and a teenage boy who gets a "funny feeling" when he looks at men. Even a straight, greasy gunslinger joins in the queering: "Heck, I ain't ashamed to admit I've bedded down with a few *hombres* myself, 'fore I got hitched."[55]

It becomes clear that the Dakota Taylor series served functional and political ends distinct from parody or satire. Two out of three of the blurbs on the back of *Rattler!* (reviews from gay publications) are almost identical: "There are few better ways to escape than by enjoying the vicarious thrills that Dakota has to offer"; and "There may be no better way to escape than into the dusty trails and sunsets of the Wild West." The books were published during the scabrous years of the AIDS epidemic, when gay men were dying like gunslingers and when an antigay movement (Measure 9, which I protested in Oregon, and Phelps's efforts in Topeka, to name two) was organizing itself into a posse. Escape was unquestionably necessary. A sexy, violent, heroic mystery would do the trick.

Queering the Western also had the political aim of affirming, or realizing, the button and bumper-sticker motto WE ARE EVERYWHERE ("Like ticks on dogs," Dakota says[56]), even in the most lonely and homophobic reaches of America's past. It's a form of rewilding, really, and one that's particularly consoling to me: My mom's sexuality seemed terribly singular to me growing up, even a hundred years after Dakota's time. I've found that looking back and realizing that certain people I knew were gay, and even that fictional characters are gay, relieves a residual loneliness and fear caused by that secret. Dakota Taylor's fearless caution is also empowering. After the first time he and Bennie make love, they discuss the issue over postcoital venison jerky:

> "It's against the law," [Bennie] said, dismally. "I'm afraid it always will be."
>
> I chuckled. "There ain't no law west of the Mississippi."
>
> "Isn't. You have terrible grammar." He smiled slightly, but he sure enough meant it. "Seriously, we could be arrested and prosecuted. It's happened already, even in America. There are cases in the law books in some eastern courts."
>
> "Crime against nature."
>
> "Yes." He acted surprised, pleased that I was smart enough to know that. "The men in the West aren't as discreet as you must be in the East, and certainly in England..."
>
> "How come nobody does anything about it?"...I leaned forward and said roughly, "See this?" I held a Colt up to the flames. They flickered off the silver barrel and it immediately warmed in my hand. "This is my law. This is the only book I go by: law book or Good Book. The law hasn't been able to jail me for killing men with this gun, and it's this gun that's going to keep them from jailing me for loving men. This is what you do about it, Junior. You fight back. And you die fighting. You're going to learn how to use it before you go back east."[57]

The epigraph to *Silver Saddles* is a quote from Sitting Bull: "We are an island of Indians in a lake of whites." The quote is out of context and has little relevance to the plot of the novel; it serves to link the lonely predicaments of gays and Indians, two groups left out as heroes in typical Westerns. Reading these three books today, I feel like an archaeologist examining arrowheads and potsherds from an insular, foreign culture. The tools are obsolete but an ingenious and artistic response to the needs and resources of their setting. They're tools I could have used once.

The blurbs say there "are few better ways" and there "may be no better way" to escape than the Western genre. The Dakota Taylor series brings into relief the purpose or appeal of the Western for all of us, whether it's a pulp Western, a gay Western, a literary Western, a Western memoir, Western history, or a commonplace of all these. The threats and the challenges we might fear in our less-than-adventurous lives—being attacked, getting lost, going broke—are very real on the arid frontier, incarnate in mob arson, rattlers, mirages, villains, Indians. There are thoughts that might be dangerous to release from the corral of our own minds in a land where the word *stranger* is laced with menace. There are ruins in our personal pasts that could unleash a curse. The Western hero is a brave voice in the face of that fear. *Hell, a little bullet wound or a rattlesnake bite will only kill you half the time. Saddle up, it'll put hair on your chest.*

My experience reading Louis L'Amour in Puerto Angel points again to loneliness and the lure of a story that makes that loneliness heroic or noble. Imagining oneself anointed as a hero, or in Phelps's case as a prophet, is really turning solitude inside out. By folding one's own lonely story into the ecology of a lonely landscape and its riding-off-into-the-sunset genre, it comes to feel bearable. *A man has to be what he is; he can't break the mold.*[58] That lonely man turns out to be indispensable for the creation of a new society.

Imagine: The wild-eyed preacher hurls his worst epithets and smoldering clods of brimstone at the low-slung slinger, who draws and fires at each one with a relaxed grin tweaking his mustache. The ivory-handled Colts twirl like a Wyoming wind farm, and a hot dust of hate settles on the dirt street between them and fizzles.

"You had enough, sky pilot?"

"Never, faggot!"

But soon the vicar's medicine bag is empty except for his Good Book. He holds it up in the air.

"Don't make me edit that testament, Rev. So help me, I'll blow the eighth verse out of each page."

The black-clad preacher snarls, drops the Bible in his bag, and scuttles off to his hole like a hunchbacked tarantula. The townsfolk gathered on the plank sidewalk start clapping. The gunslinger nods, holsters, hoists a lithe leg over his silver-inlaid saddle. Then he trots off alone in the opposite direction to wherever he came from.

Ten

Ghost Dances

10.1

This Buffalo Commonplace is no balanced, composed portrait of the Plains. The problem with this flat land is that it has no summit, no climax. But that's also a beautiful thing, a democratic and Whitmanish field that turns up surprises like little seashells in a cow pasture or even, from time to time, a whole dinosaur. From an airplane it's clear the region is profoundly empty: In 1953, a national team of meteorologists chose Ruth Harris's hometown, O'Neill, Nebraska, for its study of air-current patterns because the only impediments to the wind were a few fence posts.[1] At the same time it's full of visionaries, tiny flowers huddled low to the ground, and towns that seem bland but are tooled with outrageous flights of practicality.

In 1908, in Arthur, a tiny sand hills town southwest of O'Neill, the Catholic bishop joined forces with a Presbyterian minister to build a "church house of Twin Pulpits." The sanctuary mirrored a Protestant pulpit at one end against a Catholic altar at the other, with reversible seats.[2] Arthur, with fewer than 150 people, is studded with architectural ingenuity to

255

overcome its lack of timber—today it has two rye hay-bale buildings from the 1920s, two earth-sheltered homes, a house made of railroad ties, and a space station–like set of domes made of foam and cement. I imagine this all started with ingenious carpenters fashioning pews with seat backs that changed faiths on hinges.

Then there's the thatched-roof Shakespeare cottage and Elizabethan garden in Wessington Springs, South Dakota, and the odd town common up in Lemmon that's spired with petrified wood cemented together. In Lucas, Kansas, there's the Garden of Eden, the Populist cement sculpture built around a cement log cabin; the Garden features Adam and Eve joining hands over an arbor and Labor being crucified by a doctor, a banker, a preacher, and a lawyer. Near Regent, North Dakota, seven giant scrap metal sculptures form the Enchanted Highway. There are the little punk rock scenes hosting loud, distorted shows in basements and VFW halls. There are the growing bison herds on the Indian reservations and elsewhere. Pasting all these outcrops together in a commonplace is my rewilding project.

My effort to know the Plains newly, to build a peculiar model in my mind along frontiers of time and geography, is an attempt to avoid that lonely cliché of the ride into the sunset, or at least to ride back to town the next morning. Growing up, I didn't have a choice about whether I would fit into the land around me; I couldn't. Now, in New York, I resist even the communities to which I belong, to any sort of *scene*, clinging to a sense of self-sufficiency and singularity. To beat the solitude and sorrow I build a private frontier mythology, as if I were looking up at a night sky way out on some gravel road and redrawing the old Plains zodiac—reviewing the old myths I didn't figure into...the movie land Ruth Harris used to see at the Royal Theater after galloping around O'Neill on a tree branch...the classic frontiers of Louis L'Amour and Laura Ingalls Wilder books...the rugged idyll Dad imagined when he first came west...the hopeless backwater Mom was so happy to escape. All of these weighed on me. Looking up at that sky for myself, at the infinity of people and organisms and events that have graced the Plains, as a man grown and gone and returned visiting or studying, I could connect the dots into a whole other zodiac of heroes and villains, beasts and fables. I could reorient according to some new Polaris.

Here I could point out the fierce Gemini of Ruths Thomson and Harris—Nebraska women who learned in that young state ideals and morals that would fuel their struggles for the rest of their lives. And there's William Jennings Bryan—or is it Crazy Horse?—Sagittarius of the prairie, the archer riding against a cavalry of Hollywood Westerns. The bison Taurus of the Juárez bullring. A Scorpio pickup truck, opposite my dad's, with peeling bumper stickers on its poison tail that say, I'D RATHER GO HUNTING WITH DICK CHENEY THAN DRIVING WITH TED KENNEDY and DON'T BLAME ME. I VOTED FOR THE AMERI-CAN! (And see, there's Rush "Leo" Limbaugh on the airwaves, the real Cowardly Lion, an exotic beast from another land.) And out beyond, that's Aquarius the park ranger burning out the tumbleweeds and planting threadleaf sedge, at great expense, so we can remember the way things once were. This is why I have driven myself nearsighted with all these Plains books and farsighted crisscrossing the open Plains—why I've bypassed the Plains altogether to visit the Bronx Zoo bison or Ruth Harris in Claremont. I wanted a new horoscope, one that would reconcile somehow these opposite urges, opposites that now seem native to the place itself: coming and going, placid and furious, conservative and progressive, fitting in and fighting back, timidity and temerity. I want this the way another kid with divorced parents wants his mom and dad to get back together.

10.2

Thea, you were on the *Capital-Journal* youth staff, and you had a hyphenated last name. My *Capital Journal* was unhyphenated and so was my name, Josh Davis — or at least Mom's surname and its hyphen had been in hiding since fifth grade; I had "two middle names." You and I never met, but we should have. I only saw your column.

Oh, that the *Pierre Capital Journal* and *Topeka Capital-Journal* weren't separated by that Cornhusker-loving jock gulf of Nebraska. It would have worked out, Thea. We would have formed a Hüsker Dü–loving alliance, a loving alliance. I never had a car, but I imagine you would have, probably a late-'80s state-surplus Plymouth K-car, and we'd have wallpapered its ass with black stickers of California bands: J Church, Neurosis, Operation Ivy, Voodoo Glow Skulls. We'd drive to Sioux Falls and Rapid City on weekends for shows, even sing through the eight-hour, five-and-a-half-mix-tape haul to Minneapolis on occasion. We'd stay with my aunt and uncle there and dub dozens of cassettes from their old punk LPs.

I would have wooed you first with Dad's LPs. You'd drive me home from school and we'd pull the stylus through the familiar grooves of his few punk records. *Never Mind the Bol-*

locks. Fresh Fruit for Rotting Vegetables. Bedtime for Democracy. London Calling. He'd bought them all as novelties—except maybe the Clash—back when I was a baby and my parents ran Prairie Dog Records: 1978 to 1982, about the life span of a punk rock band. *They* broke up four years later, and I spent the next four years listening quietly to hair metal on my cassette recorder until Mom moved to Oregon.

Afterward, I lived with Dad's LP library, discovering the punk classics and other little masterpieces amid all the Southern-fried '70s rock. The punky record cut by the "Nuclear Regulatory Commission," house band at the Tennessee commune The Farm (*I wish everyone could eat white sugar / Instead of meat*). Laurie Anderson's arty *Big Science* ("O Superman!"). Tommy Tutone's *2*, featuring "867-5309/Jenny." That song, which I'd enjoyed as a toddler, acquired a kitsch appeal in high school after a punk band called Less Than Jake covered it at double speed. It turned out not to be a simple love song to Jenny but the bizarre and a little creepy reassurance some lonely guy gets from reading her phone number on the wall, *for a good time call.*

I once hypothesized that I could walk up to anybody under the age of sixty in front of the Zesto soft-serve drive-up and say, "Eight six seven," and they would instinctively reply, "Five three oh nine." After visiting Mom enough summers in Portland, I thought a similar shibboleth for Oregonians could be the nerd-ball car salesman who in his commercials year after year harangued, "If you don't come see me today, I can't save you any money." Thea, you would have loved Portland.

"Oh, pop-punk, pop-punk, pop-punk. How could that be so?" Thea wrote that day in 1994 in the *Capital-Journal*. "Punk is rebellious, true? Aye, but pop can be defined as any song that sticks in your head, according to a 2½-year-old Nirvana interview, in which the band asserts that even Black Flag 'were pop in a way.'" She showered sugary praise on Green Day's third album, *Dookie*, at the precise moment I rejected them for selling out to Reprise Records and MTV. "Like lotsa pop-punk," she wrote, "these songs have sweet tunes and embittered, luv-and-or-everything-else-gone-wrong lyrics ('In the End' and 'Basket Case' being two primo examples), which can be endearing, especially if you like to think about your feelings."[3]

Our newspapers always appreciated the teen point of view. A year earlier, I'd registered the lone dissent in a newspaper article titled, "The Death Penalty: Teen Writers Support Execution." Against five other teens whose letters spoke up for taxpayers over prisoners who had "better lives than free people," I called capital punishment "total hypocrisy."[4] Maybe I was too serious for Thea, but I think she could have brought me around to the virtues of "the kind of punk that sticks to your ears like taffy to teeth," the "perfect music to eat mayonnaise toast to," made by boys who are "adorably crusty and look far too sweet to be using the kinds of words they use." Could I be sweet and crusty? Thea said the Green Day record "melts my heart"; could she melt mine? Thea, I would have pogoed around eating mayonnaise toast and taffy even though I didn't like mayonnaise or taffy and going over the top with corny exhortations and drawing Marks-A-Lot tattoos on my arms. I would have sung the Dead Milkmen song "Punk Rock Girl" with you and meant it.

I could have used Thea's breezy affection, even a first kiss before voting age. Her sugar-high hoorays might have softened the skeptic, let him believe in punk rock instead of looking for hypocrisy in its copycat rebellion and uniform nonconformity. She could have saved me from becoming a sartorial geriatric, wearing Rockport shoes and cardigans (more Mister Rogers than Kurt Cobain in my case) at a tragically young age in order to avoid the cliché of silk-screened band patches on a black hooded sweatshirt. I sewed all my patches onto a flesh-colored chamois shirt one Portland summer at the house of Mom's friends Martha and Connie.

I had gone to my first punk show in a farm's machine shop outside Hot Springs. I stashed forty dollars from my twelfth birthday under a lamp to buy T-shirts and demo tapes. The Martians and Mr. Magoo drove sixty miles from Rapid City to play—around the eastern outsoles of the Black Hills' foothills, past Trout Haven and the pine-covered geologic break known to me as Paul Bunyan's Half-pipe but which other South Dakotans called the Buffalo Gap, where the herds once entered the shelter of the mountains in winter. While dreadlocked vegans screamed, I gleefully entered the mosh pit and even pulled a wooden chair up to its edge to dive in and crowd surf (there was no stage). When Dad drove me to Rapid City shows over the next couple of years, I would dervish my way around the slam dance despite being only a yard and a half tall.

After we moved to Pierre, which had no shows and no "scene," I began to shy from the sweat and bruises, began crossing my arms over my torso in the pit, and ultimately kept to the fringes of the Elks Lodges and VFW halls that served as all-ages nightclubs in Sioux Falls and Rapid City. By ninth grade I was playing bass in Stickman, and we started putting on the shows at the Pierre Elks Lodge. I soon postured as the half-retired punk who'd outgrown silly piercings and declarations of anarchy and hypocrisy but who still kept the important values (vegetarianism and anticonsumerism, not crustiness and hairstyles). I followed the know-it-all advice of the Dead Kennedys singer, Jello Biafra: *A hairstyle's not a lifestyle.*[5]

Thea, you should have saved me from this creeping solitude. A trip up under a Cringer T-shirt is all the convincing a teenage boy needs to join the dance. I see us skipping, elbows hooked Barrel of Monkeys–style, around the pit, or sitting in your bedroom listening to seven-inch records and reading punk zines we ordered from Gainesville, Chicago, Berkeley. Like the couple in "Punk Rock Girl," jumping up on the table and shouting, "Anarchy!"

Alas, by senior year, I gave up sweet organized rebellion in favor of a sort of straitlaced subversion, appearing in the *Capital Journal*'s pages only as student of the month or as the star of "Silent Snow, Secret Snow," a one-act play based on a short story by Conrad Aiken, about a boy with schizophrenia who hallucinates ballerina snowflakes dancing around him until he (I, in this case) crescendos to a shriek of "I hate you, Mother! I hate you, Father!"

When I was almost eighteen, with one foot out South Dakota's screen door, I fired off one parting shot to the *Rapid City Journal* editorial page (most people in Pierre subscribed to either the Sioux Falls or the Rapid City newspaper to supplement our weekday-only *Capital Journal*). My letter was aimed at the Spearfish, South Dakota, school board, which had declined to send its high school one-act to the state festival where we had performed "Silent Snow, Secret Snow." Their play, "Removing the Glove" by Clarence Coo, followed a teenager's struggle to come out to his family and friends as being left-handed. Local parents from Mountain View Baptist Church had successfully protested that the school was "promoting acceptance and nor-malcy of homosexuality."

The *Journal* published my screed on February 9, 1998:

Play Shouldn't Be Resisted

I was very disappointed to read of the resistance of Spearfish to their school's one-act play. As a cast member of Pierre High School's counterpart, I can sympathize with the amount of work the students and director put into the performance.

More disturbing, however, are the attitudes that the issue manifested in the town. To call an allegorical reference to homosexuality "pornography" is absurd; to have Christian clergy promoting hate and judgment is disillusioning; to forbid a performance teaching tolerance and love is depressing....

Sometimes I wonder why I am leaving South Dakota next year, but reading about this is a jarring reminder. Sorry to the participants for the disappointment.

—Josh Davis, Pierre

Nobody in Pierre mentioned my impolite letter to me after it was published; I was frightened yet somehow internally obligated to submit it, so I felt relieved not to have to defend it in person. Neither of my parents kept the letter, even though my dad usually saves everything. Maybe he clipped it and mailed it to my mom. I was able to find it in the archives of an online Listserv from Lambda Midwest, a gay organization based in Nebraska. Of course the name in my sign-off hid Mom's last name and the source of the rage that underlay the letter. I was balancing on an invisible hyphen. Thea, I wish you had been there with your out-of-the-closet hyphen and your glee. Thea, don't change your number.

10.3

Coda: Sailing myself seasick through months of *Capital-Journal* microfilm at the Topeka public library more than a decade later, having never met or even heard of Thea Fronsman-Cecil in the 1990s (we were in parallel universes), I come upon her review, "Green Day Knows How to Hit Heart." I can't resist stopping the machine, getting sidetracked from my mission to learn the history of Westboro Baptist Church, which I have been unable to penetrate in person. The article is dated April 19, 1994, shortly after Kurt Cobain's suicide. I wonder why Thea quotes Nirvana on Black Flag's pop qualities without even a little RIP for Aberdeen, Washington's tormented son or a punk prayer for little Frances Bean. She can't yet know how *Dookie* will open the pop-punk Elks Lodge to wholesale pillaging by the industry, how MTV will bring to light "secret" bands like the Offspring and Rancid. I will seek out more obscure subgenres like free-jazz hardcore and something called emo, and then for years I'll leave punk behind virtually altogether....I soldier on through the nauseating reels but can't forget the specter of a punk rock girl in a different Plains state capital and what might have been if it had been the same capital I lived in.

Later, I feel a bit trifling writing a love song to an imagined Thea after I find an essay the real Thea's mother wrote in the *Topeka Capital-Journal* in 2002. Sally Fronsman-Cecil and

Bill Cecil-Fronsman were pacifist and feminist activists like my parents; they met in Ashland, Oregon, in 1975, the same summer my parents met in Sioux Falls. Bill taught history at Washburn University in Topeka. Sally and Bill attended an Episcopalian church in Topeka, while Thea chose to join a Unitarian congregation. If Nebraska were in fact elbowed aside, South Dakota and Kansas superimposed, one capital city on top of another, Thea and I would without question have been family friends. Dad always knew all the radicals in town. He would have taken me to their house without calling first, "visiting"—an archaic Midwestern pastime that he kept up out of nostalgia and loneliness after my parents' homestead bit the dust. Instead of passively resisting his typical "Come on, Josh—Sally and Bill are good people," I would have skipped straight up to Thea's room to hear the latest seven-inches she'd bought in Sioux Falls / Lawrence / Rapid City / Kansas City. We might not have smooched, being family friends, but we'd have been thick as thieves.

According to Sally's article, Thea began to have health problems at age eight. With the support of her father's university health insurance, by her teenage years she rebounded to pen her hyper masterpieces for the *Capital-Journal*. But Bill Cecil-Fronsman died suddenly of a seizure in 1998, leaving Sally and Thea to cobble together medical care from various sources. "We feel as if we have fallen off a cliff into deep water and are snorkeling to survive," Sally wrote.[6]

Our leftist Plains haven unraveled before I could weave it; my vision of two antinuclear nuclear families having dinner (garden-raised, surely, and vegetarian for Thea's and my sake, on pottery dishes, with us young punks rolling our eyes at the background music) is, alas, an impossible one. "If ever there was a family that subscribed to the 1960s feminist aphorism that 'the personal is political,'" Sally wrote, "it was ours, that of the late Dr. Bill Cecil-Fronsman and its surviving members, Sally and Thea Fronsman-Cecil."

On the Fronsman-Cecil/Cecil-Fronsman end, health and money began unraveling this dinner before Thea ever heard Operation Ivy; on the Garrett/Davis/Garrett-Davis end, it had unraveled as well.

10.4

A dinosaur retakes the grasslands one slow step at a time. It is an armored herbivore like a small ankylosaur, a foot and a half long, and it hasn't set foot on the Plains in eight thousand years. OK, not a real dinosaur, but a cousin that looks almost that old: snub-nosed, walleyed, wrinkled, and green. There it is, the Bolson tortoise, on one of the mogul Ted Turner's vast bison ranches in central New Mexico. Turner has fifteen ranches in Montana, South Dakota, Nebraska, Kansas, Oklahoma, and New Mexico; he's the largest individual landowner in North America, a one-man Buffalo Commons—minus the *commons*—holding two million acres and more than fifty thousand head of bison.[7]

Why do the Plains inspire so many utopian plans, even in rational observers? Why does this semiarid country sprout (or attract) so many ornery, puffed-up visionaries and demagogues from William Jennings Bryan and Scotty Philip to Bill Janklow and Fred Phelps? My ancestors imagined that a world without booze would be a paradise. The drafters of the 1862 Homestead Act figured the Plains to be a seedbed for Jeffersonian democracy with 160-acre farms for each family; then after the biblical plague of the Dust Bowl and fifty years of boom and decline, Frank and Deborah Popper visited and saw a Buffalo Commons. Another Plains visionary, Wes Jackson, has imagined an entirely new system of agriculture, "perennial polyculture," based on combinations of perennial crops that would mimic prairie plants. This system would obviate the need to plow, fertilize, and spray every year, making a harvest perhaps more like mowing a hay field and sifting out the foodstuffs. But it has to undo virtually the entire ten-thousand-year history of annual agriculture and start from scratch.[8]

What perennial polyculture and the Buffalo Commons share even with a seeming political opposite like Fred Phelps is a radical atavism, a shocking return to some historic or prehistoric standard. Where the Buffalo Commons would restore the landscape to something resembling its state before the Homestead Act, Phelps would return the culture to a sixteenth-century Calvinist Protestant standard. Wes Jackson started the Land Institute, a humble-looking research farm just south of Salina, Kansas, with the decidedly unhumble goal of rebuilding the human institution of farming more in the image of hunting and gathering in order to save the soil from a slow, ongoing Dust Bowl. And William Jennings Bryan, I suppose, would have led us back to Eden. These visions look forward as well, and exist very much within the modern world, but they're all ghost dances of one step or another.

Perhaps it is the primordial-looking landscape, reeking of the sea floor it once was, its subterrain littered with fossils, shells, and arrowheads like shipwrecks. Or perhaps it is the vast, apparently blank space like the ocean's surface that invites conquistadors.

When I was a child in Hot Springs, one of my school's favorite field-trip destinations was the Mammoth Site on the edge of town. About twenty-six thousand years ago, in the Pleistocene epoch, a limestone cave collapsed and created a sinkhole there, and the warm artesian spring for which the town is named created a spa for mammoths. Over the centuries, the steep shale banks of the sinkhole trapped at least fifty-five woolly and Columbia mammoths to starve or drown, along with a giant short-faced bear, a llama, and a camel. (The Anthropocene spa in town—Evans Plunge—was just around a red bluff from Dad's and my little green house, and I went there frequently. The only danger it posed was a particularly tenacious species of athlete's foot.) Over time, sediments filled the sinkhole around the skeletons, and the spring bubbled up at another spot closer to where town would be, heating the Fall River. The mammoth boneyard, full of huge crescent-shaped ribs and tusks, stout limb bones, and many smaller clues, has fleshed out our models of what the continent was like in the Pleistocene epoch (long, long after Sue's time), the eighteen hundred millennia before humans arrived over the Bering Strait land bridge.

Which brings me back to the Bolson tortoise and the latest visionary idea the Plains have begotten, the most atavistic of all. Now that the Buffalo Commons have reached a flexible maturity, a group of scientists has come along to one-up the Poppers in scale, scope, and potential for controversy. The Bolson tortoise is the slow-crawling vanguard of prehistoric creatures—I think of the parade of zombies in Michael Jackson's "Thriller" video walking jerkily toward us, with the tortoise as M.J.—asking to join the bison on the range. The tortoise's advantage over the mammoths, camels, bears, and horses is that it is not extinct. A few thousand Bolson tortoises survived in the Bolsón de Mapimí desert in Mexico and were first documented in the 1970s. Barring any *Jurassic Park*–style miracles, the others would have to be replaced with extant relatives from other continents: Indian elephants substituted for Columbia mammoths, Bactrian camels and Przewalski's horses for extinct camels and horses, African cheetahs and lions for American cheetahs and saber-toothed tigers, and so on.[9]

The idea is called "Pleistocene rewilding," and it was first proposed in 2005 in the journal *Nature* by a dozen conservation biologists who had drafted a proposal at Turner's Ladder Ranch in New Mexico. It grows out of three major strains of thought. The most fundamental is the "overkill hypothesis," which explains the disappearance of the vast majority of large mammals in the Americas (and at least one large reptile, the tortoise) as the result of humans' first incursions into the wilderness with so-called Clovis spears—rather than as the result of climate cycles in the last ice age. This has come to be the dominant hypothesis for the Pleistocene extinctions, though some paleoecologists still dispute it and some modern American Indians feel they are being "blamed" for the extinctions. The overkill hypothesis effectively moves the date when North America's ecology became "unnatural" from 1492 back to about 11,000 BCE, the end of the Pleistocene epoch.[10] The second strain of thought that influenced the Pleistocene rewilding proposal is the growing appreciation for the role large animals, especially predators, play in ecosystems. Most of North America has lost even the predators that were here a few hundred years ago: grizzly bears, wolves, cougars, bald eagles. Since wolves were reintroduced to Yellowstone in 1995, the suite of wildlife has flourished up and down the food chain. Potentially, the introduction of new grazers and new predators from the more distant past could "enhance" ecosystems all over.[11] Finally, Pleistocene rewilding is an extension of the Buffalo Commons, a proposed new use for land that Americans are slowly abandoning.

In one sense the proposal isn't all that drastic. There are already wild horses, camels, elephants, lions, and cheetahs from Eurasia and Africa living in game farms and zoos across the West; Pleistocene rewilding could be seen as gradually expanding the fences of those reserves and trying to instigate and research predator-prey relationships among those species and between them and native species.

At the same time, it is stunningly radical. It obliterates the whole concept of *natural*, and envisages the ecology of the Plains—of earth—as an ant farm or a terrarium. It sweeps away the last shreds of the notion that we have left or can leave nature reserves untouched. Wes Jackson's research into perennial plant polycultures as a large-scale environmental solution begins with the acknowledgment that single-crop farm fields are the largest ecosystem on earth, and any environmental reform to reduce pollution, erosion, and carbon emissions must revolutionize the land use on farms. Pleistocene rewilding has the even broader premise that in light of climate change, energy extraction, pollution, hunting, and the spread of introduced, exotic species, the *entire* earth from arctic wilderness to Manhattan is something of a ranch or zoo.

Like the Poppers, like Bryan and Phelps and Janklow and Wovoka, the Pleistocene rewilders are not *from* the Plains. (Wes Jackson is the anomalous Plains visionary who was born and raised in Kansas, though he spent time in academia outside the region.) The lead author on the proposal and subsequent articles on Pleistocene rewilding is C. Josh Donlan, a young conservation ecologist from Cornell University whose other work includes hunting exotic predators on islands whose native wildlife they have devastated. The other authors are gray eminences of conservation ecology: the originator of the overkill hypothesis; one of the first proponents of old-fashioned rewilding (of recently native predators such as wolves and cougars); the founder of Earth First! and the Rewilding Institute; and several other prominent biologists.[12]

There are scientific questions and concerns to be considered with respect to Pleistocene rewilding. Is it dangerous to introduce predators into a foreign environment? Could they decimate other creatures the way rats and goats and snakes have decimated bird populations on the islands that Donlan also studies? Are the genetic differences between the extinct beasts and their "proxy" species large enough to change the roles they play in the food chain? Can Indian elephants survive a South Dakota winter? "Are horses that came to North America five hundred years ago native?" Donlan adds. "Maybe horses aren't quote-unquote 'horses' if they don't have predators to move them around to the water holes to serve their ecological function"—i.e., to create and maintain habitat for other plants and animals by trampling and grazing in one place before fleeing predators and doing the same at the next stop.[13] These are all questions the Pleistocene rewilders would like to research in small, experimental Pleistocene parks.

The other question, the "million-dollar question," as Josh Donlan puts it, is this: What *is* a healthy ecosystem? How is nature in a given place *supposed* to act, especially when there is no such thing as nature? Should we manage landscapes to prevent extinctions, to look pretty, to produce as many species per acre as possible? These standards sound like those of a zoo, a garden, and a farm or ranch, respectively. It seems that by being the powerful and self-conscious species that we are—by altering every inch of earth and sea and then worrying about what we've done—we have assigned ourselves the responsibility to hem and haw and argue and test and retest every decision we make with respect to the planet's ecology.

"A lot of it depends on, What benchmark do you use?" Donlan explains to me through a terrible cell phone connection from somewhere in Utah. "And I'd say that's just as much of a social question as a scientific one. When you're talking about large mammals, that's just as much an aesthetic decision as an ecological one. How much nature do people want to live with?"

Not being a scientist myself, it is the social and aesthetic questions that most interest me. As native predators (principally wolves, mountain lions, and grizzly bears) begin to return to North America, the nostalgia that urban environmentalists feel for them will be challenged. Though biologists and the *New York Times* may hail the reintroduction of wolves in Yellowstone as a success, nearby ranchers are still incensed at the new threat their cattle face. Every time a *person* is mauled by a grizzly or a cougar, a primordial fear rises in most of us and shrieks, *Kill 'em all*. Philosophers may argue that we preserve a piece of our humanity by maintaining the source of this fear, but parents shudder to think. That the fear is deep in our makeup is obvious when we realize that our chances of being mauled are probably one in a hundred million, while we actually know people who have died in car accidents and we continue happily to drive. Of the many outraged responses Donlan and the other Pleistocene rewilders received when their proposal made headlines, few were violently opposed to the exotic Bactrian camels and Przewalski's horses. It was the prospect of reintroducing the very predators with which our species evolved in African grasslands—lions and cheetahs—that was the real menace. Surely a few would escape the fences and find their way to Plains ranches and backyards. The Poppers had challenged our belief in progress and our ability to tame nature or make the desert bloom; Donlan and company seemed to be asking us to do not just that but to feed our children to the lions.

As an aesthetic decision, what would we make a Pleistocene park or an American Serengeti look like? When I was seventeen, my dad accepted a gift from his mother to take me to Tanzania. We flew on a 747 at night into an airport outside Arusha, where there were no city lights, everything outerspace black out the window except for the blue lanterns along the runway. Those lights revealed the rustling tallgrass fringe of a bestiary blanket of wild creatures sleeping or prowling. The daylight landscape was similar to western South Dakota, but there was a degree of fang and of danger profoundly foreign to the American Plains, even an expanse as big as one of the National Grasslands. In the United States, a mountain lion is a rumor or a chimera even for those who see one, but in the Serengeti we could study a yellow lioness and her cubs or a herd of elephants from a few yards away (and from the safety of a steel Land Rover).

Donlan is right. Pleistocene rewilding is an aesthetic challenge as much as an ecological one. Where the Buffalo Commons draws on the frontier myths of a thousand novels, movies, and poems, where the word *prairie* alone is a beautiful woman I can't stop gazing at and *buffalo* is our gruff masculine character,

Pleistocene rewilding has only the mute and mythless fossil record to back it up. If not *un*-American it predates America by so much as to be not-American. I wonder if we can stretch our imaginations so far, even to benefit the ecosystems of these gorgeous Plains. I think of the pratincole, a stout, dust-colored bird whose enchanting name means "grassland dweller" but which does not live in the Americas, is only native to Eurasia and Africa. It is about the size and shape of a mountain plover (which does live here, in drastically declining numbers) and some varieties have a black mark coming down from each eye like a tear streak. When I learned the etymology of its name, I wished I could say the pratincole were here, if only because its name says it belongs.

In a 2010 article about the Poppers in the Land Institute's quarterly *Land Report*, Deborah Popper spoke about "inner geographies":

> our way of experiencing place — our expectations, what we notice, what we see as significant, necessary, important. . . . We have nostalgic landscapes in our heads, literary and film ones, and the ones we daily experience. They bump against each other. At its most obvious, this affects whether the Great Plains seems right with wheat, with buffalo; whether towns are supposed to have Main Streets or strip malls on the highway. This also includes who looks right — as though they belong.[14]

Ecology aside, Pleistocene rewilding is a brilliant remapping of inner geographies.

When I mentioned offhand restoring some Plains preserves to their state thirteen thousand years ago to an environmentalist in South Dakota who works on bison restoration, he scoffed and shook his head. "How about trying to restore it to what it was a hundred and fifty years ago?" he said. I sensed a fear that Pleistocene rewilding would make all supporters of black-footed ferret and bison reintroductions look like yahoos in the way Fred Phelps makes ordinary anti–gay marriage advocates look hateful and anti-American.

When I first read the proposal, while I admired its boldness, I, too, was pretty critical. In an article Donlan published in *Scientific American*, he makes shorthand references to shopping malls and sprawl and "human encroachment" as inherently "negative influences," which seemed to me like lazy misanthropy or anti-modernity and rather extraneous to the overkill the Clovis hunters accomplished thirteen centuries ago.[15] In fact the proposal itself seemed like the culmination of a puritanical guilt over our prosperity and excess in the industrial age, as if humans' desire to eat and not be eaten were a sort of gluttony: *Let's try to undo everything that has happened on this continent since we arrived on it, for we have corrupted Eden.* There is a certain hubris in thinking we can correct these so-called mistakes.

Yet the longer I think about Pleistocene rewilding, the more appealing it becomes. For one thing, it is a much more cautious proposal than its critics fear, certainly not a wholesale takeover of the Plains and Southwest by carnivorous beasts and starry-eyed greenies. That antigovernment, anticoastal paranoia that declaims against this new proposal, that invoked the gestapo when the federal government seized the Sue fossil, and that accused the Poppers of "covering up a federal land grab" neglects to notice that for the foreseeable future Pleistocene rewilding is more of a new paradigm in zookeeping and game ranching than anything else.[16] When Frank and Deborah Popper first broached the Buffalo Commons in the relatively low-profile magazine of the American Planning Association, few Plains folk responded. It was only after North Dakota governor George Sinner brought it up and circulated it to stoke populist hometown pride against misguided know-it-alls back east that it entered the public imagination.[17] In fact, the proposal was humbly stated, incremental, and flexible — hardly an arrogant eviction notice for everyone left on the Plains.

This is where the Poppers and Wes Jackson and the Pleistocene rewilders part company with William Jennings Bryan and Fred Phelps and other demagogues. Bryan and Phelps were and are full of words and bluster but no real plans; humility and incremental change don't figure in their rhetoric or deeds. Bryan left the nuts and bolts of reform to political opponents such as Theodore Roosevelt and successors such as Woodrow Wilson and Franklin Roosevelt. For better or worse, Phelps will probably be a forgotten crank, a footnote in First Amendment jurisprudence, and his legacy may actually be to have worked against his own cause, if he has a cause other than publicity and self-aggrandizement.

The speed with which large animals went extinct in the first place suggests a remedy if unforeseen damage began to occur in a rewilded preserve. No doubt the animals would be tagged and would be easy to capture or kill, much bigger targets than the rodents and goats Donlan has had to extirpate from fragile islands.

I suppose the more important thing I like about Pleistocene rewilding is all of the questions it raises. I like the way it upsets our removed idea of nature and forces us to take responsibility for the amount of control and agency we have over what goes on in the earth's ecosystems, even as we acknowledge the simultaneous lack of control and certainty we have that our solutions to environmental problems will work or won't have side effects. When we believe that nature is simply a wilderness outside our influence, the only decision is how much of it do we want to leave alone. When we admit that perhaps the best thing for an ecosystem is to import outrageously exotic and terrifying animals, we have admitted that the Garden of Eden went extinct a long time ago. And however do we measure *best?* Two currently relevant measures of *best* might be to prevent further extinctions (one of Donlan's passions) and to sequester carbon from our warming atmosphere. By providing a secondary habitat in North America for endangered species such as Indian elephants and Przewalski's horses, Pleistocene rewilding might address the former need. There is a chance it could accomplish the latter by adding ruminants and tramplers whose grazing could stimulate increased grassland growth and thus reclaim scrublands in the Southwest that once held a greater density of plant life—that is, more carbon. A recently established Pleistocene park in Siberia is trying to reclaim tundra that was grassland until its large mammals died off and its grasses were replaced by shrubs and moss. The park's principal aim is sequestering carbon, and it seems to be working so far.[18]

I also like the way Pleistocene rewilding stretches my own inner geography of the Plains and its history and what belongs there. If any land is big enough to welcome back a mammoth, I think my Great Plains are. This landscape of motion, of coming and going, has absorbed imports from Willa Cather's Ántonia Shimerda to crested wheatgrass to my own family, twice. It takes effort to fuse the bestiary of Africa and Asia with the homesteading myth of the Plains, but it's worth a try— now we have even elected a president who made an alliterative

American dream of his "Kenya and Kansas" heritage. The Plains have been home to Sue and the Sioux, to Oz and God Hates America, to Minuteman nuclear missiles and myself. Who is to say who's native, who's exotic, and who's a pratincole?

One of the Pleistocene rewilders' most striking illustrations of the void left by missing predators is the pronghorn, the tan, swift Plains version of an antelope. (Like *buffalo*, *antelope* is a misnomer, an Old World name grafted onto a North American species.) When frightened or chased, pronghorns can run—the specific term is *pronk*, and if you've seen one springing over the terrain you know why—seventy miles per hour, but they have no predator that can run anywhere near that fast. They're still being chased by a cheetah that died off more than ten thousand years ago. What would it mean to restore the object of the pronghorn's ghost dance?

The life of a conscious beast is perpetually atavistic, haunted by a history or a prehistory to which we instinctively know how to react. The experiences of biological and cultural ancestors, and of our younger selves, guide our responses. Digging up the past at the Mammoth Site or, personally, in Hot Springs or Aberdeen or Pierre and then assembling a story about it is one thing; reconciling with what we know of that past and moving on—proving up—is another. Do I really want to resurrect the arcadia of Prairie Dog Records? Do I want to eat amaranth cookies and carob, and listen to the Allman Brothers and my parents' fights? No. I have a gut sense that sex or drugs or politics will tear up my life; this is an instinct learned from my family's secrets and my parents' divorce. But there are perhaps relics from their homestead worth rewilding in my effort to prove up: the DIY simplicity of a nonelectric solar panel; the mixture of Christian faith with wealth redistribution and pacifism; a small town's gift of civil community among like- and unlike-minded people; a life close to both working farmers and ranchers, and to a landscape with such immense gravity that it can pull creatures out of extinction and change the definition of *belong.*

Epilogue
Pratincole

It is not Central Park's Sheep Meadow or Great Lawn, a railroad trip to White Plains or out Flatbush to Flatlands, Brooklyn; not Fresh Meadows or Flushing Meadows, Queens; neither Ted Turner's Montana Grill, around the corner from Radio City (though I wonder if a grass-fed bison steak from the Plains' grandest landowner might not unroll a postage-stamp-size prairillon across my tongue), nor the Nebraska Steakhouse off Wall Street; not Harlem's Kansas Fried Chicken or Times Square's Texas Texas; not Strawberry Fields or the Dakota. These fields and meadows and lawns and plains, these protein refuges whose names stretch from Montana to Texas, do suggest the vastness of my home country. But this puny outcropping, "a little island off the coast of North America"—that's my old Brooklyn landlord paraphrasing Spalding Gray—this island cannot hold any worthwhile expanse in soil and straw, sky and clay. My eyes fix on the word *flat*, on *Nebraska* and *Cypress Hills* (the Queens cemetery that shares its name with a semi-alpine outcropping in a sea of grass in the Prairie Provinces of Saskatchewan and Alberta). Yet the names disappoint me, fail to deliver the real Great Plains, the region that preoccupies me but to which I cannot seem to return.

Today I stood in a gallery in the southwest corner of the Met, testing different vantages on *No. 13 (White, Red, on Yellow)*. Like a flag hanging down sideways, three stacked blocks of color: white, straw yellow, and red. I'm knee-deep in it, then wholly buried, looking out across two horizons in Mark Rothko's foggy, vibrating colors; or I'm squinting into a stranger's gauze-curtained window that half reveals some murky interior, half reflects my own peering face. For a moment, the stormy white is a prairie sky, wind-borne gray weather systems yanked across the ticker tape. The yellow that belts the middle and frames the canvas is the golden, amber, copper crop of grass, and the red is the blood-rich topsoil we shouldn't see....

"There is no landscape in my work," Rothko said. I wonder if at least Jackson Pollock, whose vast *Autumn Rhythm (Number 30)* hangs across the gallery from *No. 13*, would sympathize with my failure to leave Abstract Expressionism abstract and untilled. Pollock was born in Cody, Wyoming, and painted *Autumn Rhythm* in New York. Rothko's *Catalogue Raisonné*, a flagstone tablet of several hundred pages I haul home from the stacks, offers leaves and leaves of single and double horizons. Patiently, I flip through a hundred, looking for an even more perfect prairie I could see at another metropolitan museum. There is no pure blue sky / tan savanna as I hoped, but despite the artist's protest, to me they all evoke the veldt.

A hunter from South Dakota, a friendly and well-known guide, the kind of man who made me feel welcome and yet fundamentally out of place back home on the Missouri River, in Pierre—this hunter told me the prairie is the richest landscape in the world. I never once fired a gun growing up in prairie-chicken and mule-deer country. I never enjoyed the soil and straw in the way they were seemingly created to be enjoyed, harvesting other tan, freckled animals from their, *our,* habitat. Before so much of the sod was busted, he told me, elk and bear strayed from the mountains for the grass's carbohydrates. Lewis and Clark found a carpet of abundance. But let's not get carried away: plenty and paucity, hot summers, cold winters, green Aprils and bleached Augusts, all blow through the grassland. In Pharaoh's dream, seven "sleek and fat" cows wander out of the Nile into the reed grass, followed by seven more, "gaunt and thin." Pharaoh is roused, and most likely concerned, yet he drops back into sleep and sees seven "plump and good" ears of grain on a single stalk, followed by seven "thin and blighted by the east wind." A French Bible translates this "reed grass" in Genesis as *prairie.* Joseph (his great coat a *Catalogue Raisonné*) explains to Pharaoh, "The seven good cows are seven years, and the seven good ears of grain are seven years; the dream is one."[1]

Half asleep in her bed Sunday mornings, Alexandra Bergson (in *O Pioneers!*) sees a man or god, "yellow like the sunlight" with a "smell of ripe cornfields," who carries her across Willa Cather's grassland country "as easily as if she were a sheaf of wheat."[2] Psalm 65 hosannas, "Pastures of the wilderness drip, the hills gird themselves with joy."[3] And Dynamics GP 9.0, formerly Microsoft Great Plains, appears likewise provident for "managing" and "integrating" a harvest of loose leaves, hard disks, and stacks. I download a PDF on Great Plains'"Collections Management" capabilities, finding my abundant Great Plains collections unmanageable. Is it coincidence that Christ staged the loaves and fishes where "there was much grass"?[4]

Seven years of famine follow and devour the seven of abundance. In Pharaoh's dreams, the gaunt cattle eat the sleek, the

blighted grass swallows the plump. Joseph says God is instruct-
ing Pharaoh through his dream: Prepare for scarcity and drought.
The Plains are desolate, a lunar mare, the Great American Desert,
the Dust Bowl. Half a century after Columbus, Francisco Vásquez
de Coronado sought in Quivira—that is, Kansas—"houses of
stone, with many stories," Indian lords "served with dishes of gold,
and other very magnificent things." He rode seventy-seven
parched summer days from present-day New Mexico to Quivira,
drinking "more mud than water" and "cooking the food with
cow [i.e., buffalo] dung, because there is not any kind of wood
in all these plains." To the Spanish king, he reported finding
"not more than 25 villages of straw houses there & in all the
rest of the country that I saw & learned about." As consolation,
at least these twenty-five "gave their obedience to Your Majesty
and placed themselves under your royal overlordship."[5] Willa
Cather imagines that Coronado "died in the wilderness, of a
broken heart."[6]

Once Spanish Quivira and its llanos had become French-
Louisianan prairies and been purchased as American plains,
new explorers found the same desolation. The best that the
explorer Zebulon Pike (of Colorado's Pikes Peak) could say for
the Great Plains was that

from these immense prairies may arise one great advantage to the United States, viz: The restriction of our
population to some certain limits, and thereby a continuation of the Union. Our citizens being so prone to
rambling and extending themselves on the frontiers
will, through necessity, be constrained to limit their
extent on the west to the borders of the Missouri and
Mississippi, while they leave the prairies incapable of

cultivation to the wandering and uncivilized aborigines
of the country.

"[U]nfit for cultivation," "arid and destitute of timber," "a natural barrier between civilized man and the savage," "little sustenance and less shelter": later explorers agreed.[7] Isaiah warns, "All flesh is grass, and all its beauty is like the flower of the field. The grass withers, the flower fades, when the breath of the Lord blows upon it."

Actually, in the case of Canada wild rye, Indian grass, and big and little bluestem grass, "hinge" cells on the top side of the leaf contract and close when the hot breath of drought blows upon them. The leaf rolls up into a watertight hose.[8]

Alexandra Bergson looked with tremendous "love and yearning" upon her own small tract of that fertile and also barren land. "Then," Cather writes, in the face of Alexandra's determination, "the Genius of the Divide, the great, free spirit which breathes across it, must have bent lower than it ever bent to a human will before."[9] It was like a hundred thousand elbows of Kansas Jayhawks fans, "waving the wheat" after a touchdown. The Indo-European root of *prairie*—*pra*—means "to bend," which became *pratum* for "meadow" in Latin; this bent root also developed into *depravity* for "crooked." *Pratum* evolved into Madrid's Prado museum and *pratincole*, my exotic, Old World bird that nests in the hoofprints of grassland grazers. Pratincole, that is, "meadow inhabitant," from *pratum incola*—*incola* like "colony." Any prairie dweller is a pratincole, though few of the Plains hunters would use such a highfalutin half-Latin term.

We gaze on the savanna's, the pampa's, horizons and foggy masses of color, and we dream of bending its Genius triumphantly to our will. Whether we are a pioneer Alexandra Bergson or a homesick South Dakotan in New York armed with a Met admission button, collections management software, and a library card, the open Plains form a continental canvas on which to brush and drip our dreams. Our determination is admirable, but its results at times run from foolhardy to murderous. "Rain follows the plow"—the vibrations caused by the trains and the noise and settlement of the Plains were said to be shaking extra rain from the sky, and pratincolous meteorologists fired dynamite upward to yield even more precipitation. By hook or by crook, the method actually works in my great-grandfather Clyde Brion Davis's novel *Nebraska Coast;* Jack Macdougall collects a hundred fifty dollars for the rainmaker. And it wasn't only weather and environment that stood in the way of our fancies—it was other people. The stacks boast enough miserable American Indian history to bury your heart.

The best minds of Allen Ginsberg's generation "studied Plotinus Poe St. John of the Cross telepathy and bop kabbalah because the cosmos instinctively vibrated at their feet in Kansas," last home to William S. Burroughs. The grassy ocean-wasteland that repelled Coronado and me still promises some lost city of gold. The "English terms of the prairie," wrote the linguist Maximilian Schele de Vere in 1872, "almost all taken from the sea, are poetical and yet true to their meaning. Thus, besides *islands*, the prairie has also its *coves*, where small strips of grassland run into a wood as if seeking for shelter against the blazing sun and the drenching rains, and its *bays* or large openings into a forest on its borders."[10] It is not the meadows of Central Park I explore for my Atlantis but the stacks and galleries, the archives and digitized film reels, the cumulus puffs pulled across the ceiling inside the New York Public Library's lion-guarded steppes—an elevator conquistador.

Turns out GP 9.0 is a business application—"finances, e-commerce, supply chain, manufacturing, project accounting, field service, customer relationships, and human resources"— and can't digest lost cities and sod houses. I try another: a program called GNU Bison. Bison creates "lookahead left-to-right parsers" that decode code the way I might diagram a sentence, left to right, picking apart lines of incomprehensible language without me even knowing. (The combustion engine and the search engine cheapen the conquistador bit—backache drives to Willa Cather's Red Cloud, rare-book bureaucracy, and tired eyes cannot match Coronado's seventy-seven days of mud-water and "prairie coal" shit-smoke.)

"[Y]ou know it takes a long head"—real smarts—"to make a Allmyneck," brags the introduction to the 1839 *Crockett Almanac*. The editor promises the "drollest yarns about wild scrapes, terrible fights with the wild varmints of the west, both two legged and four legged, and some with no legs at all."[11] I leaf through ancient pages the color of November buffalo grass: Davy out west with his "killdevil" rum and his rifle, interspersed with sunrise-sunset tables. "You see," so-called Crockett tale-tells,

> it war when I war young I went to massacree the buffa-loes on the head of Little Great Small Deep Shallow Big Muddy River....I'd been all day till now, vagabondizing about the prairie without seeing an atom of a buffalo, when I seed one grazing in the rushes on the edge of a

pond, and a crusty old batchelder he was. He war a thousand year old at least, for his hide war all kivered with skars, and he had as much beard as would do all the dandies I've seen in Broadway for whiskers and mustashes a hull year. His eyes looked like two holes burnt in a blanket, or two bullets fired into a stump, and I see he was a cross cantankerous feller, what coodent have no cumfort of his life bekays he war too quarrelsome.[12]

In true bluestem bloodstreams, we may find optimism, self-sufficiency (prairie grasses barely flower and do not bother with bees—the inevitable wind is enough), or a good fight (from abolitionist John Brown in Kansas and William Jennings Bryan in Nebraska, to quasi-populist Rush Limbaugh beamed in on the AM): thick sod of democracy. When the sansculottes of the French Revolution set out to redefine the calendar according to republican mores, they renamed the spring months *Germinal*, *Floréal*, and *Prairial*, this last running from May 20 to June 18. To repeat, from Isaiah, "Every valley shall be lifted up, and every mountain and hill be made low; the uneven ground shall become level, and the rough places a plain." GNU Bison roams free in the commons, an open-source software grazing and parsing a sod of references laid down by a cross cantankerous fellow, who couldn't have comfort in his life because he was too quarrelsome. Something else lurks there. It is important to remember that these oceans of grass are icebergs: While your showy sequoias erect obelisks aboveground, the grassland steppes hide almost everything in the roots. Regular grass fires, million-hoof stampedes, and blizzards have trained their privacy. I cannot quite force to blossom whatever it is that underlies my searches and collections, but the plow and the search engine till it up eventually.

Under Rothko's overlapping margins, I think I see another color, but I cannot make it out. As I walk from across the gallery, the placid colors become crackly blocks. "What living and buried speech is always vibrating here... what howls restrain'd by decorum"[13]—from the sky, as most of you see the Great Plains, it is a freckled but depthless panel of dun; from the land, it is all sky. Collections management, hose-rolled leaves of grass; how could I leave out the Bard of Brooklyn? In 1879 Walt Whitman visited "our North American plains," whose "cosmical analogies" included "the Steppes of Asia, the Pampas and Llanos of South America, and perhaps the Saharas of Africa."[14] In a speech he never gave in Topeka, Kansas, Whitman wondered

> if the people of this continental inland West know how much of first-class *art* they have in these prairies—how original and all your own—how much of the influences of a character for your future humanity, broad, patriotic, heroic and new? how entirely they tally on land the grandeur and superb monotony of the skies of heaven, and the ocean with its waters? how freeing, soothing, nourishing they are to the soul?[15]

"The surface of the earth crusted, a thin hard crust," John Steinbeck wrote sixty years later in epilogue to that enchantment. When the plowed crust broke and the hot breath of drought blew, there came a wrathful dawn with "no day. In the gray sky a red sun appeared, a dim red circle that gave a little light, like dusk."[16]

*   *   *

"A child said *What is the grass?* fetching it to me with full hands," and Whitman again wonders, "How could I answer the child?...I do not know what it is any more than he." But he guesses: the democratic "flag of my disposition, out of hopeful green stuff woven"; "the handkerchief of the Lord"; "a uniform hieroglyphic"; the "uncut hair of graves."[17] In New York City, a prairie of humanity, though not without its skyscraping trees, I see each of us as a seed head waving down avenue gullies, expressionless; brownstones stretching to the horizon; free tabloids blowing in front of our faces; the vast blue sky of Grand Central Terminal constellated far above citizen-stems hoping for a break; acres of pages on research library shelves; towers of twinkling windows like frostbitten stalks, and studios their cells; outdoor walls plastered with posted bills and indoor ones with canvas horizons; a billion swaying binaries across motherboards; steel storefront gates rolling and unrolling like grassland leaves.

ACKNOWLEDGMENTS

I've been working on this book for several years, so I hope I don't forget any of the numerous people and entities who helped me get it done.

My parents gave me a singular and loving upbringing, but more recently they encouraged me in many ways to produce this book. My dad, Jay Davis, sent me bits of Plains news in reused manila envelopes practically every week, looked into case law and South Dakota political history, and corrected factual errors for me. My mom, Kathy Garrett, encouraged me to be an artist of some kind for my whole life, up through the present. Both of them agreed to dig into some regrettable and painful personal history for the sake of this project. Their willingness to come off as imperfect human beings is one of many testaments to their love and generosity toward me.

As for the book's content, thanks to everyone who's contributed information, interviews, references, and advice. Most extensively, I want to thank Ruth Harris and Pat Patterson, not only for a week's worth of interviews and hosting me at Pilgrim Place but for their broader generosity and their example as paragons of Christian faith. The family history in part two rests on the genealogical work of Ruth's cousin Lois Cole Schaffer—I'm grateful for all her archival labor. Thanks to Deborah and Frank Popper, who gave me a sheaf of articles and references when I first set out to write this, then offered notes on the nearly finished manuscript. Jeanne Ode at the South Dakota State Historical Society helped find Scotty Philip citations. Barbara Wilhelm, the Unadilla village clerk, showed me the local historical material there and directed me to my ancestors' graves. Bob Manasek guided me around Scotts Bluff. Ken Warren gave me a tour of the Land Institute. My college professor Jan Dizard introduced me to Pleistocene rewilding and, earlier, to rethinking nature in general. I was lucky to write this while living in New York City, where I could use the vast resources of the New York Public Library and the Brooklyn Public Library, as well as the excellent university libraries.

For images, thanks to Matthew Reitzel and Sara Casper at the South Dakota State Archives. Matthew found the bison-bullfight photo, and Sara helped me find the maps I used to draw the ones here. The historian Sara Evans and both Marlie Wasserman and Suzanne Kellam at Rutgers University Press helped lead me to the source of the photo of Ruth Harris in Montgomery, and Karla Donato at the General Board of Global Ministries of the United Methodist Church did the research to secure permission to use the photo. Carrie Carpenter at the Land Institute sent me the photo of Kernza and wheat roots for part three. Thanks to all three institutions for permission to use these images.

Because this book is partly an extension of the music making I've done, I want to acknowledge the collaborators who've taught me about composition and rhythm over the past eighteen years or so. ¡Viva! to Stickman, His Trusty Steed, the

Guitar Bandits, Cruisin' Euclid, the Magnets, Chautauqua, and Krylls. And *¡Viva!* to the Pierre punk rock scene, to Diseased, and to all the kids (and grown-ups) who keep it going.

My first class as an undergraduate was a seminar on Western memoirs, Western American Lives, taught by Marni Sandweiss at Amherst College. In many ways that was the seed of this book, though it took fourteen years to bear fruit. I hope this product of a later generation is a fraction as illuminating as the brilliant works we read then by Wallace Stegner, Ivan Doig, Teresa Jordan, Norman Maclean, and others. I'm also endlessly grateful to Marni for teaching me to write and do research, and for encouraging the various forms my work took over the ensuing decade and up to the present, when I have the chance to study with her again at Princeton.

This book also owes a debt to *High Country News*—"a paper for people who care about the West"—whose editors taught me reporting skills and published a couple of my early essays about South Dakota. I hope to have acquired some of the wisdom of Ed and Betsy Marston (onetime New Yorkers) in re-envisioning the American West.

This was the project I enrolled in Columbia University's MFA program to write, and it evolved thanks to the faculty who advised me there: Darcy Frey, Lis Harris, Richard Locke, Leslie Sharpe, Brenda Wineapple, and especially Patty O'Toole, who went beyond the call of professorial duty and has been a champion. As thesis readers, Paul Elie and Margo Jefferson gave me vital suggestions for reorganizing the book and finding its final form. Besides those professors and my talented classmates there, other friends, teachers, editors, colleagues, and generous acquaintances have given me feedback on sections of this book.

Thanks to Jenny Boully, Rachel Cohen, Emily Feder, Allison Lorentzen (who suggested using *Ghost Dances* as the title), Greg Lowder, Michael Beach Nichols (who traveled with me to the Plains to shoot an accompanying mini-documentary), Kevin Riordan, Nathan Schneider, Patrick Thomas, Isaac Vogel, and Brook Wilensky-Lanford.

I'm deeply grateful to Amherst College for many things, but most to the point here were the alumni fellowships from the Amherst Memorial Fund and the Henry P. Field Fellowship, which helped keep me afloat in New York.

I was also lucky enough to spend three sojourns at writers' residencies in Nebraska and Wyoming: the Cotton Mather Library in Arthur, Nebraska, operated by the Center for American Places (thanks particularly to George Thompson); the Kimmel Harding Nelson Center for the Arts in Nebraska City, just twenty-three miles from my family's old haunts in Unadilla; and the Jentel Artist Residency Program in Banner, Wyoming (Lynn Reeves, Mary Jane Edwards, the gorgeous Thousand Acres, and my five wonderful coresidents there made it a joy to take the book apart and reassemble it one last time). These three residencies gave me invaluable time to write and push through rough patches, but they also imparted a granular experience of the Nebraska sand hills, the Missouri River valley, and the edge of the Big Horns.

A few sections of the book were published in earlier forms: the material on Fred Phelps was on the great religion website *Killing the Buddha*, the epilogue was in the Minnesota journal *Dislocate*, and Scotty Philip was in the magazine *Gopher Illustrated*. Thanks to all three for publishing me and for helpful editing.

Thanks to my agent, Matt McGowan, for seeing something promising in the less-coherent draft of the book I first sent to him. He wisely connected the manuscript with the marvelous, generous, diplomatic Pat Strachan, whom I'm unbelievably fortunate to have as an editor. Will Boggess guided me through the scary logistics of publishing; and Karen Landry, a fellow copyeditor, put me to shame (but graciously...) by catching so many lazy phrasings, repetitions, and mistakes in the manuscript.

I could never enumerate all the ways Marina Libel has contributed to this project. She has been a loving partner in this world for our whole adult lives, a role model as an artist-scholar, and of course a reader, listener, and traveling companion.

NOTES

PROLOGUE
1. These three examples come from, respectively: Andrew Isenberg, *The Destruction of the Bison: An Environmental History, 1750–1920* (Cambridge, UK: Cambridge University Press, 2000), 182; David Dary, *The Buffalo Book: The Full Saga of the American Animal* (Chicago: Sage Books, 1974), 149; and Dary, *Buffalo,* 233.
2. This definition of an *edge effect,* including its metaphorical extension to human culture, comes from Richard Manning, *Rewilding the West: Restoration in a Prairie Landscape* (Berkeley: University of California Press, 2009), 44.
3. I have subsequently learned that South Dakota does have a minimal history of earthquakes, first recorded as such in 1872, with small tremors in various parts of the state very occasionally (usually under 4.5 on the Richter scale) in the twentieth century. On August 9, 2011, there was a 3.3 magnitude quake in exactly the same location as the one in my dream, but it was barely felt and caused no damage. I claim no prophetic powers.

CHAPTER 1: SUPERSTITION VS. INVESTIGATION
1. Pam Belluck, "In Little City Safe From Violence, Rash of Suicides Leaves Scars," *New York Times,* April 5, 1998.
2. There are many biographies of Willa Cather. For a straightforward account of her young life, see Phyllis C. Robinson, *Willa: The Life of Willa Cather* (Garden City, NY: Doubleday, 1983), or E. K. Brown, *Willa Cather: A Critical Biography* (New York: Knopf, 1953). The full speech is published in L. Brent Bohlke, ed., *Willa Cather in Person: Interviews, Speeches, and Letters* (Lincoln: University of Nebraska Press, 1986), 140–43.

3. The issue of Cather's sexuality is complicated, and definitively calling her a lesbian feels a bit anachronistic to me. Joan Acocella's short book *Willa Cather and the Politics of Criticism* (Lincoln: University of Nebraska Press, 2000) includes a smart and balanced discussion of Cather and how she has been interpreted by feminist and queer critics. Sharon O'Brien's biography *Willa Cather: The Emerging Voice* (Cambridge, MA: Harvard University Press, 1997) argues in favor of regarding her as a lesbian.

4. Robinson, *Willa*, 31–32.

5. See ibid., 25–26, 34–35; also Hermione Lee, *Willa Cather: Double Lives* (New York: Vintage, 1991), 18–24.

6. Willa Cather, *My Ántonia* (Boston: Houghton Mifflin, 1918), 229–30.

7. This is from the story "Two Friends," anthologized in *Cather: Stories, Poems, and Other Writings* (New York: Library of America, 1992), 673–90.

8. The first three of these suicides appear in *My Ántonia*. The remaining four (beginning with the second tramp) come from, respectively: *The Song of the Lark*; "The Bohemian Girl"; "Paul's Case"; and "Peter." The stories are collected in *Cather: Stories, Poems, and Other Writings*.

CHAPTER 2: LANDSCAPE OF MOTION

1. Richard Manning, *Rewilding the West: Restoration in a Prairie Landscape* (Berkeley: University of California Press, 2009), 7–8, 57.

2. For a narrative history of AIM and Red Power, see Paul Chaat Smith and Robert Allen Warrior, *Like a Hurricane: The Indian Movement from Alcatraz to Wounded Knee* (New York: New Press, 1996); for an account that goes beyond Wounded Knee and discusses the killings in 1975, see Peter Matthiessen, *In the Spirit of Crazy Horse* (New York: Viking, 1980); and for a local white historian's rejoinder, see Rolland Dewing, *Wounded Knee II*, 2nd ed. (Chadron, NE: Great Plains Network, 2000). For an analysis of how the Red Power movement arose and what it meant for Indian identity, see Joane Nagel, *American Indian Ethnic Renewal: Red Power and the Resurgence of Identity and Culture* (New York: Oxford University Press, 1996), particularly chapter 5, "The Politics of American Indian Ethnicity: Solving the Puzzle of Indian Ethnic Resurgence."

3. Dewing, *Wounded Knee II*, 148–49. For a thorough and balanced profile of Bill Janklow, see the series of stories by Cara Hetland and Mark Steil, "That's Just Janklow," Minnesota Public Radio online, January 21, 2004, and the earlier story by Hetland, "Bill Janklow: Love Him or Hate Him," Minnesota Public Radio online, September 5, 2003, all available beginning from the page: http://news.minnesota.publicradio.org/features/2004/01/21_hetlandc_

janklowintro/, accessed May 24, 2011. Tellingly, these articles are peppered with sources' refusals to speak on the record, even after Janklow was disgraced. He had destroyed many people's careers for defying him, and few apparently found it worth the risk to speak to a reporter.

4. See "Janklow Denies He Said Shooting Would Solve Indian Problem," *Rapid City Journal*, March 23, 1976. Despite the confusing title of this article, Janklow admitted, "With respect to a bullet in the head, I did make that statement. I [said]...that I never met anybody yet that had a bullet in their head that bothered anybody with a gun again." When my father wrote a letter to the editor in 2000 repeating this quote, Janklow responded, "I firmly believe that my strong comments deterred some of the craziest of the crazies at that time from killing other people"—a doubtful claim, in my judgment (see Jay Davis, "Race Relations Problem Is Janklow," letters, *Rapid City Journal*, April 14, 2000, and Governor William J. Janklow, "My Comments Prevented Murders," letters, *Rapid City Journal*, May 9, 2000).

5. Matthiessen, *Spirit of Crazy Horse*, 107–11. The story of Janklow's lawsuit against Matthiessen is told by Matthiessen's lawyer, Martin Garbus, in an afterword to the 1991 edition.

6. Dewing, *Wounded Knee II*, 171.

7. Associated Press, "Janklow: Foul-Mouth Student Needed Hit," *Rapid City Journal*, October 12, 1995; Steven Barrett, "Janklow to Change Adopt-a-Highway Signs," *Rapid City Journal*, August 17, 2001 (this issue blew over and the signs were never removed); Cara Hetland and Mark Steil, "'Wild Bill,' A Man of Action" and "The Pirate Saint," Minnesota Public Radio online, January 21, 2004.

8. Bob Mercer, "Janklow Calls Indian Holiday Political Move," *Rapid City Journal*, October 11, 1995.

9. Cara Hetland and Mark Steil, "The Accident and the Aftermath," Minnesota Public Radio online, January 21, 2004. In the earlier article "Love Him or Hate Him," Hetland writes, "Scott Heidepriem [a Democratic ally of Janklow's] says it's an ironic situation, because if someone else had been driving the car, Janklow would be the first to jump in and help the Scott family." (Randy Scott was the motorcyclist Janklow killed.) Equally ironic is that if someone else had been driving the car, Janklow likely would have been the first to yell, "String him up!" Also see Joe Kafka, "Janklow Has a Need for Speed," *Rapid City Journal*, August 19, 2003, which lists the twelve speeding tickets and one tailgating citation Janklow received from when computer records started in 1990 to his return to the

governorship in 1994, at which point the tickets stopped, though apparently not because he had changed his driving habits. After the 2003 accident, in a *Denver Post* op-ed, I recounted an episode a friend of mine told me about Janklow tailgating him on a city street and then, as Janklow passed him, yelling out his window that my friend was going "too damn slow"—twenty-eight miles per hour in a thirty-mile-per-hour zone; see Josh Garrett-Davis, "Janklow: Fall of a South Dakota Hero," *Denver Post,* October 21, 2003. On the earlier drug laws, see Bob Mercer, "Drug Laws Unchanged; Janklow Upset," *Rapid City Journal,* March 3, 1996.

10. Cody Winchester, "Janklow Ticketed after Going 90 mph," *Rapid City Journal,* August 9, 2011. This article recounts five traffic citations Janklow received since he was allowed to drive again after his manslaughter probation ended in 2007.

CHAPTER 3: GHOST DANCES

1. Isaiah 40:4.
2. James Mooney, *The Ghost-Dance Religion and the Sioux Outbreak of 1890* (Lincoln: University of Nebraska Press, 1991), 771–74.
3. This comes from the Book of Mormon, 2 Nephi 5:21.
4. Mooney, *Ghost-Dance,* 972.
5. Ibid., 786.
6. Ibid., 787–91.
7. Ibid., 703–04.
8. Dee Brown, *Bury My Heart at Wounded Knee: An Indian History of the American West* (New York: Holt, Rinehart and Winston, 1970), 439.
9. This comes from a letter by Indian agent James McLaughlin of the Standing Rock Agency (the Standing Rock Reservation straddles the South Dakota / North Dakota border), October 17, 1890, quoted in Mooney, *Ghost-Dance,* 787.
10. James C. Olson, *Red Cloud and the Sioux Problem* (Lincoln: University of Nebraska Press, 1965), 326. Also see Brown, *Bury My Heart,* 435–36.
11. Brown, *Bury My Heart,* 437.
12. Ibid., 439–40.
13. Paul I. Wellman, *The Indian Wars of the West* (Garden City, NY: Doubleday, 1954), 236. Also see Brown, *Bury My Heart,* 442, and Heather Cox Richardson, *Wounded Knee: Party Politics and the Road to an American Massacre* (New York: Basic Books, 2010), 1–11, which details the political conditions that led up to the massacre.
14. Brown, *Bury My Heart,* 444.

15. See, for example, Richard White, *"It's Your Misfortune and None of My Own"*: *A New History of the American West* (Norman: University of Oklahoma Press, 1991), 21–23; Pekka Hämäläinen, "The Rise and Fall of Plains Indian Horse Cultures," *Journal of American History* 90, no. 3 (December 2003); and Richard White, "The Winning of the West: The Expansion of the Western Sioux in the Eighteenth and Nineteenth Centuries," *Journal of American History* 65, no. 2 (September 1978).

16. Mooney, *Ghost-Dance*, 657.

17. Russell Means, "Marxism as a European Tradition" (speech delivered at the Black Hills International Survival Gathering, Rapid City, SD, July 1980), printed in *Akwesasne Notes* 12, no. 3 (summer 1980): 17–19. Means's speech was later reprinted under the title "For America to Live, Europe Must Die" and is widely available on the Internet, including at the site Russell Means Freedom, http://www.russellmeansfreedom.com/2009/for-america-to-live-europe-must-die-russell-means, accessed May 9, 2011.

18. For an engaging account of these family farmers' resistance to a large irrigation project, see Peter Carrels, *Uphill Against Water: The Great Dakota Water War* (Lincoln: University of Nebraska Press, 1999).

19. I recognize that it is problematic to use the Ghost Dance as a metaphor for my own response, and other responses, to injustice or tragedy. Am I, a white man, appropriating the history of Indian people, from whom so much else (chiefly, this continent) has already been appropriated by other white men? The Crow Creek Dakota writer Elizabeth Cook-Lynn has addressed this in her essay "End of the Failed Metaphor" (in *Why I Can't Read Wallace Stegner and Other Essays: A Tribal Voice* [Madison: University of Wisconsin Press, 1996], 142–48). In response to an academic panel using the Wounded Knee Massacre as a "metaphor for tragedy," she asks: "What happens to our history? What happens morally and ethically to the people in such a process? Will our children know who their relatives are? Will they be able to know themselves in the context of a new history, a literary history rather than an actual one?" From my own very different experience, I would argue that a literary history is not so inferior to an actual history—that it does not diminish the "actual" history. A literary history can in fact be particularly helpful in the process of coming to know one's heritage. My heritage as a first-generation South Dakotan, for example, is directly informed by the fact of the state's history as stolen land, and I believe I must come to terms with that history—including through metaphor and literature—in order to know who I am. It is possible that the Native children Cook-Lynn worries for would be just as

well served by a literary or spiritual history as by an empirical one—
which is not to say that one needs to give up one to have the other.

CHAPTER 4: THE THREE GUYS WHO KNEW

1. Wallace Stegner, *Wolf Willow: A History, a Story, and a Memory of the Last Plains Frontier* (New York: Penguin Classics, 2000), 8.
2. The most compelling account I've read of James J. Hill and the failed settlement of eastern and central Montana is Jonathan Raban's book *Bad Land: An American Romance* (New York: Pantheon, 1996).

CHAPTER 5: OTHER SELVES

1. James M. Robinson, *West from Fort Pierre: The Wild World of James (Scotty) Philip* (Los Angeles: Westernlore Press, 1974).
2. George Philip, "South Dakota Buffaloes Versus Mexican Bulls," *South Dakota Historical Review* 2, no. 2 (1937), reprinted in *South Dakota Historical Collections* 20 (1940): 409–30. His account is more easily found today in Cathie Draine, ed., *Cowboy Life: The Letters of George Philip* (Pierre: South Dakota State Historical Society Press, 2007), 22–40. George Philip (1880–1948) was a wry storyteller and a clever writer, and I recommend his letters to anyone interested in South Dakota lore.
3. In addition to James Robinson's book, I've gotten Scotty Philip's biography from two less idiosyncratic sources: George Philip, "James (Scotty) Philip, 1858–1911," *South Dakota Historical Review* 1, no. 1 (October 1935): 1–48; and Wayne C. Lee, *Scotty Philip: The Man Who Saved the Buffalo* (Caldwell, ID: Caxton Printers Ltd., 1975).
4. Robinson, *Fort Pierre*, 20. For a discussion of how many bison lived in North America, see Andrew Isenberg, *The Destruction of the Bison: An Environmental History, 1750–1920* (Cambridge, UK: Cambridge University Press, 2000), 23–25. A higher (perhaps less accurate) estimate of fifty million can be found in David Dary, *The Buffalo Book: The Full Saga of the American Animal* (Chicago: Sage Books, 1974), 29.
5. Isenberg, *Destruction*, 130.
6. Philip, "James (Scotty) Philip," 15.
7. "Taming the Savage," *New York Times*, April 15, 1875.
8. Philip, "James (Scotty) Philip," 18–19, 44.
9. Ibid., 25.
10. Quoted in ibid., 26–27.
11. Robinson, *Fort Pierre*, 10–11; Lee, *Scotty Philip*, 233, 289.

12. Theodore Roosevelt, letter to Ernest Harold Baynes (October 24, 1907), in *Annual Report of the American Bison Society, 1905–1907* (New York: American Bison Society, 1908), 9.
13. "Kermit Balks at Buffaloes: President's Son Refuses to Shoot Game That Is Almost Extinct," *New York Times,* September 29, 1908.
14. F. Scott Fitzgerald, *The Great Gatsby,* 1st Collier Books ed. (New York: Collier, 1992), 104.
15. Ibid., 184.
16. Joshua Garrett-Davis, "The Red Power Movement and the Yankton Sioux Industries Pork-Processing Plant Takeovers of 1975," in Richmond L. Clow, ed., *The Sioux in South Dakota History: A Twentieth-Century Reader* (Pierre: South Dakota State Historical Society Press, 2007).
17. Steve Fiffer, *Tyrannosaurus Sue: The Extraordinary Saga of the Largest, Most Fought Over T. Rex Ever Found* (New York: W. H. Freeman and Company, 2000), 24.
18. Ibid., 28–29.
19. Ibid., 104.
20. Chicoine v. Chicoine, 479 N.W.2d 891 (S.D. 1992).
21. Ibid., and Justice Henderson's opinion is at the end, on 896–98.
22. Van Driel v. Van Driel, 525 N.W.2d 37 (S.D. 1994).
23. See Fiffer, *Tyrannosaurus,* 94–95, 108–10.
24. Ibid., 192.
25. Ibid., 58, 71, 78, 128, 135, 145, 146.

CHAPTER 6: THE PEN AND PLOW

1. This comes from John D. Hicks, *The Populist Revolt* (Lincoln: University of Nebraska Press, 1961), 34–35.
2. I'm very grateful for the genealogy research that was done by my relatives on the Cole-Brion side. Almost all of this family history is built on their work. Ruth Harris and Pat Patterson got me a copy of Minnie Davis's sixty-page handwritten memoirs from Ruth's sister, Betty (Harris) May. All of Minnie's written quotes come from that document, which is undated (she died in 1953 at the age of ninety-five). A more formal packet of genealogical material came from Lois Cole Schaffer, Ruth's cousin and another strong, political (conservative Republican in Lois's case) Nebraska woman—she was mayor of O'Neill from 1984 to 1990. Lois has traced the Brions back to before the American Revolution. According to this genealogy, Minnie and her parents arrived in Unadilla on October 6, 1879.

The Horace Greeley quote is widely used; for example, see Henry Nash Smith, *Virgin Land: The American West as Symbol and Myth*, 20th anniversary ed. (Cambridge, MA: Harvard University Press, 1970), 201.

3. I got this idea of the "safety valve" from Smith, *Virgin Land*, chapter 20. The George Washington quote is on page 203.

4. In addition to Minnie's memoirs, I'm also relying here on my great-grandfather Clyde Brion Davis's memories in *The Age of Indiscretion* (Philadelphia: J. B. Lippincott Company, 1950), and the introduction to *Eyes of Boyhood* (Philadelphia: J. B. Lippincott Company, 1953), which he edited.

5. Davis, *Age of Indiscretion*, 42.

6. I visited Unadilla on September 28, 2008, and got the information about its downtown from a historical plaque on the wall there.

7. Davis, *Age of Indiscretion*, 37.

8. This is from Clyde's bio in a *Time* magazine review of his first novel, *The Anointed*, August 2, 1937.

9. Ibid.

10. This is from a short memoir of Minnie that my granddad David Brion Davis contributed to Lois Schaffer's genealogy file.

11. Davis, *Age of Indiscretion*, 17.

12. "The Best-Selling Books," *New York Times*, August 6, 1939. *The Grapes of Wrath* was number 2, and *Nebraska Coast* was number 7.

13. My granddad has written compellingly of his first stark experience with American racism against blacks, when he was serving in the military. This may have inspired, in part, his interest in slavery. See David Brion Davis, "World War II and Memory," *Journal of American History* 77, no. 2 (1990), 580–87.

14. These quotes from the Oakdale *Pen and Plow*, from December 30, 1880, and July 28, 1881, are included in Lois Cole Schaffer's family history.

15. These anecdotes, as well as the term *sky pilot*, come from Mari Sandoz, *Old Jules*, 1st Bison Book ed. (Lincoln: University of Nebraska Press, 1962), 37, 76–77. It's a tough, wonderful nonfiction portrait of her difficult father, Jules Sandoz, a Swiss homesteader in western Nebraska.

16. From Lois Schaffer's family history, an anecdote from George and Clara's daughter Georgianna.

17. *Pen and Plow*, July 14, 1881.

18. *Pen and Plow*, August 4, 1881. I am actually not certain that this article is about George Cole, since the "clergyman" isn't mentioned by name in the copy in the genealogy files. I am following Lois Schaffer's lead in saying it's our relative who was "bounced."

19. "Card of Thanks," *Pen and Plow*, February 16, 1882.
20. Lois Schaffer found George Cole's entry in the journal kept by pastors of the Methodist church in Allen, Nebraska; his bitter note was the first entry, from February 1883.
21. See, for example, Ranjit S. Dighe, ed., *The Historian's Wizard of Oz: Reading L. Frank Baum's Classic as a Political and Monetary Allegory* (Westport, CT: Praeger Publishers, 2002); Hugh Rockoff, "The 'Wizard of Oz' as a Monetary Allegory," *Journal of Political Economy* 98, no. 4 (1990), 739–60; or a critique, Bradley A. Hansen, "The Fable of the Allegory: The Wizard of Oz in Economics," *Journal of Economic Education* 33, no. 3 (2002), 254–64. Baum's quote comes from an editorial about Sitting Bull's death in the *Aberdeen Saturday Pioneer*, December 20, 1890 (nine days before the almost total annihilation at Wounded Knee).
22. Davis, *Age of Indiscretion*, 38.
23. From Bryan's first major speech in Congress, on a bill that would reduce the tariffs on wool, March 16, 1892, in *Speeches of William Jennings Bryan: Revised and Arranged by Himself* (New York: Funk and Wagnalls, 1909), 60.
24. For an excellent recent account and assessment of Bryan's life and political legacy, see Michael Kazin, *A Godly Hero: The Life of William Jennings Bryan* (New York: Knopf, 2006).
25. There are digitized recordings of two of Bryan's speeches, both from 1908, available from the Internet Archive (http://www.archive.org) and from the University of California, Santa Barbara's Cylinder Preservation and Digitization Project (http://cylinders.library.ucsb.edu).
26. Sandoz, *Old Jules*, 113.
27. Davis, *Age of Indiscretion*, 194, 202.
28. Willa Cather, "The Personal Side of William Jennings Bryan," in William M. Curtin, ed., *The World and the Parish: Willa Cather's Articles and Reviews, 1893–1902* (Lincoln: University of Nebraska Press, 1970), 789, 784.
29. *Pen and Plow*, October 26, 1882. I don't know the local results in the suffrage vote.
30. Davis, *Age of Indiscretion*, 38.
31. Ibid., 194–95.
32. George E. Mowry, *Theodore Roosevelt and the Progressive Movement* (Madison: University of Wisconsin Press, 1946), 11; William Jennings Bryan, *The First Battle: A Story of the Campaign of 1896* (Chicago: W. B. Conkey Company, 1896), 361; *Speeches of William Jennings Bryan*, 43.

CHAPTER 7: RUTH HARRIS

1. My interviews with Ruth Harris took place in Claremont, California, May 21–25, 2007. All of Ruth's quotes are from those interviews, except where noted.
2. William Jennings Bryan, "In the Beginning—God," in *In His Image* (New York: Fleming H. Revell Company, 1922), 17.
3. See Sandra L. Myres, *Westering Women and the Frontier Experience, 1800–1915* (Albuquerque: University of New Mexico Press, 1982), chapter 8. Each of these states had local political quirks, and it was by no means an easy task to pass women's suffrage, but all of the states that enfranchised women before the federal constitutional amendment were in the West. I got the more specific Kansas dates from Leo E. Oliva, "Kansas: A Hard Land in the Heartland," in James H. Madison, ed., *Heartland: Comparative Histories of the Midwestern States* (Bloomington: Indiana University Press, 1988), 260.
4. Quoted in Lynne Cheney (!), "It All Began in Wyoming," *American Heritage* 24 (April 1973).
5. Clyde Brion Davis, *The Age of Indiscretion* (Philadelphia: J. B. Lippincott Company, 1950), 43.
6. Mari Sandoz, *Old Jules*, 1st Bison Book ed. (Lincoln: University of Nebraska Press, 1962), 375; the European immigrant who could no longer play the violin is also in *Old Jules*, 78.
7. Ruth shared with me the letters she wrote home from China, many of which her mother kept and gave to her.
8. Ephesians 4:16.
9. Ruth wrote a short autobiography as the first chapter (pages 15–44) in Sara M. Evans, ed., *Journeys That Opened Up the World: Women, Student Christian Movements, and Social Justice, 1955–1975* (New Brunswick, NJ: Rutgers University Press, 2003). This quote comes from page 22.
10. Ibid., 27.
11. Kenneth J. Dale, *Lest We Forget: A Bit of Family History with a Focus on Some 19th Century Nebraska Pioneers* (Claremont, CA, 2004); Reverend C. F. Erffmeyer, *Fifty Years and More: An Autobiography* (Holton, KS, 1939).
12. This painting is at the South Dakota Art Museum in Brookings, South Dakota.
13. Report of the Committee on Socio-Political Concerns, Methodist Student Movement, in Box 1 of the Ruth M. Harris Papers, Record Group No. 171, Special Collections, Yale Divinity School Library.
14. "By Dread Alone?" *Communique* 15, no. 5 (United Student Christian

Council, March 1959), 1. This, too, was in Box 1 of the Ruth M. Harris Papers at Yale.

15. From the bulletin/schedule of events for the 18th Ecumenical Student Conference on the Christian World Mission, Athens, Ohio, 16–18. Box 2, Ruth M. Harris Papers.
16. "Virginia Negroes Rally," *New York Times*, January 1, 1960.
17. Evans, *Journeys*, 33.

CHAPTER 8: A BUFFALO COMMONPLACE

1. E. B. White, *Here Is New York* (New York: Little Bookroom, 1999), 25–26.
2. Tom Baldwin, "How Do You Build a Paper Clip into a House? First, Swap It for a Fish Pen..." *Times* of London, July 12, 2006. For other incentives towns have used, see, e.g., Calvin Woodward, "This Land Can Be Your Land," Associated Press, August 26, 2005, about Ellsworth, Kansas, and other towns giving away lots or houses.
3. Andrew Isenberg, *The Destruction of the Bison: An Environmental History, 1750–1920* (Cambridge, UK: Cambridge University Press, 2000), 23–25, 33–35. See also Pekka Hämäläinen, "The Rise and Fall of Plains Indian Horse Cultures," *Journal of American History* 90, no. 3 (December 2003).
4. Isenberg, *Destruction*, 103–07.
5. Ibid., 109.
6. Ibid., 136–38.
7. David Dary, *The Buffalo Book: The Full Saga of the American Animal* (Chicago: Sage Books, 1974), 114, 119; Isenberg, *Destruction*, 159.
8. Dary, *Buffalo*, 118; Isenberg, *Destruction*, 164.
9. Deborah Epstein Popper and Frank J. Popper, "The Great Plains: From Dust to Dust," *Planning*, American Planning Association, December 1987, 12–18.
10. See figure 5 in Paul Mackun and Steven Wilson, "Population Distribution and Change: 2000 to 2010," 2010 Census Briefs (Washington, DC: U.S. Census Bureau, March 2011), which is available on the Census Bureau's website. On North Dakota's current energy boom, see, e.g., Eric Konigsberg, "Kuwait on the Prairie," *The New Yorker*, April 25, 2011.
11. The journalist Timothy Egan made this same demographic/ecological juxtaposition after the 2000 census, in "As Others Abandon Plains, Indians and Bison Come Back," *New York Times*, May 27, 2001. I've added the figures from the 2010 census.
12. See, for example, A. G. Sulzberger, "As Small Towns Wither on Plains, Hispanics Come to the Rescue," *New York Times*, November 13, 2011.

13. Vine Deloria Jr., *Custer Died for Your Sins* (Norman: University of Oklahoma Press, 1988), 161.
14. Dary, *Buffalo*, 233–34; Judith Hebbring Wood, "The Origin of Public Bison Herds in the United States," *Wicazo Sa Review* 15, no. 1 (Spring 2000), 157–82. This article meticulously charts the transfer of small numbers of bison around in the early days of their resurgence.
15. Wood, "Origin," 171.
16. Isenberg, *Destruction*, 175, 182.
17. Ibid., 183.
18. Wood, "Origin," 176.
19. Ibid.
20. Dary, *Buffalo*, 232.
21. Wood, "Origin," 177.
22. "A New Park to Save the Plains," *Kansas City Star*, November 15, 2009. See also Tom Parker, "Revisiting the Buffalo Commons," *Marysville Advocate* (Marysville, KS), December 15, 2010. More elaborate, nuanced versions of the original proposal can be found in Deborah E. Popper and Frank J. Popper, "The Onset of the Buffalo Commons," *Journal of the West* 45, no. 2 (2006), 29–34; Deborah E. Popper and Frank J. Popper, "Great Plains: Checkered Past, Hopeful Future," *Forum for Applied Research and Public Policy* (Winter 1994), 89–100; and Deborah E. Popper and Frank J. Popper, "The Buffalo Commons: Metaphor as Method," *Geographical Review* 89, no. 4 (October 1999), 491–510.
23. I visited Scotts Bluff National Monument and interviewed Bob Manasek on August 30, 2007.
24. Susan J. Tunnell and James Stubbendieck, "Restoration of Threadleaf Sedge: Final Report," submitted to Scotts Bluff National Monument (Department of Agronomy and Horticulture, University of Nebraska–Lincoln, July 2005).
25. There is an effort to designate a prairie wilderness in the Buffalo Gap National Grassland in western South Dakota. The idea has been introduced in Congress on multiple occasions and is supported by the South Dakota Wild Grassland Coalition, as well as, unsurprisingly, my father.

CHAPTER 9: LEAVES OF GRASS

1. The site now says church is at twelve p.m., but my visit to Westboro took place August 6, 2006. An extensive archive of faxes, press releases, etc., are available on the site http://www.godhatesfags.com, but some of the material I've used here is no longer archived there as of May 2011.

2. See FAQ, "What do you think of the Religious Right?" http://www.god hatesfags.com/faq.html, accessed May 5, 2011.
3. Associated Press, "Phelps Supporters Flee Service," *Topeka Capital-Journal*, February 23, 1994, 8A.
4. Westboro Baptist Church, press release, August 11, 2000.
5. See FAQ, "Why do you focus on homosexuals?" http://www.god hatesfags.com/faq.html, accessed May 5, 2011.
6. Westboro's appearance at Matthew Shepard's funeral is well documented and has been dramatized in the play *The Laramie Project*. Not all of these websites are extant, and Westboro has replaced some with sites such as http://www.jewskilledjesus.com and http://www.beastobama.com.
7. Westboro Baptist Church, "Take a Good Look, America," press release, February 25, 2006, among many others.
8. *Snyder v. Phelps* was argued before the Supreme Court on October 6, 2010, and decided March 2, 2011. The decision is available at http://www.supremecourt.gov/opinions/10pdf/09-751.pdf.
9. Joe Taschler and Steve Fry, "The Transformation of Fred Phelps," *Topeka Capital-Journal*, July 8, 1994.
10. "Repentance in Pasadena," *Time*, June 11, 1951.
11. Joe Taschler and Steve Fry, "Fate, Timing Kept Phelps in Topeka," *Topeka Capital-Journal*, July 9, 1994.
12. The series was called "Hate for the Love of God," and it ran from July 8, 1994, to July 15, 1994. Several individual articles are cited separately in this chapter.
13. Joe Taschler and Steve Fry, "Phelps' Law Career Checkered" and "As a Lawyer, Phelps Was Good in Court," *Topeka Capital-Journal*, July 10, 1994; also Monograph on Westboro Baptist Church, February 14, 2004.
14. Taschler and Fry, "As a Lawyer."
15. Westboro Baptist Church, "Open Letter to President Obama," February 9, 2009.
16. Taschler and Fry, "As a Lawyer."
17. Westboro Baptist Church, "All Nations Must Immediately Outlaw Sodomy...," press release, December 3, 2002.
18. Taschler and Fry, "Phelps' Law Career."
19. Ibid.
20. See FAQ, "Why do you preach hate?" http://www.godhatesfags.com/faq.html, accessed May 5, 2011.
21. I called Westboro and spoke with this woman on August 8, 2006.
22. Westboro Baptist Church, "Thank God for IEDs," press release, August 3,

2006. See also Mary Clare Jalonick, "Kansas Church Group Will Picket at Baucus Funeral," Associated Press, August 4, 2006, and "Baucus' Nephew Remembered by Hundreds," Associated Press, August 7, 2006.

23. Joe Taschler and Steve Fry, "Phelps Flock: Afterlife Is Prearranged," *Topeka Capital-Journal*, July 13, 1994.

24. Summary of *The Sovereignty of God*, Ligonier Ministries website, http://www.ligonier.org/store/sovereignty-of-god-paperback, accessed May 5, 2011.

25. Matt Sedensky, "A Sermon of Hatred and Doom from a Kansas Minister Eager to Preach It," Associated Press, May 30, 2006.

26. See FAQ, "What do you think of the Religious Right?" http://www.god hatesfags.com/faq.html, accessed May 5, 2011.

27. Joe Taschler and Steve Fry, "No Sparing of the Rod, Sons Recall," *Topeka Capital-Journal*, July 11, 1994.

28. Ibid.

29. Sedensky, "A Sermon of Hatred."

30. Kristen L. Hays, "We Weren't Beaten, Phelps Siblings Say," *Topeka Capital-Journal*, July 15, 1994.

31. Joe Taschler and Steve Fry, "Phelps Controlled Children's Lives, Sons Say," *Topeka Capital-Journal*, July 12, 1994.

32. Joe Taschler and Steve Fry, "Life in a 'War Zone,'" *Topeka Capital-Journal*, July 8, 1994.

33. Sedensky, "A Sermon of Hatred."

34. Taschler and Fry, "Life in a 'War Zone.'"

35. Fred Phelps, "Touch Not Mine Anointed," August 6, 2006, transcribed by me.

36. Taschler and Fry, "The Transformation."

37. Jodi Wilgoren, "Vote in Topeka Today Hangs on Gay Rights and a Vitriolic Local Protester," *New York Times*, March 1, 2005.

38. Mona Gambone, "Others Deserving," letter, *Topeka Capital-Journal*, July 18, 1994.

39. Associated Press, "Lesbian Candidate Holds Off Foe as Topeka Votes for Gay Rights," March 2, 2005.

40. Mark Phelps, "A Letter from a Son Who Left," *Topeka Capital-Journal*, July 8, 1994.

41. Cap Iversen, *Silver Saddles*, Dakota Series #2 (Boston: Alyson Publications, 1993), 19.

42. Ibid., 62.

43. Cap Iversen, *Arson!*, Dakota Series #1 (Boston: Alyson Publications, 1992), 61.

44. Ibid., 233.
45. Iversen, *Silver Saddles*, 209.
46. Iversen, *Arson!*, 78; *Silver Saddles*, 188.
47. Iversen, *Silver Saddles*, 150.
48. Cap Iversen, *Rattler!*, Dakota Series #3 (Boston: Alyson Publications, 1995), 21.
49. Walt Whitman, *Leaves of Grass*, 1st ed. (1855) (Digireads, 2008), 35.
50. These quotes come from, respectively: Iversen, *Arson!*, 225; ibid., 192; ibid., 202; *Silver Saddles*, 36; *Rattler!*, 100.
51. Iversen, *Arson!*, 55; *Silver Saddles*, 115.
52. Iversen, *Rattler!*, 12.
53. Iversen, *Arson!*, 17.
54. Ibid., 113.
55. Iversen, *Rattler!*, 212–13.
56. Ibid., 159.
57. Iversen, *Arson!*, 214–15.
58. This is adapted from the 1953 Western movie *Shane*.

CHAPTER 10: GHOST DANCES

1. Heinz H. Lettau and Ben Davidson, eds., *Exploring the Atmosphere's First Mile; Proceedings of the Great Plains Turbulence Field Program, 1 August to 8 September 1953, O'Neill, Nebraska* (New York: Pergamon Press, 1957).
2. I read about this church in a local history of Arthur, written by Ted Frye, which was held in the Cotton Mather Library, Center for American Places, Arthur, NE.
3. Thea Fronsman-Cecil, "Green Day Knows How to Hit Heart," *Topeka Capital-Journal*, April 19, 1994.
4. Erin Andersen, "The Death Penalty: Teen Writers Support Execution," *Rapid City Journal*, February 15, 1993.
5. This line comes from the song "Chickenshit Conformist" on the Dead Kennedys album *Bedtime for Democracy*.
6. Sally Fronsman-Cecil, "A Price Too High," *Topeka Capital-Journal*, November 3, 2002.
7. "Ranches," http://www.tedturner.com/ranches.asp. The Bolson tortoise was reintroduced at the Armendaris Ranch.
8. For more information about the Land Institute, see http://www.landinstitute.org.
9. There is a good account of this proposal in William Stolzenburg, *Where the Wild Things Were: Life, Death, and Ecological Wreckage in a Land of Vanishing*

Predators (New York: Bloomsbury, 2008), 168–83. See also J. C. Hallman, "Pleistocene Dreams," *Science & Spirit* (May/June 2008), 24–33.

10. The original Pleistocene rewilding article is by Josh Donlan, Harry W. Greene, et al., "Re-wilding North America," *Nature* 436 (2005), 267–69. A more fleshed-out version of the proposal is C. Josh Donlan et al., "Pleistocene Rewilding: An Optimistic Agenda for Twenty-first Century Conservation," *American Naturalist* 168, no. 5 (November 2006), 660–81; and a critique can be found in Dustin R. Rubenstein et al., "Pleistocene Park: Does Re-wilding North America Represent Sound Conservation for the Twenty-first Century?" *Biological Conservation* 132 (2006), 232–38. A crucial book on the overkill hypothesis is by another of the Pleistocene authors: Paul S. Martin, *Twilight of the Mammoths: Ice Age Extinctions and the Rewilding of America* (Berkeley: University of California Press, 2005). There are still plenty of scientists who attribute the die-offs to climate change, disease, or competition for resources between bison and other large herbivores. For a Native repudiation of the overkill hypothesis (also a Native version of "intelligent design" pseudoscience), see Vine Deloria Jr., *Red Earth, White Lies: Native Americans and the Myth of Scientific Fact* (New York: Scribner, 1995).

11. Stolzenburg, *Wild Things*, 134–56.

12. I'm referring, respectively, to Paul S. Martin, Michael Soulé, and David Foreman.

13. I interviewed Josh Donlan by telephone on August 30, 2008.

14. Jake Vail, "Hope Is a Thing with Roots," *Land Report* 96 (Spring 2010): 22.

15. C. Josh Donlan, "Restoring America's Big, Wild Animals," *Scientific American* (June 2007), 73.

16. Anne Matthews, *Where the Buffalo Roam: The Storm Over the Revolutionary Plan to Restore America's Great Plains* (New York: Grove, 1992), 150. This is a very well-written account of the Poppers' first few years after proposing the Buffalo Commons.

17. "In the Eye of the Storm: The Poppers and the Great Plains," *PEI News*, Princeton Environmental Institute (Winter 2003–04): 3–4.

18. Sergey A. Zimov, "Pleistocene Park: Return of the Mammoth's Ecosystem," *Science* 308 (May 2005), 796–98.

EPILOGUE: PRATINCOLE

1. Genesis 41.

2. Willa Cather, *O Pioneers!* (Boston: Houghton Mifflin, 1913), 206.

3. Psalm 65:12.

4. John 6:10.

5. "Coronado's Report to the King of Spain, Sent from Tiguex on October 20, 1541," Archives of the West, accompanying the documentary series *The West* (directed by Stephen Ives), http://www.pbs.org/weta/thewest/resources/archives/one/corona9.htm, accessed May 8, 2011.

6. Willa Cather, *My Ántonia* (Boston: Houghton Mifflin, 1918), 244.

7. After Pike, these four quotes come from, respectively, Major Stephen H. Long, Captain Randolph B. Marcy (two), and Horace Greeley—all (including Pike) quoted in Walter Prescott Webb, *The Great Plains*, 1st paperback ed. (Lincoln: University of Nebraska Press, 1981), 156–59.

8. John Madson, *Where the Sky Began: Land of the Tallgrass Prairie*, rev. ed. (Iowa City: University of Iowa Press, 1995), 57.

9. Cather, *O Pioneers!*, 65.

10. M. Schele de Vere, *Americanisms: The English of the New World* (New York: Scribner, 1872), 103.

11. Ben Harding, "Introduction," *The Crockett Almanac: Containing Adventures, Exploits, Sprees and Scrapes in the West, and Life and Manners in the Backwoods* 2, no. 1 (Nashville, TN: Ben Harding, 1839), 2. (This is a pretty rare comedic pamphlet; I found it in the Columbia University Rare Book and Manuscript Library.)

12. "Col. Crockett's Adventure with a Grizzly Bear," in ibid., 3–6.

13. Walt Whitman, *Leaves of Grass* (Boston: Small, Maynard and Company, 1908), 35.

14. Walt Whitman, *Specimen Days in America* (London: Walter Scott, 1887), 234.

15. "The Prairies, and an Undeliver'd Speech," in ibid., 219.

16. John Steinbeck, *The Grapes of Wrath* (New York: Penguin Classics, 1992), 1, 2.

17. Whitman, *Leaves of Grass*, 33.

INDEX

317

ABOUT THE AUTHOR

Josh Garrett-Davis has an MFA from Columbia and is currently a PhD student in American history at Princeton. *Ghost Dances* is his first book.